ISBN 978-1-4400-7928-3
PIBN 10108196

1 MONTH OF
FREE
READING

at
www.ForgottenBooks.com

By purchasing this book you are eligible for one month membership to ForgottenBooks.com, giving you unlimited access to our entire collection of over 700,000 titles via our web site and mobile apps.

To claim your free month visit:
www.forgottenbooks.com/free108196

Similar Books Are Available from
www.forgottenbooks.com

LINCOLN, GARFIELD, McKINLEY.

A History

OF THE

Republican Party

BY

Geo. W. Platt.

———

"And summon from the shadowy Past,
The forms that once have been."

———

C. J. Krehbiel & Co.,
CINCINNATI, O.
1904

Copyright, 1904,
By GEO. W. PLATT.
All rights reserved.

Inscribed

to the Memory of

the three Martyred Republican Presidents

LINCOLN, GARFIELD, McKINLEY.

PREFACE.

Early in February, 1900, the writer delivered an address before the Stamina Republican League of Cincinnati on "The Origin and Rise of the Republican Party." The interest in the subject shown by the audience and the many words of approbation led to a deeper consideration of the history of the Party, and the address was repeated on a more elaborate plan before many other organizations in Cincinnati and vicinity.

It soon became apparent that the great majority of every audience had very vague recollections of the tragic events which led to the organization of the Party, and of its early history, owing perhaps to the fact that they belonged to a generation that had followed the enactment of those events. It was also clear that those who had lived in the momentous decade before the Civil War were deeply interested and stirred by a new recital of

the history of that period, and thus it was suggested that a History of the Republican Party
might prove of interest and value.

Like the place of Homer's birth that of the Republican Party is in dispute, but it is believed that
the facts herein narrated are supported by the
weight of evidence.

It is hoped that this work does not display so
much partisanship as to make it uninteresting to
members of other political parties in the United
States.   GEO. W. PLATT.

Cincinnati, February, 1904.

CONTENTS

LIST OF ILLUSTRATIONS.

A
HISTORY
OF THE
REPUBLICAN PARTY.

A HISTORY

OF THE REPUBLICAN PARTY.

CHAPTER I.

FORMATIVE CAUSES.

"*Resolved,* That the Constitution confers upon Congress sovereign power over the territories of the United States for their government, and that in the exercise of this power it is both the right and duty of Congress to prohibit in the territories those twin relics of barbarism, polygamy and slavery."

Republican National Platform, 1856.

Near the beginning of Mr. Conway's small volume entitled "Barons of the Potomack and Rappahannock" occurs the sententious remark that "a true history of tobacco would be the history of English and American Liberty." With whatever truth there is in such sweeping statements it may also be said that "a history of Slavery in this country would be the history of the Republican Party." This is distinctly so, at least to the close of the Civil War, for we are to notice that while the party originated in a desire to oppose the extension of slavery, the cause of its origin disappeared in less than ten years after the birth of the organization. But the results of that cause remained for

(5)

many years, and justified the assertion in the Republican platform of 1860 that "a history of the nation during the last four years has fully established the propriety and necessity of the organization and perpetuation of the Republican Party, and that the causes which called it into existence are permanent in their nature." From its primary position as an opponent of slavery extension, the new party became the champion of abolition, and in the chaos brought on by the Civil War, and in the Reconstruction period which followed, it was kept in power, notwithstanding the disappearance of its direct formative cause, and the justification for its continued existence was found in the urgent necessity of the hour. Gradually but firmly it became a strong State and National Party, solving the many vexed problems which followed the great conflict, restoring public credit, reducing the enormous war debt; and when the slavery question and its direct consequences had been eliminated from national politics, taking up new political ideas and economic policies, for the welfare of the entire country, until now, after half a century of existence, during which time it has written some of the brightest pages of American history, the Republican Party stands out as one of the greatest and most consistent of political parties in all the world's history.

Taking the popular vote as a criterion of permanent growth, the vote for the Republican presidential candidates, beginning with 1,341,264 for Fremont in 1856, reached the maximum of 7,208,244 for McKinley in 1900, and only once (in 1892) during this entire period did the popular vote for the Republican presidential candidate fail to show an increase over the vote of the preceding election.

The events of the momentous decade before the Civil War (during which period the Republican Party was firmly established), the election of Mr. Lincoln, the Civil War and Reconstruction, the story of the national development along commercial and financial lines since that period, present the most interesting and vivid chapters of American history. Throughout its history of fifty years, covering the period just mentioned, the Republican Party has a remarkable record for solid and consistent action, resulting universally in national prosperity and honor, and on the three occasions since its formation (1856, 1884 and 1892), when the voters turned away to listen to the teachings of Democracy, the invariable result has been national disaster and humiliation and a retarding of progress.

The Republican Party was organized in the early months of 1854, and the direct formative causes leading to its establishment were the repeal of the Missouri Compromise and the efforts on the part of the South, under the leadership of that ambitious politician, Stephen A. Douglas (with his specious doctrines of non-intervention on the part of the Government, and popular sovereignty), to force slavery into the Territories of Kansas and Nebraska, which, by the Compromise of 1820, should have been forever dedicated to freedom. By these efforts it was seen that the South was attempting to make slavery a national instead of a sectional institution, and the situation early in 1854

(after the long series of triumphs of the Slave Power)
seemed almost hopeless as far as concerned political opposition to these radical measures was concerned. At this
time, and, indeed, for many years past, the Democratic
Party was firm and united in its support of slavery, and
the course of the Whig Party, intimidated by its southern
members, and fearful of civil strife, had been one of subserviency to the exacting demands of slavery. The Whig
Party had proven itself totally incapable of meeting the
great question of the hour, and after the election of 1852
was on the verge of absolute dissolution.

The astonishing repeal of the Missouri Compromise
early in 1854, coming, as it did, in a time of comparative
peace on the slavery question, obliterated old party lines in
the North completely, and left disorganized groups of anti-
Nebraska Whigs, anti-Nebraska Democrats, Free-soilers,
Abolitionists, and Know-Nothings, all of whom represented every extreme of the northern views of slavery. But
underneath these views was the belief that slavery was a
great moral wrong, and that its extension, at least, should
be opposed, and from these seemingly discordant elements
it became, in fact, an easy matter to organize, in a short
time, a strong opposition party to the new aggression of the
slave interests.

The Republican Party was at first one of defense only;
it was a combination of the existing political elements opposed to slavery, and its first stand was conservative, not to
abolish slavery, but to firmly oppose its extension. The
Party at first had no intention of interfering with slavery

in the States in which it then existed, but the idea of allowing slavery, with its manifest evils, to be extended into
other States and Territories at the will of the South was
not to be silently borne. The early views of the party, up
to the Civil War, were well expressed by Mr. Lincoln in his
last great public utterance before his election as President
in November, 1860 (The Cooper Union Speech, February,
1860): "Wrong, as we think slavery is, we can yet afford
to let it alone where it is, because that much is due to the
necessity arising from its actual presence in the nation;
but can we, while our votes will prevent it, allow it to
spread into the national territories and to overrun us here
in these free States?"

It will be of interest, before taking up the history of
the immediate casual events which made necessary this new
political party, to consider the early history of that great
institution, slavery, which, from the very beginning of
American history to the close of the Civil War, and indeed
for many years after, was the chief disturbing element in
the country; to consider how this institution established itself in other countries, how it insidiously began its growth
in the Jamestown colony, and how it gained in strength
and political power, until, at the opening of the Revolution
it owned half a million slaves, and after Independence had
been gained, forced recognition in the Constitutional Convention and there domineered the North into the first of a
series of humiliating compromises on the slave question.,
And from that time on, with increasing force, pressed its
obnoxious doctrines upon the press, the pulpit, platforms

and political parties of the country, until, after many years of bitter contention, it was met in 1854 by the organization of a determined opposition political party, which, after one failure, brought about its political overthrow, an event followed by a last tremendous struggle for the mastery, in which slavery was wiped out forever in the life-blood of those who upheld and those who opposed it.

CHAPTER II.

"Slavery is as ancient as War, and War as human nature."

Voltaire.

"That execrable sum of all villainies, commonly called the slave trade."

John Wesley, 1792.

The earliest records of the human race begin with accounts of slavery. The first slave was probably a war captive whose life had been spared, and slavery probably originated when the nations emerging from the savagery of early times discovered that the prisoner captured in war could render to the conqueror more service alive than dead; and it became a very early custom that all persons captured in war and not ransomed by their fellows should remain the property of the conqueror to be used by him at will or sold to others. It is seen that slavery in its inception was in some degree an innocent and humane institution, because it saved many lives and resulted in much development in building, agriculture and the crude manufacturing of early times.

It is convenient to divide the history of slavery into two epochs, ancient and modern, although there are times in the history of several nations when ancient slavery assumed the modern form. The ancient slaves were the pris-

(11)

oners captured in war, the hereditary slaves, and persons who, by the laws of their country, became slaves by the commission of crime or inability to meet their debts. Modern slavery assumed a more brutal aspect. Here the slave was not the result of wars, but the direct object of them, and we find nations engaged in the shameful traffic of deliberately declaring war upon a foreign and inoffensive people for the purpose of obtaining possession of their bodies to carry them away for sale in foreign countries. The modern slave for four centuries was a distinct article of commerce, quoted and bargained for in the markets and reckoned on as a medium of exchange.

For the history of ancient slavery we turn first to Egypt, and find abundant evidence of the use of slaves from the very earliest times. Egypt thrived, and its native population was overflowing; but notwithstanding this, thousands of slaves were brought into the country by the early Wars of Conquest. Most of these slaves, for lack of other work, were put to labor on vast monuments, buildings, shrines and temples. The great Pyramid of Gizeh, near Memphis, the smaller pyramids near it and the ruins near Thebes, and the Karnak, still remain as mysterious and wonderful records of the skill of the Egyptian builders, and as mute evidence of the use of vast numbers of slaves.

In the quaint diction of early biblical history is told the manner of the Egyptian use of slaves. We learn how Joseph was treacherously sold by his brethren into Egyptian captivity, but gaining favor, was placed in the house of his master, and how, in later years, when famine waxed sore in the land of Canaan, Joseph's father, Jacob, and his brethren and their flocks went into Egypt and prayed to Pharaoh for permission to dwell there, and partly through the influence of Joseph were given permission to live in the country of Goshen. The Israelites grew and multiplied until the land was filled with them, but new Kings ruled in Egypt, hostile to them, and their lives were made bitter with hard bondage and compulsory work in mortar and brick, "and they built for Pharaoh treasure cities, Pithom and Raamses."

When the Hebrews, under the guidance of Moses, left Egypt, they took slaves with them, and in their subsequent history we find a record of the use of two classes of slaves, the Hebrew born and those of alien blood. The Hebrew slave usually became such by selling himself on account of his poverty, or because it was imposed upon him as a punishment for crime. He could claim his liberty at the end of six years, but not so with the alien, who was in bondage for life. Jerusalem was built, and after many years captured by Nebuchadnezzar, King of Babylon, who razed the city and carried the upper classes of the Hebrews captive to Babylon, where they remained in a condition of servitude until the destruction of Babylon by Cyrus the Great, King of Persia, who, as a political measure, permitted the Hebrews to return to their homes and rebuild Jerusalem. Egypt went down to rise no more before the new power of the Persians, who, in turn, gave way to the Greeks, and they to the Romans. Throughout the history of the ancient people, the Egyptians, the Syrians, Babylonians, Phœnicians, Medes and Persians, slavery developed in the same general way; the prisoner of war was held in slavery and reduced to the lowest caste, and this we find true in China, Ancient India and in the history of the Aztecs.

Slaves were used in Greece, especially so at Athens, where, at the height of the city's power, there were four times as many slaves as citizens. The slaves took a prominent part in the domestic and public economy, being used as agricultural laborers, and as artificers and servants, and by the State as policemen and soldiers. Sparta possessed very few slaves, probably only enough to supply the demand for domestic servants. With the rapid progress of the Greeks came an increased use of slaves, and the wars not being sufficient to supply the demand, an open slave trade was soon established. In Greece arose to its height that peculiar form of slavery practiced by the early Hebrews, wherein foreigners violating laws, and Greeks themselves, if unable to meet their debts, were sold with their families into slavery. This brought about such a threatening state of affairs that by the wise laws of Solon this form of slavery was abolished. This peculiar slavery also existed in the early days of Rome, but in the third century before Christ it was also abolished.

In the Roman Empire slavery existed from the earliest times, and was carried to an excess not known before or since in the history of slavery. The wonderful and rapid rise of the Romans in power, domain and wealth led to a moral and political degeneracy which demanded the increased use of slaves in all branches of domestic and public life. Here, as in Greece, the Wars of Conquest bringing in, as they did, vast numbers of slaves, failed to supply the demand, and here again, as in Greece, the slave trade, with its acts of piracy, was established to obtain a supply, and the occupation of the professional slave hunter and slave dealer became fully recognized and were the forerunners of similar acts in the history of Negro slavery many centuries later. The abuses brought on by the Roman system of slavery led to such decay and corruption in the Empire that it became an easy prize for the Teutonic tribes, and Rome of the West fell to rise no more, about the middle of the fifth century.

Then probably began the Feudal system, which practically abolished the ancient form of slavery, and in its place the lower classes of the population were put in the semi-servile condition of serfs and villeins to their Feudal Lords. This system spread in Germany, France, England and Russia, but by the time of the capture of Constantinople in 1453 by the Turks, Feudalism, the last relic of slavery in Western Europe, was almost extinct, and was gradually assuming a very mild form in the other countries, when suddenly and unexpectedly slavery was revived and perpetuated in a new, its modern form, by a singular and interesting series of events which brought about the ruthless bondage of an entire people to nations whom they had never offended.

Portugal, Spain and England were mainly responsible for fastening the evils of Negro Slavery on the New World. The Portuguese first began the modern traffic in negro slaves; the Spaniards introduced them into America, and the English engaged in and encouraged, more than any other nation, the infamous slave trade, to supply the New World demand.

In a strange way Christianity was indirectly responsible for the beginning of negro slavery in its modern form. For many centuries prior to the discovery of America the Mohammedans and Christians had been arrayed against each other in western Europe, and the struggles for the mastery had aroused the most implacable hatred between the foes, and the almost inevitable fate of the captives, whether taken by Christian or Mohammedan, was slavery for life. Fifty-one years before the discovery of America some Portuguese sailors, coasting along the shores of Morocco, took captive a few Moors and brought them to Portugal. This event led to the beginning of modern slavery, for in the following year, 1442, these captive Moors, at their own request, were exchanged for negroes, which they procured from Africa. It appears that Prince Henry of Portugal had made many ineffectual attempts to convert these Moors, and their obstinate refusal made acceptable an exchange for negroes, "for whatever number he should get he would gain souls, because they might be converted to the Faith, which could not be done with the Moors," said the Prince. With what sincerity this argument was advanced cannot be known, but it is certain that the beginning of modern slavery was justified by this crafty philanthropy, not only in Portugal but later in the Spanish Colonies, where the same argument was advanced by Columbus and accepted by the Spanish Monarchs to ease their minds while it filled their treasuries. It is also certain that in a very short time, whether to be Christianized or not, shipload after shipload of the unfortunate Africans were brought to Portugal and a regular slave trade, with all its sickening horrors, was established, the Crown receiving one-fifth of the proceeds as its royal share. Soon Spain engaged in the traffic, and then the event happened, the discovery of America, which startled Europe, and opened up a vast new country to whatever good or evil its conquerors might choose to plant.

Strangely enough the very events which led to the discovery of the New World operated to firmly establish the beginning of what was to be its greatest curse. With the capture of Constantinople in 1453 by the Turks and the cutting off of that way to the Indies, increased efforts were made to discover a new route, and the first attempts were down the west coast of Africa. The Portuguese were the most active mariners at that time and took the most prominent part in these new voyages, and while they did not meet with complete success, they discovered a country thronged with the people, who, by the circumstances already related, were practically doomed to slavery. So promising was this base of supplies that about the year 1485 the Portuguese established a Colony at Benin, on the west coast of Africa, for the purpose of more actively carrying on the slave trade, and this was the first of those permanent fortified places established in Africa by the Christian countries of the world as stations where, by the blackest of cruelties and

crimes, they might obtain large and immediate supplies of
this new article of commerce. From the time of the establishment of this first Colony to the year 1807, when Great
Britain and the United States prohibited the slave trade
(a period of 322 years), Africa was desolated and her people abducted, sold and murdered by the Christian people of
the earth; and indeed for many years after its prohibition
the slave trade was carried on, notwithstanding that it became piracy to do so, punishable by death, so profitable had
the business become and so rapacious and insensate those
who engaged in it.

Thus was the slave monster, a gigantic and hideous
Frankenstein, created by the Christian nations, and long
after, when it obtained its full growth, it was to fright
them, retard their progress and result in dreadful retribution. The slave district began with the River Senegal on
the west coast of Africa and continued a distance of fully
3000 miles to Cape Negro. The enormous sum of cruelty
and wickedness which attended the slave trade throughout
this vast territory can never be known, but may be partially
imagined when we know that at its height fully 80,000 persons were torn from their homes annually, with all the attendant horrors of rapine, murder 'and the worst crimes of
mankind.

The evil thus begun and fostered in Europe needed only
a new impetus to make it grow beyond all bounds; owing to
economical conditions, it would probably have died out in
western Europe had it not been for the discovery of America, which almost immediately opened up a new and enor-

mous market for slaves. The first Spanish settlement in the West Indies was called Hispaniola, now the Island of Haiti, and this Colony became the scene of the first use of negro slaves in the New World. A cruel fate seemed to be working out the enslavement of the African, for it is almost certain that Columbus in his first voyages did not take with him any slaves, and there seemed to be no thought of using them in this new Colony during the first few years after the discovery. The first negroes were brought to Hispaniola about eight years after Columbus landed, but they were few in number, and it was probably not contemplated to use them in the fields and mines, for the Spaniards had an immense and almost inexhaustible supply of free labor at hand in the native population, who, by the avarice of the Spaniards, were almost immediately enslaved and compelled to work in the mines and on the farms. So greedy were the Spaniards to acquire sudden wealth, and so numerous the natives, that their lives were reckoned of no value, and so heartlessly cruel and inhuman was their treatment that the population of the island, which is given as about 800,000 in 1492, had decreased, it is estimated, one-third four years later, and twenty years later the native population is given as only 14,000. These figures are probably greatly exaggerated, but making all allowances they tell a frightful story.

The benevolent Las Casas, aroused by the frightful cruelties to the natives and their rapid destruction, began his successful opposition to Indian slavery; but, without knowing or intending it, his success was at the fearful cost of the Africans, who now began to be imported in large numbers to take the place of Indian slaves, and it was shortly discovered that one negro could do the work of four or five natives. Thus a new and growing market opened for slaves, and the slave trade of the New World became so profitable that Charles V. of Spain, desiring to reap the greatest benefit from it, granted, for a consideration, an exclusive right for eight years of supplying four thousand slaves per year to the Spanish Colonies. This seems to have been the first monopoly on the slave trade, but soon other nations were attracted by the ease and profit of the business, and the Dutch and English began early to engage their energies in the trade, and the latter, with their superior methods, greatly increased its profit and popularity. William Hawkins was the first Englishman to begin the slave trade, and made a trip to Guinea in 1530. In 1562 his son, John Hawkins, who was knighted later for his services by Queen Elizabeth, followed in his father's steps and carried away three hundred slaves to San Domingo. This voyage was repeated in 1564 and 1567 with great profit, and soon England had entered and was committed fully to the business. One hundred and fifty years later the traffic in negro slaves was considered the most profitable branch of British commerce.

Thus it is seen that prior to the discovery of America negro slavery had begun in western Europe, and, like some dread scourge, lay in wait for new fields in which to operate; and we have seen how it was permitted to enter so early into the history of the New World. From the islands of the West Indies the Spaniards went to the mainland, and with them went slavery; and as more territory was discovered the use of slaves was more in demand and they were brought over in almost incredible numbers. This history is not further concerned with the development of slavery in other countries, or with the horrifying details of the slave trade which grew up to supply the enormous demand of the New World, except as it affected this country.

How slavery became established in the United States, how it dominated the first attempts of the Colonies to organize a strong Federal Government, and how, after a series of compromises, seeking to settle a question which could only be settled by its abolition, it resulted in the organization of a great opposition political party, the first success of which was followed by the bloodiest civil war in all history, will now be the direct subject of our inquiry.

CHAPTER III.

BEGINNING OF SLAVERY IN THE UNITED STATES.

"I do not say who was guilty of this........but there was the evil, and no man could see how we were to be delivered from it."

Frelinghuysen.

Ayllon, a Spaniard, who attempted to find the northwest passage, landed in Virginia as early as 1526, near the same place where the English eighty-one years later founded their colony, and began to build a town, using negro slaves in the work, but this settlement was abandoned. Negro slaves were also used in Florida prior to the Jamestown settlement. These appear to be the first use of negro slaves in territory subsequently a part of the United States. But we are not concerned with these events except as curious historical facts, because they had no influence on the history of the country, and are of no more importance or interest than the discovery of America by the Norsemen before Columbus. But toward the end of August, 1620, an event occurred of the greatest moment to the history and welfare of the country, and which was to have a far-reaching and lasting effect upon the political and social life of the United States. In that month, about thirteen years after the English founded their settlement, a Dutch ship, in great distress for food, entered the James River, and after

(22)

some negotiation with the settlers, exchanged twenty negroes for a supply of food. This was the beginning of negro slavery in the United States, and thus was the disturbing element planted which was to distract the nation for so many weary years, and the opposition to which was finally to culminate in the founding of the Republican Party.

Not many months after these slaves were landed the Pilgrims established their settlement on the New England shores and began that political and social life whose subsequent development made them an enemy to slavery. If there is one scene or period in American history representing the very genesis of the Republican Party, it is the landing of the Pilgrims in December, 1620; just as the settlement at Jamestown, Virginia, was the point from which radiated, by subsequent economical and social developments, the principles of the Democratic Party. Thus it is seen at this early period that slavery and freedom were planted almost side by side to progress along unconsciously until economical conditions and demands were to make them openly antagonistic; and. here began that remarkable balancing of power between slavery and freedom, which was to be maintained in later years, after the Union had been formed, by a series of compromises, and indeed also by a balancing of progress along economical lines.

The Virginians at first neither sought nor needed negro slaves; this is proven by the circumstances under which the first slaves were landed, and also by the fact that slavery grew very slowly. In 1622 there were only twenty-two negro slaves in the Colony, and in 1648, twenty-eight years after the first acquisition, there were only three hundred in Virginia; not that the settlers were averse to using them, but because another class of cheap labor was obtainable in the great number of criminals which were sent from England to work out their freedom in the New World, and by other white persons who voluntarily sold themselves and became indented or bond servants for a period of years in payment of their passage to America, or for other considerations. The use of this class of labor began very shortly after the first settlement, but toward the close of the seventeenth century the use of indented servants became less as negro slaves became more numerous.

Negro slaves were introduced into every one of the other Colonies when they were founded, or a short time afterwards, and to the close of the Revolution negro slaves were used in every Colony. The North was for slavery as long as it was necessary and profitable, and the early settlers in New England found no scruple in using as slaves the Indians captured in war; and when negro slavery appeared later, the shrewd Yankees made money in the slave trade along the coast to the South and to the West Indies. The modern Newport, R. I., was the great slave mart of New England, and it is said that the first slave ship used by American colonists was fitted up in a New England port.

Prior to 1715 the number of slaves in America was not so great, but after that year they increased in large numbers, not only by an active demand which sprang up for them, but also by the infamous Asiento Clause in the

Treaty of Utrecht between England and Spain, whereby the former for a period of thirty years, from 1713 to 1743, took the exclusive right of importing and selling 144,000 negroes into the Spanish Colonies at the rate of 4,800 per year, and more could be brought in on the payment of a small tax. This made England the greatest slave nation in the world, and her interest demanded, and Parliament saw to it, that nothing adverse to the use of slaves should happen in the American Colonies. The growth of slavery in America from 1715 to 1775, and the slave population in the Colonies at these two periods, were as follows:

	1715	1775
New Hampshire	150	629
Massachusetts	2,000	3,500
Rhode Island	500	4,373
Connecticut	1,500	5,000
New York	4,000	15,000
New Jersey	1,500	7,600
Pennsylvania . . . . }	2,500	10,000
Delaware . . . . }		9,000
Maryland	9,500	80,000
Virginia	23,000	165,000
North Carolina	3,700	75,000
South · Carolina	10,500	110,000
Georgia		16,000
	58,850	501,102

Of the half million slaves in this country at the opening of the Revolution, 450,000 were in the Southern Colonies. The reasons for this are found in the difference in economical conditions and political and social customs which separated the Northern and Southern Colonies before the Revolution. The Northern group devoted themselves mainly to fishing, commerce and farming. The soil, especially in New England, was unpromising for the production of great staples, and the result in the North was concentration of the people, growth of town life, distribution of political power, great freedom of speech and press, and a wide discussion of political principles. The South devoted herself wholly to the production of three great staples, rice, indigo and tobacco, and the result in the South was just the reverse of that in the North. Great plantations were established, few cities of any importance sprang up, manufacturing did not thrive, the South importing almost every article of use or luxury. Political power was in the hands of a few, and the three great staples demanded cheap labor, working under the most destructive conditions. Thus, influenced almost entirely by environment and economical and political development, the North became the scene of freedom to individuals and protection to industries, because these things were absolutely essential to the existence and happiness of the people; and the South, by the same necessity, was dedicated to slavery and free trade.

It must not be thought that the colonial period was without any development of opposition to slavery. The German Quakers of Pennsylvania in 1688 took a stand against the use of slaves in their community, and they subsequently became the most active opponents to slavery and the slave trade. Their efforts, however, had little effect except in Pennsylvania, but it is important to mark their

action as the beginning of the abolition movement in this
country. There are records in the Southern Colonies of
taxes placed upon the importation of slaves prior to the decade before the Revolution, but it would appear that these
taxes were more for revenue than as prohibitive means,
and that they were of no value in diminishing the demand
and the number of negroes imported. However, in 1769, a
distinct sentiment crystallized in Virginia against the further importation of slaves, and the Legislature passed a
law prohibiting it, but this was vetoed by the Royal Governor, acting under orders from the Crown; the same thing
occurred in Massachusetts two years later. In 1772 Lord
Mansfield proclaimed the law, "As soon as a slave sets foot
on the soil of the British isles he becomes free." This decision had a marked influence on the anti-slavery sentiment, which was now strong in the Colonies, and the ap-
proach of the Revolution, with its spirit of national independence and of individual right to life, liberty and the
pursuit of happiness, seemed to promise freedom to a people who had already suffered three centuries of terrible
bondage.

CHAPTER IV

THE EARLY FEDERAL GOVERNMENT.

"The policy to sustain which Mr. Lincoln was elected President in 1860 was first definitely outlined by Jefferson in 1784. It was the policy of forbidding slavery in the National Territory."

John Fiske.

The history of slavery from the opening scenes of the Revolution to the meeting of the First Congress affords a curious example of the direct influence of self-interest upon the opinions of mankind. The opening of the Revolution saw an emphatic and unanimous expression against slavery and the slave trade, and a general spirit of emancipation was abroad. Two years later this had changed, for when the Declaration was promulgated there was no mention of anti-slavery sentiments in it, and as Independence became more and more assured, the feeling against slavery seems to have weakened, and finally, when a serious attempt to perfect the Union was made, the slave question was decided by expediency and not by principle.

In 1773 and 1774, when the colonists spoke their final defiance against Great Britain, and the latter launched her retaliatory measures, the climax was reached. It is to be kept in mind that at this time slavery existed in every one of the Colonies. The First Continental Congress, representing all the Colonies except Georgia (who agreed to con-

(28)

THE WHITE HOUSE WASHINGTON D. C.

cur), met at Philadelphia in September, 1774, to determine what should be done in this grave crisis. It turned
out to be largely a Peace Congress, but a protest, several ad-
dresses and a non-importation and non-consumption agreement was signed. One of the Articles of this agreement
provided that "We will neither import nor purchase any
slave imported after the first day of December next, after
which time we will wholly discontinue the slave trade, and
will neither be concerned in it ourselves, nor will we hire
our vessels or sell our commodities or manufactures to
those who are concerned in it." This important and far-
reaching resolution received the unanimous support of all
the Colonies. Would that its spirit had been kept alive!

Almost two years after the First Continental Congress
met (the Revolution having been started in the meantime)
the Declaration of Independence was adopted, but there
was no expression in it against slavery or the slave trade.
The original draft of that instrument contained a fierce
denunciation of England's part in the slave trade:

> "He has waged cruel war against human nature
> itself, violating its most sacred rights of life and
> liberty in the persons of a distant people who
> never offended him; capturing and carrying them
> into slavery in another hemisphere, or to incur a
> miserable death in their transportation thither.
> This piratical warfare, the opprobrium of Infidel
> Powers, is the warfare of the Christian King of
> Great Britain. Determined to keep open a mar-
> ket where men could be bought and sold, he has
> prostituted his negative by suppressing every leg-

islative attempt to prohibit or restrain this execrable commerce."

These burning words were from the pen of Jefferson, who
had been the most active in his opposition to slavery. They
were omitted from the Declaration, out of compliance to
South Carolina and Georgia, but they voiced unquestionably the sentiment of a large majority of the Continental
Congress. This was the first fatal concession to South
Carolina and Georgia, and we shall find them again united
and influencing the other Southern Colonies to maintain a
bold stand for slavery at the most critical period in the nation's history.

On the same day in June, 1776, that the Committee was
appointed to draft the Declaration of Independence, Con
gress resolved that "A Committee be appointed to prepare
and digest the form of a Confederation to be entered into
between the Colonies." The work of this Committee was
the Articles of Confederation, which were presented in
November, 1777, for ratification by the States. These
Articles contained no anti-slavery sentiments, and we are
only concerned with them in noting the unexpected and
most important results which came up before the ratification was completed. Several of the States claimed a right
to the territory west of the Alleghanies to the Mississippi
under their original charter. Their claims were conflicting, and Maryland refused to ratify the Articles of Confederation until the land-claiming States should relinquish
all their rights to Congress. For a number of years these
States were obdurate, but Maryland held out resolutely and

bravely, and finally, by her firm action and the magnanimity of New York and Virginia, the question was settled by the cession of the disputed lands to Congress. The acquisition of the Northwest Territory is one of the great turning points in American history, for we shall see that the subsequent development of this territory was of no less importance than the saving of the Union from annihilation by the slave power.

Thomas Jefferson was the most urgent against slavery of all the founders of the nation. His statesmanship foresaw the evils negro slavery would bring upon the nation's social and political development, and his nature was stirred by the great moral wrong. Long before the Declaration of Independence he worked untiringly in Virginia to bring about a sentiment against the slave trade, and his efforts met with success. His fierce denunciation of England's part in the slave trade was stricken from the Declaration, but he did not give up the fight, although the material interests of the South thwarted his plans for the moment. When, by the unforeseen results attendant upon the ratification of the Articles of Confederation, that imperial domain reaching from Pennsylvania to the Mississippi and from the Ohio to the Lakes became national territory, Jefferson, with the prescience of a mighty genius, saw an opportunity to deal a death blow to slavery. This magnificent public domain, subsequently to be divided into the States of Ohio, Indiana, Illinois, Wisconsin and Michigan, was given to the nation on condition that it should be cut up into States, to be admitted when they had a certain population, and that the land should be sold to pay the debts of the United States. Throughout this vast region there were very few people, and there had been no social, political or economical development, and so the only opposition which could come in Congress to any measure for the future government of the Territory would be from the original States. No sooner had the cession been fully made than Jefferson suggested a plan which, if it had succeeded, would have confined slavery North and South to the mountain boundaries of the original States. His plan for the government of this new territory, among other things, provided that after the year 1800 slavery should be prohibited in it. He went beyond this and advocated and urgently solicited Virginia, North Carolina, South Carolina and Georgia to cede their rights in the land west of the Mountains, and he would have had slavery prohibited in this territory also after the year 1800. His plan was no more or less than to prohibit slavery after the year 1800 in all land between the Alleghanies and the Mississippi, from the Lakes to Florida.

On April 19, 1784, Jefferson's Ordinance came up for consideration. North Carolina moved that the clause prohibiting slavery after 1800 be stricken out; South Carolina seconded the motion, which was put in the form, "Shall the words moved to be stricken out stand?" Six States voted that the clause should stand, three were opposed to it, but as the Articles of Confederation required the votes of nine States, the motion was lost and the Ordinance, with the slavery clause taken out, was then adopted.

The following year Congress made inducements so attractive that in a short time several companies were organized and bought large tracts in the new National Territory; and as they purposed settling on their purchases at once, Congress agreed upon a more elaborate plan of government and laws than those set forth in the Ordinance of 1784. The famous Ordinance of 1787 was the result of this agreement. Mr. Jefferson was not present at the time of its adoption, having been sent as Minister to France, but the influence of his work and sentiments were felt, and his ideas were adopted in a new form. The new Ordinance repealed the old one, and among other things provided that the Territory should be cut up into not less than three nor more than five States, all of which were to be admitted into the Union when they had a population of 60,000 free inhabitants. The States which might be formed were forever to remain a part of the United States, and it was declared that the Ordinance was to be considered as a compact between the original States and the people and States of the new territory, and forever to remain unalterable unless by common consent. Most important and far-reaching of all was the Article,

"There shall be neither slavery nor involuntary servitude in the said territory, otherwise than in the punishment of crimes, whereof the party shall have been duly convicted; Provided always, that any person escaping into the same, from whom labor or service is lawfully claimed in any one of the original States, such fugitive may be lawfully reclaimed, and conveyed to the person claiming his or her labor or service, as aforesaid."

With slavery forever prohibited in such a large territory, with the Ordinance beyond repeal, and secession condemned, the Ordinance of 1787 stands out as one of the
most remarkable and most important enactments in American history. What the Declaration of Independence and
the War had obtained, and the Constitution was to make
more perfect—the Union—the development of the country
under the Ordinance of 1787 was to preserve. The South
yielded to the strong anti-slavery clause in this ordinance
because a fugitive slave clause was added to it, and because
she had a plan of making the territory west of Virginia,
North Carolina, South Carolina and Georgia slave territory.
This was done shortly afterwards, when two years later
South Carolina and North Carolina, and Georgia in 1802,
ceded their western claims to Congress on the express condition that it should be slave soil, and Congress accepted
the territory on that condition; Kentucky being admitted
as a slave State in 1792.

While the national greatness and safety were being
worked out in the West, affairs were in a miserable condition in the East, owing to the radical defects in the Articles of Confederation which had been in operation since
1781. The cup of bitter national humiliation was being
drained to the dregs, but fortunately the best men of the
country finally succeeded in calling a Convention to revise
the Articles. The Convention met at Philadelphia in May,
1787, and by September had adopted a new Constitution.

The great struggle between the North and the South began in the Constitutional Convention. Slavery and the

conflicting commercial interests were the difficult questions
which divided the country and resulted in the first of the
Compromises that held off the Civil War for so many
years. It was decided to have an equal representation of
States in the Senate and an unequal representation in the
House, based upon population; but should slaves be
counted as population? This and the other slavery questions which came up in the Convention threatened to dis-
rupt the proceedings entirely. There were at this time
about 675,000 slaves in the country, of which number fully
625,000 were in the South. South Carolina, henceforth to
be so active for the interests of the South, immediately
claimed that these slaves should be considered as population to be counted in fixing the representation in the House.
The North argued that the slaves were chattels and should
not be counted, for it was seen at a glance that if this enormous number of slaves were to be counted on any basis,
the political power of the South would be greatly increased.
South Carolina made open and repeated threats to withdraw from the Confederacy, and the situation was serious,
because, without her and the other Southern Colonies, who
would unquestionably be influenced by her, the work of the
Convention would not be ratified, and there would be no
Union. The inexorable necessity of the hour demanded a
compromise, and it was decided that in apportioning the
Representatives there should be added to the whole number
of free persons three-fifths of all other persons. This was
equivalent to saying that five slaves in the South should be
counted the same as three white persons in the North.

In regard to the slave trade there was a sentiment in all the States except Georgia and South Carolina against it, because five slaves counted as three whites, and because almost all of the eminent men North and South were at this time opposed to Slaverv itself as not only a moral wrong, but as something which would injure the development of the country. The Southern planters insisted upon a continuation of the slave trade, but at the same time they were fearful that the North might tax their exports. The second great 'Compromise was affected, and it was agreed that the importation of such persons as any of the States might think proper to admit should not be prohibited by Congress prior to 1808, but a tax on each person so admitted might be imposed, not exceeding $10, and that no tax or duty should be laid on articles exported from any State. A Fugitive Slave Clause very similar to that contained in the Ordinance of 1787 was also added.

By these Compromises, especially the one giving representation for slaves, the South was given that tremendous political power which she wielded so long to threaten and coerce the North to her bidding. The Slave Power was politically enthroned, not to be finally dislodged until the election of Mr. Lincoln. At this early period, however, it was firmly and honestly believed that in a very short time slavery would disappear in all of the Colonies, as it was already dying out rapidly in the North, and it was fully believed that after 1808, when the slave trade should be prohibited, slavery would become extinct. It must be remembered that at this time cotton was not a staple of the South, and there was nothing seriously present or threatened, in the social or economical development of the South, which made slavery absolutely necessary. Nobody foresaw how greatly cotton was to add to the wealth and standing of the South, and nobody foresaw the great injury which the Constitution was to do the North.

When Washington was inaugurated, April 30, 1789, the United States reached from the Atlantic to the Mississippi, and from the Lake of the Woods, the Great Lakes, the St. Lawrence and St. Croix Rivers southward to Florida, which then extended to the Mississippi and was owned by Spain.

All of the threatening phases of the slave question had been compromised by the various provisions in the Constitution, and the common territory of the nation had been practically partitioned between Freedom and Slavery, with the Ohio River as the dividing line. With some exceptions the Northern States still possessed a large number of slaves, New York and New Jersey having the greatest number (33,000 out of the 40,000 still in the North), but not only in these States, but throughout the North, emancipation was making rapid progress.

The population of the country was scattered along the Atlantic seaboard, but the migration to the west of the Alleghanies had set in strongly both north and south of the Ohio River; the settlers from Virginia and the States south of her carrying with them, westward, the prejudices and customs of their mother States, while the settlers north of the Ohio River took with them into the wilderness the energy and thrift of the East, and its spirit of freedom and emancipation for all individuals, laying the foundation of those great States which, in later years, untrammeled by the commercial conservatism of the East, were so outspoken and sturdy in their expressions against slavery. The first census, taken in 1790, showed a population of 3,929,827, classed and divided between the North and South as follows:

	White.	Free Negroes.	Slave.
North	1,900,976	27,109	40,370
South	1,271,488	32,357	657,527

These figures are interesting because of the political effect that the population of the two sections had upon the representation in the House.

The South was still devoting herself to the raising of tobacco, rice, indigo, and several lesser staples, but since the close of the Revolution, owing to the dying out of the indigo plant, a new staple had received considerable attention. Cotton had been cultivated in Virginia by the early settlers, but little attention had been paid to it, and only enough was produced for domestic use; but after the close of the Revolution it gradually came to be cultivated in all the Southern States, and it was quickly discovered that being an indigenous plant it grew very rapidly, and the climate, soil and the great number of slaves at hand were favorable toward making it, with some attention, a most promising and valuable product.

The development of cotton manufacture had been gradual but certain to this period, which saw the triumph and use of the mechanical inventions of Hargreave, Arkwright, Crompton and Cartwright. The steam engine was introduced to supply motive power, and only one thing stood in the way of an enormous production of the new staple. The separation of the seed from the cotton fibre was a tedious and time-consuming task; one negro could only remove the seeds from about two pounds of cotton a day, and consequently only a small amount could be sent to market.

In 1790 not a pound of cotton was exported from the United States. In 1793, Eli Whitney, of Massachusetts, who was temporarily in Georgia, invented his Cotton Gin, one of the earliest and most remarkable of the many great inventions of Americans. This invention was productive of most important and far-reaching consequences. It caused an industrial revolution in the South by making cotton the great staple. The production increased by leaps and bounds, bringing great wealth and increasing social and political power to the South. With the earlier form of the new invention the seeds could be removed from about one hundred pounds of cotton a day. In 1792, 192,000 pounds were exported to Europe; in 1795, after Whitney's invention, nearly six million pounds were exported. The value of the export in 1800 was $5,700,000; in 1820, it was $20,000,000. These figures represented enormous wealth in those days.

Whatever sentiment in the South against slavery had survived the Constitutional period now disappeared completely. Cotton brought about a new view, and from being an evil to be eradicated in some way in the course of time, it was now regarded as absolutely necessary to the social and political welfare of the South. The strongest of human passions, avarice, ambition and worldly interest now bound the South closer than ever to slavery. The slaves produced cotton—which was wealth—and wealth brought independence and social distinction; besides the slave was a political advantage of great importance, because five of them, without any voice in the matter themselves, counted as three white persons. Under these auspices grew the Slave Power, soon to be a bold, threatening and overbearing faction in the nation.

While the South and the Slave Power were thus being prepared for great wealth and political standing, circumstances were working in the North to counteract and balance, in a way, this development. New England was beginning to feel the first impulses of a great industrial development; interest in commerce and manufacturing was awakening, and inventive genius, called into action by economical necessity, was at work, and the use of machinery and mechanical inventions was increasing. New England was shortly to be covered with cotton and other factories.

The war between France and England opened to the United States almost a monopoly on the West Indies trade in 1793, and it was the North that received the greatest benefit from this trade. Congress in 1791 had established the United States Bank at Philadelphia, with branches in all of the important cities, and this aided the North more than the South. In short, the North was developing that capital, energy, ingenuity and thrift and use of mechanical inventions, the lack of which was the greatest weakness of the South. The settlement of the Northwest Territory by pioneers from the northern States is also to be kept in mind.

This great manufacturing and commercial development, and the movement of the population westward, also awakened in the North a lively interest in internal improvements, and the steamboat, railroad and telegraph were soon to add their tremendous influences and advantages to this section of the country. The various pursuits and the development of the North increased and attracted population, and the balance between the North and the South, which was so nearly even in 1790, grew steadily in favor of the North, until at the opening of the Civil War the North had nineteen million free people against eight and one-quarter million in the South, the South at that time having four million slaves.

CHAPTER V.

"The Missouri question marked a distinct era in the political thought of the country.   suddenly and without warning the North and the South, the free States and the slave States, found themselves arrayed against each other in violent and absorbing conflict."

James G. Blaine.

Shall there be Slave States other than Louisiana west of the Mississippi River? This question coming suddenly before the people in 1818, laying bare the inherent antagonisms of the North and South, aroused the entire country to a white heat of excitement; and only after a most bitter and alarming struggle resulted in the third great Compromise on the slavery question.

From the time of Whitney's invention to the Missouri Compromise, three important events happened in the history of slavery: The first Fugitive Slave Law passed in January, 1793; the acquisition of the Louisiana Territory in 1803, and the abolition of the slave trade in 1807.

The call for legislation to enforce the Fugitive Slave provision in the Constitution came, strangely enough, from the North. A free negro had been kidnapped in Pennsylvania in 1791 and taken to Virginia. The Governor of Virginia refused to surrender the kidnappers, claiming

(42)

there was no law on the subject. Upon the matter being brought to the attention of Congress by the Governor of Pennsylvania, a Fugitive Slave Law and also an Extradiiton Law for fugitives from justice were enacted. While the fugitive from justice was surrounded by the safeguards of a requisition accompanied by a certified copy of an indictment or affidavit charging the crime, these safeguards were not given to the slave, but he could be forcibly seized by the owner or his agent and taken before a magistrate. There was no trial by jury, and the only requisite for conviction was an affidavit that he had escaped. The harshness of this procedure was resisted from the very first by the northern people, but this law was on the statute books until the second and last law on the subject was passed as a part of the Compromise of 1850.

When the time came at which Congress could abolish the slave trade, a law was promptly passed, after considerable angry debate as to its terms, prohibiting the slave trade after December 31, 1807. In fact, it was necessary to even effect a compromise on this subject on the point as to what should be done with any slaves that might be imported contrary to the law; and it was decided that they should belong neither to the importer nor any purchaser, but should be subject to the regulations of the State in which they might be brought. As far as it restrained the South, the law abolishing the slave trade proved to be more of a dead letter than the Fugitive Slave Law did in the North, because the slave trade was carried on with more or less openness until the Civil War, it being estimated that about fifteen thousand slaves were brought into the country annually. The abolition of the slave trade caused several of the border States to devote their attention to slave breeding, which, with the increased demand and the large advance in prices, became a profitable industry in Virginia, Maryland and Kentucky.

The acquisition in 1803 of the Louisiana Territory, the wonderful and romantic exploration of it by Lewis and Clark in 1804-5, the closing of the Indian Wars and the second war with England, and hard times in the East, caused that tremendous rush of population to the West, which resulted in the admission of so many new States prior to 1820, and opened anew the slavery question. Vermont, admitted in 1791, Kentucky 1792, Tennessee 1796, Ohio 1803, Louisiana 1812, Indiana 1816, Mississippi 1817, Illinois 1818, and Alabama 1819, had raised the number of States to twenty-two; eleven free and eleven slave; the early custom of admitting a free and slave State together having been strictly followed. The admission of these States effectively partitioned all of the territory east of the Mississippi between Freedom and Slavery, with the exception of the Michigan Territory (subsequently divided into Michigan and Wisconsin), and the new Territory of Florida, purchased from Spain in 1819. West of the Mississippi only one State had been admitted, and the rest of the land was known as the Missouri Territory. The tide of population passing down the Ohio, or through the States, had crossed the Mississippi into the Missouri country, and Missouri, in 1818, petitioned Congress for permission to

THE CAPITOL, WASHINGTON, D. C.

form a Constitution and enter the Union. Nothing was
said about slavery, but it was known that the great majority
of the Missouri settlers were slave owners or sympathizers.
as those who held anti-slavery opinions were content to remain in the States formed out of the Northwest Territory,
and it was therefore certain that Missouri would be a slave
State.

The Bill authorizing Missouri to act was taken up in
the House on February 13, 1819, and immediately Mr.
Tallmadge, of New York, moved that the further introduction of slavery in Missouri be prohibited, and that children
born in the State after its admission should be free at the
age of twenty-five years. Instantly and unexpectedly an
exciting, violent debate took place between the North and
South. Neither professed to understand the position of the
other, but the North was more sincerely astonished, because
for the first time she realized what the South had intended
for many years, that slavery should be made a permanent
institution in the original States, and that it should be
forced into the Missouri Territory as a matter of political
necessity; because the extension of slave area had by this
time become absolutely necessary for the interests of the
South.

It was a plain proposition that if the South lost control
of the legislative reins at Washington, slavery would eventually be doomed by adverse legislation and by the admission of free States. At the time the Missouri question
came up, the North, by reason of her larger population,
controlled the House, but the Senate was controlled by the

South. The censuses taken in 1800 and 1810 had shown that the North was increasing two to one in population over the South, and the coming census, it was feared, would show a much larger increase in favor of the North; in fact, when the census for 1820 was published the division of the population was as follows:

	White.	Free Negroes.	Slaves.
North 5,030,371		99,281	19,108
South 2,831,560		134,223	1,519,017

With a great moral weakness to justify, the South now knew herself to be growing physically weaker, and her skillful leaders, always alert on every phase of slavery, saw quickly that the South must insist upon more slave territory, not only to maintain the equilibrium in the Senate, but to counteract the growing population in the North. Therefore the Missouri question was pressed with violence, threat and strategy. The South was determined that Missouri should come in as a slave State or the South would secede from the Union; the North not only argued that slavery was a great wrong, not to be encouraged by its extension, but was equally determined that the South should have no more political advantage because of her slaves. "This momentous question," wrote Jefferson, "like a fire-bell in the night, awakened and filled me with terror."

With the two Sections dead-locked, nothing could take place but the most acrimonious debates, accompanied by threats and defiances. The House adopted the Tallmadge Amendment, but it was rejected by the Senate. Neither branch would recede from its position, and amid scenes of the greatest excitement in Washington and throughout the country, the Fifteenth Congress adjourned.

The Sixteenth Congress met on December 6, 1819, and the Missouri question came up immediately. A compromise that the territory west of the Mississippi should be divided in the same manner as that east of the river was rejected by the North. Fortunately or unfortunately, there is some difficulty in deciding which, Maine applied at this time for admission, and the South in the Senate refused to admit Maine unless the North would admit Missouri, and out of the situation rose the Missouri Compromise. By a close majority the Senate joined Maine and Missouri in the same Bill, and then Senator Jesse B. Thomas, of Illinois, moved that, excepting Missouri, slavery should forever be prohibited in all the Louisiana Territory north of 36 degrees 30 minutes north latitude, this being the southern boundary of Missouri. The Bill was taken to the House toward the end of January, 1820, but it refused to concur. The Senate stood fast, and after some further angry debate the House yielded early in March, 1820; Maine came into the Union, and Missouri was permitted to draft a Constitution, which, if acceptable, would admit her to statehood.

But the difficulty was not over, for when Missouri presented her Constitution it was found to contain a provision that the Legislature should pass a law preventing free negroes from settling in the State. The North violently opposed this provision and refused to admit Missouri, and the situation was even more serious than when the original subject was considered. The intense excitement spread from Washington throughout the country, and many felt that the Union would be dissolved. The debate continued until the middle of February, 1821, without solution, and Congress was to adjourn early in March. Maine had already been admitted, and her representatives were in Congress. The South felt that she had been betrayed. Finally a second compromise on the Missouri question was reached, through the efforts of Henry Clay, and Missouri was admitted upon condition that no law should ever be passed by her to enforce the objectionable provision in her Constitution.

While it was true that the North received in area decidedly the best of the bargain, the Missouri Compromise was a distinct victory and gain for the South, because she obtained a present, tangible and important advantage in the admission of a slave State and the establishment of slavery in the heart of the Louisiana Territory. The North obtained nothing but a hazy, speculative advantage, and as the subsequent history of this Compromise proved, the South intended to keep it only as long as it served her interests.

On the subject of the sacredness of the various Compromises on slavery, it is interesting to note that a strong attempt was made to set aside the Ordinance of 1787. After Ohio had been admitted the rest of the Northwest Territory was organized under the name of the Indiana Territory, and as many of the settlers were slavery sympathizers, they very early (1802), under the lead of William Henry Harrison, asked Congress to at least temporarily suspend the operation of the Ordinance of 1787. This was refused, but Governor Harrison and a large number of the settlers persisted until 1807 in their efforts; fortunately Congress took no action, and in 1816 Indiana came in as a free State. There was a struggle to make Illinois a slave State, by amending her Constitution, which continued until 1824.

The Compromise of 1820 practically settled the slavery question for twenty-five years, for the question only came up in a serious form when new territory was acquired and the manner of its division arose. No more States were admitted until 1836, when Arkansas became a State, to be balanced by the admission of Michigan in 1837. From 1820 to 1845 the main issues before the people were those relating to the Tariff, Re-chartering the Bank of the United States, and Internal improvements.

The greatest political excitement, having an important bearing upon the feeling between the North and South, was the opposition of the South to the protective Tariffs of 1824 and 1828, and to the question of Internal improvements. As a culmination of her opposition, South Carolina passed a Nullification Ordinance in 1832, based upon the doctrine of State rights as advocated by John C. Calhoun, but the difficulty was settled by Clay's Compromise Tariff Bill of 1833. The opprobrium of nullification and secession, however, does not rest entirely with the South; the Federal Press of New England and many Federal leaders in Congress deliberately discussed and planned a Secession Movement in 1803-4 because they thought that the purchase of the Louisiana Territory was unconstitutional and that it would give the South an advantage which the North would never overcome. This movement, however, never gained strength enough to be serious.

One result of the Missouri Compromise, most important in its political effect, was that it created a solid South. and divided the North into various opinions as to what should exactly be done to meet the evil. It was this uncertainty on the part of the North and the lack of organization on the direct subject of slavery opposition that permitted the South to hold out so long after she had been greatly outnumbered in population and left far behind in material progress.

CHAPTER VI.

"If we have whispered Truth,
  Whisper no longer;
Speak as the tempest does,
  Sterner and stronger."

"Song of the Free," *Whittier*, 1836.

Great changes in the political and economical life of a nation seldom take place abruptly. The forces responsible for a change or modification of conditions are generally at work long before the final result. Nations, like individuals, grope for the truth, forming different opinions, trying different plans—now radical, now conservative—often failing to see and grasp the solution when it is at hand, but all the while bringing about conditions which, when the crisis comes, form a solid and decisive basis for action. Such is the history of this country with reference to slavery for the three decades prior to the Civil War. From 1833 to the organization of the Republican Party, and after that event to the promulgation of the Emancipation Proclamation, public opinion was incessantly agitated by the organized efforts of the Abolitionists, although they differed among themselves and divided as to the best plan under which to act.

While the Northerners grouped into the Whig and

(51)

Democratic Parties, and condemned the constant agitation of the slavery question as disturbing the public peace and jeopardizing party success, still they could not help recognizing the cogency of the abolition argument; and as year after year went by, and the aggressions of the slave power continued, a steady change went on in the North and the anti-slavery sentiment became more and more pronounced. When active political opposition to slavery finally began it found the North not exactly unanimous as to what should be done, but with her mind almost made up on one point, that slavery should at least be restricted to the territory it then occupied; it required a great political shock, such as came in 1854, to amalgamate this sentiment. From this standpoint the opinions in the North reached out to the ex· treme views of Garrison and his followers, that slavery should be stamped out regardless of all consequences.

The Quakers, who, from the early colonial days, had been strongest in their expressions against slavery, formed the first Anti-Slavery Society in the United States at Philadelphia in 1775. The Revolution interrupted their work, but at its conclusion they resumed their efforts patiently and incessantly, year after year, in their attempts to arouse the public mind to the enormity and dangerousness of the slave evil. Although other States organized anti-slavery societies immediately after the Revolution, the Pennsylvania Society took the leading part, and was comparatively alone for many years in the work. In the First Congress this Society presented a Memorial, asking Congress to exercise its utmost powers for the abolition of slavery. The subject was the occasion of a heated debate, and Congress decided that under the Constitution it could not, prior to 1808, abolish the slave trade; but that it had authority to prevent citizens of the United States from carrying on the African slave trade with other nations (a law to this effect was subsequently passed); and that it had no authority to interfere with the emancipation of slaves or their treatment in any of the States. The Pennsylvania Society watched Congress closely and worked along patiently year after year, meeting with failure after failure. This early Abolition movement had among its supporters the foremost men of the day—Washington, Jefferson, Franklin, Hamilton, Jay and Henry are some of the illustrious names connected with the movement, just as in England the names of Burke, Fox and Pitt are recorded against the iniquity. When the purchase of the Louisiana Territory came before Congress, the Pennsylvania Society petitioned that measures should be taken to prevent slavery in the new territory, but the Federalists were more engrossed with a discussion of Constitutional questions, and the opportune moment went by without any action on the matter.

The agitation connected with the Missouri question brought about the formation of a stronger anti-slavery sentiment in the North, and a group of fearless men sprang up to devote their lives and energies to an Abolition movement. They were radical in their views, progressive in their methods and absolutely fearless in their denunciations. Benjamin Lundy, a Quaker, may be said to be the father of the Abolition movement. In 1821 he began the publication of *The Genius of Universal Emancipation,* the first Abolition paper; he was joined at Baltimore in 1829 by William Lloyd Garrison, henceforth to be the most zealous, unceasing and uncompromising of all the Abolitionists. Garrison, extreme in his views, left Lundy, and in January, 1831, at Boston, without capital and with little help, started *The Liberator,* and placed at its head, "The Constitution of the United States is a covenant with death and an agreement with Hell," which declaration was printed in every edition of the paper until President Lincoln's Emancipation Proclamation went into effect, when it was changed to "Proclaim liberty throughout the land unto all the inhabitants thereof."

As a result of Mr. Garrison's activity many new abolition societies were formed, and on December 4, 1833, a National Convention of them was held at Philadelphia, and the American Anti-Slavery Society was organized, with Beriah Green as President and Lewis Tappan and John G. Whittier as Secretaries. This Convention decided to petition Congress to suppress the domestic slave trade between the States, and to abolish slavery in the District of Columbia and in every place over which Congress had exclusive jurisdiction. It admitted that Congress had no right to interfere with slavery in any State, but its plan was to circulate extensively anti-slavery tracts and periodicals, not only in the North but throughout all of the slaveholding States, and to organize anti-slavery societies in every city and village where possible, and to send forth its agents to lift their voices against slavery. It frowned on the work of the American Colonization Society, which had been organized in 1816, for the purpose of colonizing parts of Africa with American negroes, as tending to deaden the public conscience on the question.

With this energetic organization the anti-slavery move- ment now gained rapidly in strength, but its political work for many years was confined to a fruitless interrogation of candidates and to sending hundreds of petitions and me- morials to Congress. Anti-slavery pamphlets and papers were also sent broadcast North and South. On seeing *The Liberator,* with its extreme views, and on reading the anti- slavery pamphlets, the South was enraged beyond all bounds. A North Carolina Grand Jury indicted Garrison, and Georgia offered a large reward for his arrest and con- viction. On July 29, 1835, all anti-slavery papers were taken from the postoffice at Charleston, S. C., by a mob and destroyed. The following year Mr. Calhoun, in the Senate, demanded the suppression of the right of petition on any matter connected with slavery, and in 1838 the House adopted the infamous Atherton Gag-Rule, "Every Peti- tion, Memorial, Resolution, Proposition or Paper touching or relating in any way or to any extent whatever to slavery or the abolition thereof, shall, on presentation and without further action thereon, be laid upon the table without being debated, printed or referred." This remarkable rule was adopted year after year in the House until 1844, when it was repealed through the efforts of John Quincy Adams, who for ten years fought nobly for the Right of Petition, although he was not entirely in sympathy with the Abolitionists.

During this period the sentiment against the Abolitionists was very strong in the North. In many places mobs seized upon and destroyed their papers and printing presses, and broke up their meetings and mobbed the speakers. James G. Birney's paper, *The Philanthropist,* was twice mobbed in Cincinnati. On November 7, 1837, the Abolition cause was baptized in blood by the murder of Elijah P. Lovejoy, who was shot while defending his paper and press from the attack of a pro-slavery mob at Alton, Illinois. The following month Wendell Phillips delivered his first abolition speech against the aggressions of the Slave Power and the murder of Lovejoy. The continued despotism of the Slave Power, its attempts to muzzle the freedom of speech and press, to deny the Right of Petition, to obstruct the mails, and to obtain an Extradition Law for the trial of citizens in slave States on charges of circulating anti-slavery documents, and the use of violence against all who dared raise their voices against the slavery dogmas, aroused the abolition societies to more radical action, and a group of Abolitionists now formed, determined on political action. This was one of the causes of the disruption of the American Anti-Slavery Society and the withdrawal of Garrison and his followers, who refused to take part in any election held under the pro-slavery Constitution.

The great leaders of the Whigs and Democrats in the North, who were aspirants to the presidency, dared not

take any active stand against the growing demands of the
Slave Power, and both parties bowed abjectly to the monster and passed in silence these gross violations of constitutional rights. Both parties deprecated the slavery agitation, especially the Whigs, who were highly incensed because it jeopardized their candidates more than it did those
of the Democrats. The failure of the two great political
parties to act led to the first political organization of the
anti-slavery sentiment. At Warsaw, New York, on November 13, 1839, the Abolitionists held a convention and
nominated James G. Birney, of New York, for President,
and Thomas Earl, of Pennsylvania, for Vice-President.
This was subsequently called the "Liberty Party," and was
the first of the three anti-slavery parties to appear in national politics. Its platform demanded the abolition of
slavery in the District of Columbia and in the territories;
stoppage of the interstate slave trade, and opposition to
slavery to the fullest extent of Constitutional powers. Mr.
Birney did not desire the nomination, and in the election
of 1840, that resulted in the defeat of Van Buren by Harrison, the Abolitionists received only 7069 votes out of a
total of two and one-half millions. The membership of
the abolition societies at this time was about 200,000; the
failure to show strength at the polls may be accounted for
by reason of the refusal of many to vote at any election
held under the Constitution, and also that many feared the
dissolution of the Union, and preferred, if they voted at
all, to remain with the Democratic or Whig Parties in the

hope that their party would take some decisive action on the question.

While the Slave Power in the United States was making violent efforts to perpetuate itself and stifle all opposition, all the other civilized countries of the world were abolishing slavery. Great Britain abolished it in all her colonies in the year 1833 at a cost of one hundred millions of dollars; but the United States, already showing itself to be the most progressive nation in the world, could not throw off the evil, and it remained a cause of bitter distraction until overthrown politically by the success of the Republican Party and removed by Secession, War, the Emancipation Proclamation, and the amendments to the Constitution.

Although the Abolition cause seemed hopeless after the election of 1840, they persisted in their work, and soon a series of events happened—Texas Annexation, the Mexican War, and the Wilmot Proviso, which, independent of their efforts, brought about a direct issue between the North and South on the great question—an issue to be finally decided only by the Civil War. The work of the early Abolitionists, however, had an influence of inestimable value and weight on the immediate success of the Republican Party when it was organized.

CHAPTER VII.

COMPROMISE OF 1850.

"That as an express and fundamental condition to the acquisition of any territory from the Republic of Mexico by the United States, neither slavery nor involuntary servitude shall ever exist in any part of said territory."

Wilmot Proviso, August 8, 1846.

From the campaign of 1844 to the Civil War the slavery question dominated all others in politics, North and South. During this period almost every legislative question was decided with reference to its effect on slavery. Press, Pulpit and Platform felt the baleful influence of its presence, and aspirants to the presidency and to lesser political honors sacrificed principle, conscience, and the support of their friends to obtain the favor of the aggressive and dominating Slave Power. The Democratic Party during this entire period took a bold stand on the question; an anti-slavery wing of the party appeared in the North, but at no time was it successful in changing the party platforms. The Whig Party, with its strong pro-slavery wing in the South, and with its northern members desirous of party success, omitted entirely any mention of slavery in its platforms, and although the anti-slavery members of the party were outspoken in their private views of slavery, they attended the party conventions and acquiesced in the plat-

(59)

forms until 1852, when there was a general desertion of
the Whig platform and candidate. The refusal of the
Whig Party to make a direct issue of the slavery question
doomed it, sooner or later, to dissolution; and although the
party was successful in 1840 and in 1848, its disintegra-
tion really began after the election of 1840.

To say that the result of the "Log Cabin and Hard
Cider" campaign was a bitter disappointment to both
Democrats and Whigs is putting it mildly. The Democrats
were deeply chagrined at the defeat of their candidate by
a "clap-trap" campaign, and the disappointment of the
Whigs came with the death of President Harrison and the
succession of Tyler, who played directly into the hands of
the Democrats and the Slave Power, bitterly antagonizing
the party that elected him.

The Texas question now came up to disturb politics and
again bring slavery directly before the people. Texas had
gained her independence from Mexico, and had applied, in
1837, to be received into the Union, but the offer was declined by President Van Buren. The tragic death of Mr.
Upshur, Secretary of State, on February 28, 1844, and the
appointment of Mr. Calhoun to that office, made possible
the completion of a long conspiracy to admit Texas, and to
further extend the slave area by a war with Mexico. A
Treaty of Annexation was immediately prepared (April
12, 1844) and presented to the Senate, but was subsequently rejected. It then became apparent that the South
intended to make a political issue of the Texas question,
and there was great alarm in the North, for the admission

of Texas meant a slave area capable of being divided into five or six slave States.   In addition, it meant war with Mexico over disputed boundaries, and the fact that Mexico had not fully recognized the independence of Texas, and the result of that war would unquestionably be the acquisition of more area contiguous to the South.

Mr. Clay and Mr. Van Buren at this time were the only ones prominently mentioned as possibilities for the Whig and Democratic nominations for the presidency; both published letters in which they opposed the annexation of Texas.   Mr. Van Buren's letter cost him the Democratic nomination, for when the Convention met at Baltimore on May 27, 1844, he was unable to obtain a sufficient vote under the two-thirds rule, and the South forced the nomination of James K. Polk of Tennessee.   This division on the slavery question in a Democratic Convention is of great historical importance as a link in the chain of events which led to the final great political division between the North and South.   The Democratic Platform was emphatic in its support of slavery and the condemnation of the Abolitionists; it advocated the annexation of Texas and the occupation of Oregon, and the Democrats went into the campaign with the rallying cry of "Fifty-Four Forty or Fight," in the North—a promise of more free soil—and in the South the "Annexation of Texas."

Mr. Clay's letter had made him stronger than ever with his party and he was nominated unanimously.   The Whig Platform, however, was absolutely silent about the Texas question, and there was absolutely no mention of any opposition to slavery; the whole question was totally ignored. Mr. Clay would have defeated Polk had he not been led into the blunder of writing another letter on the Texas question, in which he largely withdrew from his earlier position; this alienated great numbers of the Northern Whigs and threw thousands of votes to the candidate of the Liberty Party. This party, in a convention at Buffalo the preceding year, had again nominated James G. Birney for President. Its platform was long and elaborate, and contained strong denunciations of slavery and pledged the party to work for its abolition. The Liberty Party polled a total of 62,300 votes, defeating Clay, who lost New York, the pivotal State, with its thirty-six electoral votes, by 5,106, the Liberty Party casting 15,812 votes in that State. Texas annexation followed the election, but the pledge in regard to Oregon was cast aside. "Fifty-four Forty or Fight" was nothing more than a campaign cry, never intended to be followed up, and, in truth, could not have been without a war with England.

With the great Texas victory achieved, the South now turned herself to the acquisition of more territory, and war with Mexico was declared May 11, 1846. The Whig Party in the North was strongly against the Mexican War, and a strong element also expressed itself in the northern Democratic ranks as against it; the opposition became so threatening that, as a new House was to be elected in the Fall of 1846, the Administration decided to end the War, if possible, and Congress was asked to give $2,000,000 to be used in negotiating a Treaty with Mexico, fixing the dis-

puted boundaries. Immediately David Wilmot, of Pennsylvania, introduced a Proviso, which had been prepared
by Jacob Brinkerhoff, of Ohio (both Democrats, and both
afterwards members of the Republican Party), to the effect
that slavery should be prohibited in any territory acquired
from Mexico. This Proviso carried in the House, but the
Senate adjourned its session without coming to a vote on it.
The Proviso appeared again often in Congress, but was
never adopted; it caused more excited debate between the
North and South than anything that had ever been introduced by the anti-slavery element in Congress. Although
defeated, it served to amalgamate the anti-slavery forces,
and from that day they rallied around it as representing
the fixed and unalterable sentiment of the North; on it the
Free-Soil Party entered the Campaign of 1848 and it was
the underlying principle in the organization of the Republican Party in 1854. As a counter-balancing action to the
Wilmot Proviso, Mr. Calhoun, in February, 1847, introduced in the Senate a long resolution to the effect that Congress had no power to prohibit slavery in any territory, and
that any attempt to do so would be a violation of constitutional rights and lead to a dissolution of the Union. No
vote was ever taken on this resolution, and it was nothing
more than a deliberate attempt to force the issue with the
North.

The Thirtieth Congress met December 6, 1847, and had
among its members Abraham Lincoln, of Illinois, and Andrew Johnson, of Tennessee, the former elected as a Whig
and the latter as a Democrat; in the Senate Stephen A.

Douglas, of Illinois, took his seat for the first time in that body. Opposition to the war was strong, and it was finally closed by the Treaty of Guadalupe Hidalgo, signed February 2, 1848; by its terms vast stretches of new territory were acquired by the United States. This land had been free soil by the Laws of Mexico since 1827, but the South, as a matter of course, expected, and had planned, to make it slave soil, and she was determined to oppose to the utmost any attempt to keep slavery out of this new territory; the North was equally determined that it should remain free. The campaign of 1848 came on with the question undecided. The Democratic Convention nominated Lewis Cass, of Michigan, and adopted a platform similar to those of 1840 and 1844, but nothing was said about slavery in the new territory. The Whigs nominated Major-General Zachary Taylor, of Louisiana, for President, and Millard Fillmore, of New York, for Vice-President, and their Convention adjourned without adopting any platform at all.

The failure of the two great parties to take up the prohibition of slavery in the new territory was regarded with great indignation by many members of both parties in the North, especially so by the Whigs; in addition, an element of political revenge crept into the situation to help the anti-slavery sentiment. The defeat of Van Buren in the Democratic Convention of '44, and the anti-slavery sentiment in the Democratic Party, had divided it, in New York, into two factions known as "Barnburners" and "Hunkers"; the former being those who were opposed to the extension of the slave area, and were likened to the Dutchman who burned his barn to rid it of rats; and the latter were "Administration Democrats"—"Northern men with Southern principles," who "hankered" after office. Samuel J. Tilden and Benjamin F. Butler were two of the leading "Barnburner" leaders. When the Democratic National Convention convened in 1848, both "Barnburners" and "Hunkers" applied for admission; the Convention offered to permit the New York vote to be cast between them. This was refused by the "Barnburners," and they withdrew and held an enthusiastic meeting in New York, and soon became known as "Free-Soil Democrats." A National Convention was called to meet at Buffalo, August 9, 1848. The old Liberty Party had already held their Convention in November, 1847, and had nominated John P. Hale, of New Hampshire, for President, but Mr. Hale withdrew and the Liberty Party joined in the new movement and attended the Free-Soil Convention. Mr. Van Buren was nominated for President, and Charles Francis Adams, of Massachusetts, for Vice-President. The Free-Soil Platform was, of course, strongly antagonistic to the Slave Power, and concluded with the stirring words, "We inscribe on our banner, 'Free Soil, Free Speech, Free Labor and Free Men,' and under it will fight on and fight ever, until a triumphant victory shall reward our exertions."

The Free-Soil Party was the second predecessor of the Republican Party, and it was a curious circumstance that in this campaign it was to have at its head a man who had been a Democratic President. The Free-Soilers of New

York later nominated Senator John A. Dix for Governor, and the split in the Democratic Party in that State was complete, and lost the election for the National ticket. Many Whigs hesitated between Taylor and Van Buren, but Horace Greeley, in the *New York Tribune,* advocated the election of Taylor. The vote in New York, which was again the pivotal State, was: Taylor, 218,603; Cass, 114,-318; Van Buren, 120,510. The total Free-Soil vote was 291,263. It was a strange and fateful effect that made the Liberty Party in 1844 divide the Whigs and give the victory to the Democrats; and in 1848 the Free-Soil Party, a successor of the Liberty Party, divided the Democrats and gave the Whigs the victory.

The Campaign of '48 assumes another important aspect, in that Mr. Lincoln took an active part in it; it fixed his ideas on slavery, and impressed him with the utter hopelessness of reconciling the North and South on this question. Mr. Lincoln had made his debut in the House in December, 1847, with the famous "Spot Resolutions." In the Spring of '48 he urged his Illinois friends to give up Clay and support Gen. Taylor. He attended the Whig Convention at Philadelphia and was well satisfied with the nominations and the prospects of victory. Late in July he made a strong speech for Taylor on the floor of the House, attracting the attention of the campaign managers to such an extent that he was sent to New England where he delivered a number of speeches, pleading with the New Englanders not to join the Free-Soil movement, but to vote with the Whig Party. Here he saw the strength of the anti-

slavery movement, and what he heard made him think
deeper on the great question of the hour.   After listening
to one of Governor Seward's speeches at Boston, in September, he said, "Governor Seward, I have been thinking about
what you said in your speech ; I reckon you are right.   We
have got to deal with this slavery question, and got to give
more attention to it than we have been doing."   Later in
the campaign Mr. Lincoln stumped Illinois for Taylor.

When the Thirty-first Congress convened for its first
session, on December 3, 1849, all was confusion and uncertainty in regard to the situation.   A great many felt that
the crisis had been reached at last, and that nothing but a
civil war could result.   The South feared that its long cherished plan of more slave territory was to be frustrated, and
the anxiety in the North that the territory acquired from
Mexico might be made slave was equally great.   An event
now occurred that brought matters directly to an acute
crisis and necessitated a settlement or a war.   Gold had
been discovered in California early in 1848, and instantly
there was a tremendous influx of population, with the result that late in 1849 California was ready for admission
into the Union, not as a slave State, as the South fondly
hoped, but as free soil.   With the convening of Congress
came the President's message, and it was a severe blow to
the South, for it advocated the admission of California as
a free State.   The South now indeed saw its plan rapidly
weakening.   Violent opposition was at once made to the admission of California as disturbing the equal balance between the two sections, and in addition the South com-

plained bitterly of the difficulty of capturing slaves who escaped into the free States. She also complained of the constant agitation of the slave question, and now demanded that the territories should be open to slavery, and asserted that any attempt to enforce the Wilmot Proviso or to abolish slavery in the District of Columbia would lead to an immediate dissolution of the Union.

Such was the acute situation in December, 1849, and the men, scenes and debates which attended the solution of this grave crisis present a remarkable and dramatic picture. All eyes now turned to Mr. Clay, the great Compromisor, then in his seventy-third year. In January, 1850, he began his efforts to bring about what proved to be the last compromise between the North and the South. Four great speeches were delivered on the resolutions introduced by him. Mr. Clay, so feeble that he had to be assisted up the Capitol steps, spoke early in February. On March 4th Mr. Calhoun, too weak to speak himself, had his speech, full of antagonism and foreboding, read by a colleague. Three days after Calhoun's speech, Webster delivered his famous "Seventh of March" speech, in which he sacrificed the support of thousands of friends, and demoralized the entire North by condemning the Abolitionists and advocating the passage of the Compromise measures. On March 11th Mr. Seward delivered his "Higher Law" speech, denouncing the Compromise. The great triumvirate, Clay, Calhoun and Webster, appeared in this debate for the last time before the American public. Calhoun died on the last day of March. Late in '51 Clay resigned his seat in the

Senate and died at Washington, June 29, 1852. Webster took the office of Secretary of State, received a few votes in the Whig Convention and refused to support General Scott in the election of 1852, and died broken-hearted October 24, 1852.

The Compromise of 1850, as finally agreed on, provided that Utah and New Mexico should be organized into territories without reference to slavery; California to be admitted as a free State; $10,000,000.00 to be paid Texas for her claim to New Mexico; a new Fugitive Slave Law; and the slave trade to be abolished in the District of Columbia. The compromise was viewed with great indignation by the North, and was in many respects extremely unsatisfactory to the South, who was now certain that her plan of extension of slave area was lost. The political leaders of both parties now argued and pretended that the slavery question was absolutely settled, inasmuch as there was no further territory to be partitioned, and that Clay's Compromise had included all possible phases of the subject. But it was apparent to those who looked beneath the surface that the situation was not settled at all; nobody in the North, however, looked for such a startling and rash course as was adopted by the South in 1854, and which resulted, in that year, in the formation of the Republican Party.

CHAPTER VIII.

BIRTH OF THE REPUBLICAN PARTY.

"Resolved, That of all outrages hitherto perpetrated or attempted upon the North and freedom by the slave leaders, and their natural allies, not one compares in bold and impudent audacity, treachery and meanness with this, the Nebraska Bill, as to the sum of all its villainies it adds the repudiation of a solemn compact, held as sacred as the Constitution itself for a period of thirty-four years."

Adopted at First Meeting, Ripon, Wis., February 28, 1854.

The new Fugitive Slave Law (passed as a part of the Compromise) was unreasonable and extremely harsh in its terms, and did more than anything else to continue the bitterness between the North and the South. Opposition to it appeared in the North almost immediately after its passage, and it was clear that, because of its terms, it would prove to be more of a dead letter than the original law of 1793. The fact of the matter was that the South forced its passage in the harshest terms conceivable, with the sinister plan of compelling the North to violate it so that bad faith could be charged; and the North did not hesitate to violate a law so repugnant to constitutional and natural rights and human sympathy. Personal Liberty Laws were passed in many Northern States, practically nullifying the Act; and as a result of it, the Underground Railroad, which had been organized about 1839 by the Quakers, did its most effective

(70)

work. This mysterious organization had a chain of stations, leading from the slave across the free States into Canada, to assist in the escape of fugitive slaves. Mrs. Stowe, moved by the wrongs and sufferings of the fugitives, published "Uncle Tom's Cabin" in the summer of 1852, and it had a telling effect in creating and solidifying the anti-slavery sentiment in the North.

The campaign of 1852 found the Democrats united; but the Whigs had no promising candidate, and were sorely disorganized, with a stronger anti-slavery element than ever before in its midst. The Democrats nominated Franklin Pierce, of New Hampshire, for President, and their platform contained the following emphatic promise: "The Democratic Party will resist all attempts at renewing in Congress, or out of it, the agitation of the slavery question in whatever shape or color the attempt may be made." The Whig Party nominated General Winfield Scott, of Virginia, for President, and their platform also contained a resolution pledging the party to the Compromise Measures as a settlement in principle and substance of the slavery question. The Free-Soil Party, though it had received little support at the polls, still retained a strong organization, and nominated John P. Hale, of New Hampshire, for President, and George W. Julian, of Indiana, for Vice-President, and denounced both the Whig and Democratic Parties as "hopelessly corrupt and utterly unworthy of confidence." The electoral vote gave Pierce 254 and Scott only 42, but the popular vote was much closer: Pierce, 1,601,474; Scott, 1,386,580; Hale, 156,667.

President Pierce's first message went to Congress December 5, 1853, and he congratulated the country on the settlement of the slavery question; but in the following month, notwithstanding the express promises made in both the party platforms of the preceding election, the event came that stunned the North, and as the realization of its enormity grew, aroused her to the wildest excitement and the most bitter denunciation, finally resulting in direct and emphatic political action in the organization of the Republican Party.

On January 4, 1854, Senator Douglas introduced a Bill organizing the Territory of Nebraska. Twelve days later Senator Dixon, of Kentucky, gave notice that he would move an Amendment, repealing the Missouri Compromise, thereby permitting slavery in the new Territory. Senator Douglas then reported (January 23d) a new Bill, making two territories out of the same territory of the first Bill, the southern part to be called Kansas and the northern part to be called Nebraska, and the Missouri Compromise, "being inconsistent with the principle of non-intervention by Congress with slavery in the States and Territories, as recognized by the legislation of 1850, commonly called Compromise Measures, is hereby declared inoperative and void; it being the true intent and meaning of the Act not to legislate slavery into any Territory or State, nor to exclude it therefrom, but to leave the people thereof free to form and regulate their domestic institutions in their own way." The Bill passed the Senate March 3d, but the South was not certain of its success in the House, and final action was postponed until May 24th, and this iniquity became a law on May 30, 1854. While setting forth the doctrine of non-intervention and popular sovereignty the Bill was in effect the forcing of slavery into the Territories, and that this was the plan became practically assured when it was discovered that throughout the summer and fall of 1853 the people of western Missouri had been deliberately planning to settle in the territory west of them (now called Kansas) and to make it slave soil. The whole plot, as revealed by the legislation to which Douglas gave his support, was to force Kansas into the Union as a slave State, thereby counterbalancing the admission of California, which had destroyed the equilibrium between the two sections.

A storm of indignation swept over the North in the opening months of 1854, gaining in intensity and fury as the baseness of the new scheme of the Slave Power was fully realized. Thousands of letters poured in on Congressmen protesting against the passage of the Act, and hundreds of memorials and petitions were presented to the Senate and the House. The newspapers all over the North, beginning late in January, contained constant articles calling on the people to hold meetings and protest against the Nebraska outrage, and hundreds of these meetings were held in churches, schoolhouses and public halls, and the anti-Nebraska sentiment dominated everything. Douglas received the brunt of all this opprobrium, and was compared to

Benedict Arnold. The foreign element was the strongest
in opposition to the Nebraska measure, and the German
newspapers and the Germans, North and South, were the
most emphatic in their denunciation, and the success which
the new political party was to have must be attributed
largely to them. The Western States, Ohio, Indiana, Illinois, Wisconsin, Michigan and Iowa, were the leaders in
the anti-Nebraska movement, and also in the organization
of political opposition. The election of 1852 had badly demoralized the Whig Party, and now the Kansas-Nebraska
measures swept it away almost entirely in the Western
States, but the Eastern States, while condemning the Douglas Bill and adopting resolutions similar to the Republican
platforms of the West, were loath to give up their party
organization, and the Whig Party continued in several of
them until after the election of 1856. During the period
between 1852 and 1854 it probably occurred to many in the
North, who watched and analyzed the popular sentiment
and vote, that the Whig Party would soon be swept away,
and that the dissatisfied masses of Abolitionists, Free-
Soilers, Anti-Nebraska Whigs, Anti-Nebraska Democrats and Know-Nothings must and would unite into a
party under a new name with a platform acceptable to the
anti-slavery elements in politics. The Douglas Bill demanded political action in the North, but how was a new
party to be formed ? Who would lead it, and what would be
the success of the new movement ?

We come now to the organization and first meetings of
the Republican Party. Alvan E. Bovay was the founder of

the Republican Party. Not only were the name and early principles of the party clearly outlined and decided on in his mind, and talked about by him long before any action was taken by any other person, but he took the first practical steps looking to the dissolution of existing parties, and with patience and much difficult work brought about the first meeting and pointed out clearly and unanswerably the course to be taken.

Mr. Bovay was born in July, 1818, at Adams, New York; graduated from Norwich University, Vermont, and was Professor in several eastern schools and colleges, and later was admitted to the New York bar. In October, 1850, he went West with his family, and settled at Ripon, Fond du Lac County, Wisconsin, and soon became the recognized leader of the Whig Party. He studied the political situation carefully, and with his liberal education and the principles of freedom taught by life in the West, he imbibed a hatred for the institution of Slavery, and saw clearly that, at least, its extension must be opposed to the utmost. He remained with the Whig Party, "following its banners, fighting its battles faithfully, at the same time praying for its death," as he expressed it in later years. He was fortunate in numbering among his close friends Horace Greeley, the editor of the *New York Tribune,* the greatest exponent of the northern views of slavery. The *Tribune* in 1854 had a circulation of about 150,000 per week, and therefore wielded a vast influence on public sentiment in the North. In 1852, while the Whig Convention was in session, Mr. Bovay dined with Mr. Greeley in New York

City, and the conversation turned to the prospects of General Scott, the Whig nominee. Mr. Bovay predicted his overwhelming defeat, and that the Whig Party would be utterly demoralized in the North, and that it would become necessary to organize a new party out of the debris. He there suggested to Greeley the name "Republican" for the new party, but Greeley received the proposition with little enthusiasm because he not only believed that Scott would be elected but that the Whig Party should not be dissolved. Mr. Bovay says that he advocated the name Republican because it expressed equality—representing the principle of the good of all the people; that it would be attractive to the strong foreign element in the country because of their familiarity with the name in their native lands, and that in addition the name possessed charm and magnetism. After the defeat of General Scott, Mr. Bovay corresponded with Mr. Greeley often in regard to the political situation. He was fully determined to do his utmost to organize a new party and call it Republican, and he talked over the matter persistently with all his neighbors in the little village of Ripon, and waited for the time to act. That time came with the violent agitation caused by the Kansas-Nebraska Bill, and Mr. Bovay achieved the result he had planned so long. After talking over the matter with two friends, Jehdeiah Bowen, a Free-Soil Democrat, and Amos Loper, a call was issued for a mass meeting to be held in the Congregational church in Ripon, February 28, 1854, with the object of ascertaining the public sentiment. This little frontier village had a small population, and the coun-

ALVAN E. BOVAY.
Founder of the Republican Party.

try around it was sparsely settled, but so earnest was the political thought of the time that the meeting was a great success, and the church was crowded with men and women, and even some children, who were attracted by the seriousness of their elders. Deacon William Dunham, of the church, acted as Chairman of this meeting, and there was a full and free discussion of the situation and the best action to be taken. Mr. Bovay pointed out that the only hope of defeating the extension of slavery was to disband the old parties and unite under a new name. Before the meeting had progressed very far the sentiment was practically unanimous. Those who hesitated were overcome by the enthusiasm and logical arguments of the speakers. The name Republican was suggested at this meeting, but no action was taken on it for the reason that this was looked upon as merely a preliminary meeting to be followed by a later one. As the Kansas-Nebraska Bill had not yet passed the Senate nothing further could be done at this meeting, and after adopting the following well-worded and prophetic resolutions, the meeting adjourned to await the action of Congress

"WHEREAS, The Senate of the United States is entertaining, and from present indications is likely to pass, Bills organizing governments for the Territories of Kansas and Nebraska, in which is embodied a clause repealing the Missouri Compromise Act, and so admit into these Territories the slave system with all its evils, and

"WHEREAS, We deem that compact repealable as the Constitution itself; therefore

"*Resolved,* That of all outrages hitherto perpetrated

or attempted upon the North and freedom by the slave leaders and their natural allies, not one compares in bold and impudent audacity, treachery and meanness with this, the Nebraska Bill, as to the sum of all its other villainies it adds the repudiation of a solemn compact, held as sacred as the Constitution itself for a period of thirty-four years;

"*Resolved,* That the northern man who can aid and abet in the commission of so stupendous a crime is none too good to become an accomplice in renewing the African slave trade, the services which, doubtless, will next be required of him by his Southern masters, should the Nebraska treason succeed;

"*Resolved,* That the attempt to withdraw the Missouri Compromise, whether successful or not, admonishes the North to adopt the maxim for all time to come, 'No more Compromises with Slavery';

"*Resolved,* That the passage of this Bill, if pass it should, will be a call to arms of a great Northern Party, such an one as the country has not hitherto seen, composed of Whigs, Democrats and Free-Soilers, every man with a heart in him united under the single banner cry of 'Repeal! Repeal!'

"*Resolved,* That the small but compact phalanx of true men who oppose the mad scheme upon the broadest principle of humanity, as well as their unflinching efforts to uphold the public faith, deserve not only our applause but our profound esteem;

"*Resolved,* That the heroic attitude of General Houston, amidst a host of degenerate men in the United States Senate, is worthy of honor and applause."

The Senate, as we have already seen, passed the Kansas-Nebraska Bill on March 3d. Mr. Bovay and his coworkers lost no time in signing and publishing the following call for a second meeting:

"A Bill expressly intended to extend and strengthen the institution of Slavery has passed the Senate by a large majority, many Northern Senators voting for it, and many more sitting in their seats and not voting at all, and it is evidently destined to pass the House and become a law unless its progress is arrested by a general uprising of the North against it;

"Therefore, we, the undersigned, believing the community to be nearly unanimous in opposition to the nefarious scheme, would call a public meeting of the citizens of all parties to be held in the schoolhouse at Ripon, on Monday evening, March 20th, at 6:30 o'clock, to resolve, to petition and to organize against it."

Through the efforts of Mr. Bovay, the meeting on the night of March 20th was largely attended, and the little schoolhouse on the prairie was filled with men, all voters, "We went in," wrote Mr. Bovay, "Whigs, Free-Soilers and Democrats; we came out Republicans, and we were the first Republicans in the Union." It is true, however, that this meeting did not formally adopt the name Republican, but it was discussed, as it had been for months in the village, and was practically agreed upon, but the meeting felt that it would be better not to use the name until a more pretentious movement of a national character was made. The meeting lasted well into the night, and the "cold March wind blew around the little building and the tallow candles burned low" as these pioneers in this frontier town made history. A motion was duly made and carried that the Town Committees of Whigs, Free-Soilers and Democrats be dissolved and a new Committee to represent the new party be appointed. The first Republican Committee was composed of Alvan E. Bovay, Jehdeiah Bowen, Amos A. Loper, Jacob Woodruff and Abraham Thomas, all courageous, outspoken and fearless men of the West, whose very names seem towers of strength, speaking the unalterable purpose of the new party.

These preliminary meetings of the new party having been held and a plan of action outlined, Mr. Bovay directed all his efforts toward having some National recognition of the name of the party. Two days before the first meeting at Ripon he wrote Mr. Greeley a strong letter, urging him to publish an editorial and adopt the name. Mr. Greeley gave the matter but little attention, and several months went by before he took any notice of the suggestion, and then it was only taken up in a half-hearted way, but what he said was enough to settle the matter. In the *Tribune* of June 24, 1854, appeared an article expressing indifference as to what name should be chosen to represent the Anti-Nebraska sentiment in the North, but the article concluded, "We think some simple name like Republican would more fitly designate those who have united to restore the Union to its true mission, the champion and promulgator of liberty rather than the propagandist of slavery."

Another event had occurred to strengthen the adoption of the name Republican for the new party. On the morning after the final passage of the Kansas-Nebraska Bill, a meeting of the Anti-Nebraska members of Congress was held in Washington, and the general political situation **and** its hopelessness was fully discussed. At this meeting the feasibility of the new party was talked over, and the members present decided to lend their aid to such a movement, and the name Republican was discussed and adopted.

In point of time, Michigan has the honor of being the first State to hold a Convention and formally adopt a platform containing the principles of the new party and using the name Republican. Late in May, and throughout June, 1854, a call was published and copies circulated for signing among the voters of Michigan, in which all citizens, "without reference to former political association," were called to assemble in Mass Convention on Thursday, July 6th, at 1 p. m., at Jackson, Michigan, "there to take such measures as shall be thought best to concentrate the popular sentiment in this State against the aggressions of the Slave Power." The meeting was overflowing in numbers and most enthusiastic and earnest in sentiment. A long and outspoken platform was unanimously adopted, setting forth something of the history of slavery, and denouncing it as a great moral, social and political wrong. The platform condemned the repeal of the Missouri Compromise; pledged the party to opposition to slavery extension; demanded the repeal of the Fugitive Slave Law, and demanded an Act to abolish slavery in the District of Columbia; spoke words of cheer to those who might settle in Kansas, and concluded·

"*Resolved,* That, in view of the necessity of battling for the first principles of Republican Government and against the schemes of aristocracy, the most revolting and oppressive with which the earth was ever cursed or man debased, we will co-operate and be known as Republicans until the contest be terminated."

The State Central Committee was chosen and the first Republican State Ticket in the United States was nomi nated, headed by Kinsley S. Bingham for Governor. One week later, on July 13th, chosen as the anniversary of the day on which the Ordinance of 1787 was adopted, State Conventions of the Anti-Nebraska members of all parties were held in Ohio, Wisconsin, Indiana and Vermont. In Wisconsin and Vermont the name Republican was distinctly adopted, and in these two States, as well as in the others mentioned, platforms similar in sentiment to that of Michigan were agreed on. In Massachusetts the Convention met on July 20th and adopted the name Republican and an Anti-Nebraska platform, and nominated Henry Wilson for Governor, but the peculiar political situation in this State led to the election of the Know-Nothing candidates, but as far as opposition to slavery was concerned, the Know-Nothings in Massachusetts were Republican in sentiment, for they selected Henry Wilson for United States Senator.

Ohio was the first State to suggest a State Convention of the Anti-Nebraska sentiment; a preliminary meeting was held at Columbus March 22d, and was attended by Whigs, Free-Soilers and Democrats. The political situation was thoroughly discussed, and afterwards, as the passage of the Kansas-Nebraska Bill became assured, a call was issued for a State Convention to be held on July 13th. At this Convention the name Republican was not formally adopted, but throughout the State in the Congressional Districts that name was common. In New York the Whigs refused to give up their party organization, but an Anti-Nebraska platform was adopted and the Whig candidate was elected on it. New York joined the Republican party in 1855, and Mr. Seward took his place as a leader of the party in that State. Maine was engrossed with local issues, and did not adopt the Republican organization in 1854, but returned Anti-Nebraska Congressmen. Pennsylvania also held to her old organizations, but returned Anti-Nebraska Congressmen, and the same situation occurred in Illinois. In Iowa the situation was peculiar, but nevertheless emphatic for the new organization. The Whigs held their Convention in that State on February 22d, before the Nebraska Bill had passed the Senate, and before the sentiment in the North had reached an acute stage. But before the election in August the Whig candidate, John W. Grimes, declared himself in favor of the Republican platform and name, and he was practically elected as a Republican Governor, the first in the United States. The South, of course, was solid for the Democratic Party, and no attempt at a Republican organization was made in the Southern States. In the other Northern States not already mentioned the sentiment gradually, but with some slowness, solidified in favor of the new party.

The presence of the American, or Know-Nothing Party, which had come into politics in 1852 as a secret organization, with the prevailing principle of "America for Americans," and which obtained its popular name of "Know-

Nothing" because of the invariable answer of its members that they "knew nothing" of the organization, confused the political situation in 1854 and 1855, and makes it difficult to correctly analyze and state the political situation.

It is seen that the Republican Party was strong in the States which had been organized out of the Northwest Territory, but that the East and New England, while fully endorsing the platforms of the new party, entered reluctautly into the movement to adopt its name and organization. In the East there were four distinct parties, the Whigs, Democrats, Know-Nothings and Republicans, but in the West there were but two, the Democratic and Republican. There can be no question, however, that the sentiment of the Know-Nothing Party, which controlled many of the elections in the East during 1854 and 1855, was strongly Anti-Nebraska, and the success of that party in the North may safely be counted as expressing the sentiment of the new party.

The close of 1855 found the Republican Party well organized in Michigan, Ohio, Wisconsin, Vermont, Connecticut, New Hampshire, Iowa, Maine, Pennsylvania, Massachusetts, New York and Indiana. In the several other States not mentioned it was rapidly gaining strength, and the prospects for the presidential campaign of 1856 looked fairly bright, and if the remnants of the Whig Party would retire from the field, and if the Anti-Nebraska Know-Nothings would vote with the new party, the chances for victory were exceedingly good. The struggle in Kansas between the free settlers from the North and the pro-slavery

SCHOOLHOUSE AT RIPON, WISCONSIN, WHERE THE REPUBLICAN
PARTY WAS BORN.

citizens from Missouri was now growing in bitterness, and reports of violence and blood-shed, which came from the scene of the conflict, set the North on fire with indignation and tended materially to solidify sentiment in favor of the Republican Party.

The Thirty-fourth Congress, which had been elected the preceding year, convened December 3, 1855, and the extent of the great political revolution which had taken place in the North was seen more clearly. The proud Democratic majority of 89 in the preceding House had been swept away, and the Thirty-fourth Congress, as near as it could be classified, which was indeed difficult, was made up of one hundred and seventeen Anti-Nebraska members. seventy-nine Democrats, and thirty-seven Pro-Slavery Whigs and Know-Nothings. After a contest of nine weeks. Nathaniel P. Banks, of Massachusetts, was chosen Speaker over the Southern candidate, and although during this first session of the Thirty-fourth Congress the opponents of slavery were without a party name or organization, the election of Banks was clearly a victory for the young party. Altogether the progress of the party in a period of less than two years had been most satisfactory, and if a strong presidential candidate could be obtained, and if great party leaders would appear, it was evident that the new party would stand an even chance of succeeding in the presidential election of 1856, and early preparations were made for the first great national political contest over the slavery question; a contest certain to be exciting and bitter in its events and portentous in results.

CHAPTER IX.

FIRST REPUBLICAN NATIONAL CONVENTION.

"Free Soil, Free Men, Free Speech, Fremont."

Republican Rallying Cry, 1856.

The opening of 1856 found the country in a turmoil of political excitement and anxiety. Late in January, President Pierce, in a special message, recognized the pro-slavery Legislature of Kansas, and called the attempt to establish a Free-state Government in that Territory an act of rebellion. This continued subserviency of the Administration to the Slave Power so aroused the North that two days later the Anti-Nebraska members in the House forced through a resolution by a vote of one hundred and one to one hundred, declaring that the Missouri Compromise ought to be restored, but nothing further could be done with the resolution. The House at this time was dead-locked over the election of a Speaker, which was not settled, as we have seen, until February 2d. The situation in Kansas was daily growing more acute, and had the natural effect of creating great bitterness both in the North and the South, and this general unsettled and threatening state of affairs and public opinion confronted the political parties on the eve of another presidential campaign.

The Republican State leaders had decided on an at-

(86)

tempt at a National Organization and Convention, and on January 17, 1856, the following call was issued:

"To the Republicans of the United States:

"In accordance with what appears to be a general desire of the Republican party, and at the suggestion of a large portion of the Republican Press, the undersigned, Chairmen of the State Republican Committees of Maine, Vermont, Massachusetts, New York, Pennsylvania, Ohio, Michigan, Indiana and Wisconsin, hereby invite the Republicans of the Union to meet in informal Convention at Pittsburg on the 22d of February, 1856, for the purpose of perfecting the National Organization, and providing for a National Delegate Convention of the Republican Party at some subsequent day, to nominate candidates for the Presidency and Vice-Presidency, to be supported at the election in November, 1856.

"A. P. STONE, of Ohio,
"J. Z. GOODRICH, of Massachusetts,
"DAVID WILMOT, of Pennsylvania,
"LAWRENCE BRAINARD, of Vermont,
"WILLIAM A. WHITE, of Wisconsin."

Because of lack of time the names of the other State Chairmen mentioned in the body of the call were not obtained but they all approved it by letter. The Pittsburg Convention was to be merely preliminary to the National Convention, but it developed unexpected enthusiasm, and it was seen by the friends of freedom that at last a great National Party was in the field, determined to oppose slavery to the utmost, and to remain until the victory should be won.

Twenty-four States, sixteen free and eight slave, sent their representatives to the Pittsburg meeting. Lawrence

Brainard, of Vermont, called the Convention to order, and the delegates chose John A. King, of New York, for temporary Chairman. After a prayer by Owen Lovejoy, brother of the murdered Abolitionist, the Committee on Permanent Organization reported the venerable Francis P. Blair, of Maryland, for President of the Convention, who accepted the honor and read an elaborate paper on the situation, which was listened to with marked attention. The names of eighteen prominent Republicans were presented for Vice-Presidents and five for Secretaries. A Committee was appointed to draft an address to the people of the country. Earnest, hopeful and enthusiastic speeches were made by Horace Greeley, Zachariah Chandler, Preston King, David Wilmot, Joshua R. Giddings, George W. Julian, and others, and a strong Freedom letter was read from Cassius M. Clay. The Committee on Resolutions reported a lengthy address to the people of the United States, setting forth the crimes and continued aggressions of the Slave Power, and closing with three Resolutions, demanding the repeal, and pledging the party to labor for the repeal, of all laws which allowed the introduction of slavery into territory once consecrated to freedom, and declared its purpose to resist by all constitutional means the existence of slavery in any of the Territories of the United States; pledging the Republicans to the support, by every lawful means, of the brethren in Kansas, and to use every political power to obtain the immediate admission of Kansas as a free State; and denounced the National Administration and pledged the party to oppose and overthrow it. A National Committee, headed by Edwin D. Morgan, of New York, was then chosen and the preliminary Convention adjourned on February 23d to await the call of the National Committee

From Washington, on March 29, 1856, the National Committee issued this call for the First National Convention:

"The people of the United States, without regard to past political differences or divisions, who are opposed to the repeal of the Missouri Compromise, to the policy of the present Administration, to the extension of slavery into the Territories, in favor of the admission of Kansas as a free State, and restoring the action of the Federal Government to the principles of Washington and Jefferson, are invited by the National Committee, appointed by the Pittsburg Convention on the 22d of February, 1856, to send from each State three delegates from every Congressional District, and six delegates at large, to meet at Philadelphia on the 17th day of June next, for the purpose of recommending candidates to be supported for the offices of President and Vice-President of the United States."

Pursuant to this call, the first Republican National Convention convened at Philadelphia, in the Musical Fund Hall, on June 17, 1856, the anniversary of the battle of Bunker Hill, and was called to order by Edwin D. Morgan, Chairman of the National Committee. Every Northern State, and also Delaware, Maryland, Kentucky and Virginia, and the Territories of Minnesota, Kansas, Nebraska and the District of Columbia, were represented by full delegations, and there were probably between eight hundred and one thousand delegates in attendance. Robert Emmet, of New York, formerly a Democrat, was made temporary chairman, and accepted the honor in an eloquent and stirring speech. After prayer, Committees on Credentials, Resolutions and Permanent Organization were then appointed. The latter committee reported Henry S. Lane, of Indiana, as President of the Convention, and the names of twenty-four Vice-Presidents and a number of Secretaries. The first National Platform of the Republican Party was then reported by David Wilmot and was adopted with thunders of applause and amid scenes of the highest enthusiasm.

REPUBLICAN NATIONAL PLATFORM, 1856.

This convention of delegates, assembled in pursuance of a call addressed to the people of the United States, without regard to past political differences or divisions, who are opposed to the repeal of the Missouri Compromise, to the policy of the present administration, to the extension of slavery into free territory; in favor of admitting Kansas as a free State, of restoring the action of the Federal government to the principles of Washington and Jefferson; and who purpose to unite in presenting candidates for the offices of President and Vice-President, do resolve as follows:

Resolved, That the maintenance or the principles promulgated in the Declaration of Independence and embodied in the Federal Constitution is essential to the preservation of our Republican institutions, and that the Federal Constitution, the rights of the States, and the union of the States, shall be preserved.

Resolved, That, with our Republican fathers, we hold it to be a self-evident truth, that all men are endowed with the unalienable rights of life, liberty and the pursuit of happiness, and that the primary object and ulterior designs of our federal government were to secure these rights to all persons within its exclusive jurisdiction; that, as our Republican fathers, when they had abolished slavery in all our national territory, ordained that no person should be deprived of life, liberty or property without due process of law, it becomes our duty to maintain this provision of the Constitution against all attempts to violate it for the purpose of establishing slavery in any Territory of the United States, by positive legislation prohibiting its extension therein; that we deny the authority of Congress, of a territorial legislature, of any individual or association of individuals, to give legal existence to slavery in any territory of the United States while the present Constitution shall be maintained.

Resolved, That the Constitution confers upon Congress sovereign power over the territories of the United States for their government, and that in the exercise of this power it is both the right and the duty of Congress to prohibit in the territories those twin relics of barbarism—polygamy and slavery.

Resolved, That while the Constitution of the United States was ordained and established by the people in order to form a more perfect union, establish justice, insure domestic tranquillity, provide for the common defense, promote the general welfare, and secure the blessings of liberty, and contains ample provisions for the protection of life, liberty and property of every citizen, the dearest Constitutional rights of the people of Kansas have been fraudulently and violently taken from them; their territory has been invaded by an armed force; spurious and pretended legislative, judicial and executive officers have been set over them, by whose usurped authority, sustained by the military power of the government, tyrannical and unconstitutional laws have been enacted and enforced; the right of the people to keep and bear arms has been infringed; test oaths of an extraordinary and entangling nature have been imposed as a condition of exercising the right of suffrage and holding office; the right of an accused person to a speedy and public trial by an impartial jury has been denied; the right of the people to be secure in their persons, houses, papers and effects against unreasonable searches and seizures, has been violated; they have been deprived of life, liberty and property without due process of law; the freedom of speech and of the press has been abridged; the right to choose their representatives has been made of no effect; murders, robberies and arsons have been instigated and encouraged, and the offenders have been allowed to go unpunished; that all these things have been done with the knowledge, sanction and procurement of the present administration; and that for this high crime against the Constitution, the Union and humanity, we arraign the administration, the President, his advisers, agents, supporters, apologists and accessories, either before or after the fact, before the country and before the world; and that it is our fixed purpose to bring the actual perpetrators of these atrocious outrages and their accomplices to a sure and condign punishment hereafter.

Resolved, That Kansas should immediately be admitted as a State of 'the Union, with her present free constitution, as at once the most effectual way of securing to her citizens the enjoyment of the rights and privileges to which they are entitled, and of ending the civil strife now raging in her territory.

Resolved, That the highwayman's plea that "Might makes right," embodied in the Ostend circular, was in every respect unworthy of American diplomacy, and would bring shame and dishonor upon any government or people that gave it their sanction.

Resolved, That a railroad to the Pacific Ocean, by the most central and practicable route, is imperatively demanded by the interests of the whole country, and that the Federal government ought to render immediate and efficient aid in its construction; and, as an auxiliary thereto, to the immediate construction of an emigrant route on the line of the railroad.

Resolved, That appropriations by Congress for the improvement of rivers and harbors of a national character, required for the accommodation and security of our existing commerce, are authorized by the Constitution and justified by the obligation of government to protect the lives and property of its citizens.

Resolved, That we invite the affiliation and co-operation of freemen of all parties, however differing from us in other respects, in support of the principles herein declared, and believing that the spirit of our institutions, as well as the Constitution of our country, guarantees liberty of conscience and equality of rights among citizens, we oppose all legislation impairing their security.

The time now came to ballot for a candidate for President, but he had been practically decided on some time before the Convention met. The merits of four men had been thoroughly discussed in connection with this honor—Salmon P. Chase and Judge John McLean of Ohio, William H. Seward, of New York, and John C. Fremont of Cali-

JOHN C. FREMONT,
First Republican Candidate for President.

fornia. Senator Chase had been too open in his opposition to slavery to be available, and his name was withdrawn; Mr. Seward, influenced by Thurlow Weed, did not wish the nomination, and this fact became known several months before the Convention. McLean, of the United States Supreme Court, was strongly favored by many, because it was felt that he alone of the candidates mentioned could carry Pennsylvania, which had already been figured as the pivotal State. The candidate deemed most available was John C. Fremont, whose political experience had been brief, a term from California in the United States Senate, and he would therefore arouse no bitter personal antagonism by reason of his political record. He had been a Democrat, but was in accord with the principles of the Republican Party; in addition, he had a good record in the Army, and was widely known for his explorations in the Rockies. His wife was the daughter of Senator Thomas C. Benton, of Missouri, and altogether he was an attractive and, it appeared at the time, a shrewdly selected candidate.

There were no formal nominating speeches, but the names of all who had been discussed as candidates had been mentioned in the many enthusiastic speeches which were made during the Convention. An informal ballot gave Fremont 359; McLean 190; Sumner 2; Seward 1. A formal ballot was then immediately taken and Fremont received the entire vote of the Convention except 37 for McLean, 1 for Seward, and the Virginia vote, which was not cast because its delegation was not organized; the nomination was then made unanimous. The next day an informal ballot was taken for Vice-President. William L. Dayton, of New Jersey, received 253 votes; Abraham Lincoln, 110; N. P. Banks, 46; David Wilmot, 43; Charles Sumner, 35, and some votes each for Henry Wilson, Jacob Collamer, Joshua R. Giddings, Cassius M. Clay, Henry C. Carey, John A. King, Thomas Ford, Whitefield S. Johnson, Aaron S. Pennington and Samuel C. .Pomeroy. Mr. Lincoln was not a candidate for the office, and was named without his knowledge, and he was greatly surprised, several days later, when he learned of it. When his name was put in nomination—the second mentioned—inquiries as to who he was came from all parts of the hall. Mr. Lincoln's speech before the Bloomington Convention, in Illinois, had turned the eyes of the Republican Party in that State to him as its leader, and the Illinois Delegation to the National Convention knew well enough who he was, but his time had not yet come. Mr. Dayton received the nomination for Vice-President on the formal ballot and it was made unanimous. After appointing a committee, headed by Henry S. Lane, of Indiana, to notify the candidates of their nominations, and listening to a number of enthusiastic speeches, the Convention adjourned on June 19th. In one of the speeches reference was made to "Free Speech, Free Press, Free Soil, Free Kansas," when one of the delegates interrupted, "and Fremont"; the utterance and its amendment, with some abridgment, became one of the rallying cries of the campaign.

The selection of Mr. Fremont had also been influenced by the fact that he was looked upon with favor by those delegates who withdrew from the American or Know-Nothing Convention. The Know-Nothings had held their Convention on February 22d, and had nominated Millard Fillmore for President and A. J. Donelson for Vice-President. The delegates from New England, Ohio, Pennsylvania. Illinois and Iowa, being unable to secure an Anti-Slavery Extension Plank in the Platform, seceded and soon afterwards nominated Fremont for President, and William F. Johnston, of Pennsylvania, for Vice-President.

On September 17th the remnant of the Whig Party met at Philadelphia and adopted the nominees of the American Party, Fillmore and Donelson. This Convention and their votes in the ensuing election marked the last appearance of the Whig Party in politics.

The Democrats held their Convention in Cincinnati on June 3d, before the Republican Convention was held, and nominated James Buchanan, of Pennsylvania, for President, and John C. Breckinridge, of Kentucky, for Vice-President. President Pierce and Senator Douglas were both candidates for the presidential nomination, but were withdrawn on the fifteenth and sixteenth ballots because the South had already selected a candidate. Mr. Buchanan had been absent as Minister to England during the turmoil over the repeal of the Missouri Compromise. In addition, he came from a Northern State, and was therefore doubly attractive as a candidate; for the South, with its 112 electoral votes, needed 37 more votes to elect their candidate, and Pennsylvania, with 27 votes, was looked on as the pivotal State.

The Democratic Platform, as usual, denounced the Abolitionists, and repeated its hollow promise of 1852, that the party would resist all attempts at renewing the agitation of the slavery question. It denounced the Republican Party as "sectional, and subsisting exclusively on slavery agitation," and it contained the following remarkable and artfully worded plank:

"*Resolved,* That we recognize the right of the people of all the Territories, including Kansas and Nebraska, acting through the legally and fairly expressed will of a majority of actual residents, and whenever the number of their inhabitants justifies it, to form a Constitution, with or without domestic slavery, and be admitted into the Union upon terms of perfect equality with other States."

The ambiguous part of this plank was the insertion of the right of the inhabitants to form a Constitution with or without domestic slavery. Mr. Douglas and the other Democratic speakers argued in the North that this meant that the people of the Territory had the right to decide for or against slavery, but the South looked upon it as fully protecting slavery in any Territory until a Constitution could be formed. In the North and South the plank obtained votes for the party, but the votes were cast in the respective sections on diametrically opposed grounds.

The political situation in this campaign was somewhat complicated at first by the presentation of so many candidates, for, in addition to the candidates already named, the Abolitionists presented a ticket, as did also a number of

Americans, who seceded from the second convention of that party, but the situation gradually resolved itself into a contest between Buchanan, Fremont and Fillmore. No electoral tickets were presented for Fremont in the slave States, and the fact that Fillmore could not carry any of the free States weakened him in the South, and it was seen that Buchanan would receive the solid electoral vote of the South, and that the contest would therefore be between Buchanan and Fremont for the Northern electoral votes.

The struggle in Kansas was inseparably connected with the campaign of 1856. That struggle was virtually the opening of the Civil War, and while the North and South fought out the issue with bullets in Kansas, in the other States of the two sections the contest was no less bitter, although the means were less destructive. Before either of the great political conventions were held, Lawrence, Kansas, was captured and sacked by the Pro-Slavery Party, and on the following day (May 22d) Charles Sumner was struck down in the Senate by Preston S. Brooks, of South Carolina, because of his speech, "The Crime against Kansas." These events picture the feeling between the North and South which existed during this campaign. The South had probably already felt that if they went into the campaign solely on their cause they would be defeated, hence the nomination of a Northern Democrat from a necessary State, and the artful construction of their platform. The enthusiasm of the Republicans was probably more for their cause than for the candidate. The Democrats in the North evaded the issue of slavery as much as possible, and denounced the candidacy of Fremont as sectional, and that his success would mean the dissolution of the Union, a weighty argument with thousands of voters, especially those who were attached to the South by financial and commercial bonds. The speeches of the Southern leaders and the press of the South abounded in threats of disunion in the event of Fremont's election. The Republicans, unhampered by a southern wing and advocating the restriction of a great moral wrong, went into the campaign with the earnestness and enthusiasm of a religious crusade. They carried on a clean campaign of education, and tons of political literature were scattered broadcast over the country.

The young men of the North were especially attracted to the Republican Cause, and it was recognized that their vote would be a great aid; and the influence of the women of the country was distinctly with the new party. The clergy, the religious press and most of the eminent professors and educated men of the North also lent their potent forces to the new party.

The issues presented in the campaign of 1856, like those of 1860, were the most remarkable in our political history, and a canvass attended by such circumstances and so portentous in results could not but be exciting in the highest degree, and the bitterness of the situation grew in intensity as the days of the fall elections approached. All eyes now turned with anxiety on the few State elections which were to be held in the North prior to the presidential election in November, because they would unquestionably foreshadow the final result. Iowa came first, and, in August, went Republican, and was joined in September by Maine and Vermont, both overwhelmingly Republican. These successes were to the highest gratification of the members of the new party, and now came the final test, the October elections in Pennsylvania, Indiana and Ohio. The first of these States, with its twenty-seven electoral votes, was the most important. Thousands of dollars were poured into the campaign funds of the State by both sides, the Democratic Committee having the greater amount to spend and having the better organization. Several hundred speakers, representing both sides, traversed the State in all directions. The Democrats used the disunion argument with great effect, and added to it the campaign cry of "Buck, Breck and Free Kansas," and on October 14th Pennsylvania went Democratic by a very narrow majority. Ohio, as was expected, went Republican, but Indiana was lost, and the result of the presidential issue was thus practically known before the election, on November 4th. Fremont received the electoral votes of Maine, New Hampshire, Massachusetts, Rhode Island, Connecticut, Vermont, New York, Ohio, Michigan, Iowa and Wisconsin, one hundred and fourteen in all. Buchanan received the vote of all the slave States and Pennsylvania, New Jersey, Indiana, Illinois and California, a total of one hundred and seventy-four votes; the eight votes of Maryland going to Fillmore the only State won by the Know-Nothings. The popular vote gave Buchanan 1,838,169; Fremont 1,341,264; Fillmore 874,534. The popular vote of South Carolina is not included as the electors in that State were chosen by her Legislature.

When the first wave of bitter disappointment passed away, the Republicans saw the enormous headway that had been made and they immediately began to prepare for the national contest four years hence. The Democrats had lost ten States which they carried in 1852, and their electoral vote of 254 in 1852 had shrunken to 174. The South elected Buchanan, and he became the tool of the Slave Power, and, as subsequent events developed, it was fortunate that the Republicans were not successful in the campaign.

WILLIAM H. SEWARD.

CHAPTER X.

"Can the people of a United States territory in any lawful way, against the wish of any citizen of the United States, exclude slavery from its limits prior to the formation of a State Constitution?"

Lincoln to Douglas, Freeport Debate, August 27, 1858.

The Buchanan Administration began on March 4, 1857, and the Slave Power, through the Democratic Party, found itself in complete and absolute control of every branch of the Government, legislative, executive and judicial. Two days after the inauguration came the famous Dred Scott decision. The arguments in this case had been heard before the election, but the court adjourned until after the election. The decision, delivered by Chief Justice Taney, fixed the legal status of the negro in the United States, and declared that he could not claim any of the rights and privileges of a citizen, and "had no rights which the white man was bound to respect, and that the negro might justly and lawfully be reduced to slavery for his benefit." Then, traveling out of the record, the Court declared that the Missouri Compromise was unauthorized by the Constitution. and was null and void, and that Congress had no right to keep slavery out of any Territory. It was apparent at once that this decision completely nullified Douglas' doctrine of

(101)

popular sovereignty, and the South lost no time in abandoning that doctrine, and declaring that she would insist as a Constitutional right that slaves taken into any Territory must be protected like any other property. The North was stunned for the moment by this sweeping decision; the South was jubilant beyond all bounds, and instantly prepared to take advantage of the new dogma to the utmost. While under this decision the Slave Power seemed all triumphant, it was, in fact, to produce its destruction, and slavery was to lose its power by the very thing which seemed to strengthen it. The Dred Scott decision was bound to produce a split in the Democratic Party and the moment that occurred the success of the Republican Party was assured. The South spread thousands of copies of the decision throughout the country, and when the North recovered from the shock and saw what a revolution the decision would cause in the Democratic Party, it joined in giving it the utmost publicity.

The attempt to force Kansas into the Union as a slave State under the infamous Lecompton Constitution now began. In that Territory the Free-State settlers had rapidly been gaining in strength, and the Slave Power, in desperate straits, resorted to trickery. Several attempts of the Free-State Legislature to meet were prevented by the Federal troops, but finally, in 1857, the Free-State men voted at the regular election and obtained control of the Territorial Legislature; but before they could act, a pro-slavery Convention, previously chosen, concluded its work at Lecompton and submitted the Lecompton Constitution to the people, not permitting them, however, to vote for or against the Constitution, but "For the Constitution with Slavery," or "For the Constitution without Slavery." The Free-State men refused to vote at this election, and the Lecompton Constitution was adopted, with Slavery.

When Congress assembled, on December 7, 1859, President Buchanan, in his message, approved the Lecompton Constitution, and recommended the admission of Kansas under it. It had been rumored for some time that Senator Douglas would oppose the Administration in its attempt to force the Lecompton Constitution upon the people of Kansas, and this, indeed, proved to be true, when, on December 9th, Douglas announced his opposition to the action of the Administration as contrary to his doctrine of popular sovereignty. It is unnecessary to go into the motives that actuated Senator Douglas, but it may be stated that his re-election to the Senate was to depend on the election in Illinois in 1858, and unless he did something to counteract the feeling against him he was almost certain of defeat. The apostasy of Douglas was as a thunderbolt to the South, but the North received it with great delight, and in the early months of 1858 Douglas was easily the most popular man in the North. The new Legislature in Kansas met in December and ordered another election at which the people of the Territory could vote for or against the Lecompton Constitution, and on January 9, 1858, that Constitution was rejected by ten thousand majority. Notwithstanding this emphatic condemnation by the people of the Territory, the Administration persisted in its course to force Kansas in under the Lecompton Constitution. The Senate was for the admission of Kansas, but the House opposed it, and in a joint conference the infamous English Bill was agreed on, in which the people of Kansas were offered a bribe in the form of large land grants if they would accept the Lecompton Constitution. This they subsequently refused to do by a large majority, and Kansas remained a Territory until 1861. The Dred Scott decision and the attempt to force in Kansas under the Lecompton Constitution helped the Republican Party greatly, and its prospects were brighter in 1858 than they had been in 1857, in which year there was a reaction from the enthusiasm created by the presidential campaign of the preceding year.

A legislature was to be chosen in Illinois in 1858 which would select the successor to Senator Douglas. Douglas' action in opposing the Administration had aroused public interest in him in the North, and many of the Republican leaders desired that he should have no opposition in Illinois, but the Republicans of that State were not of that opinion. The Democratic Convention in Illinois met in April and endorsed Douglas; the Republican Convention, on June 16th, resolved "That Abraham Lincoln is the first and only choice of the Republicans of Illinois for the United States Senate, as the successor of Stephen A. Douglas." In his speech that evening to the Convention Mr. Lincoln made the remarkable and daring statement, "A house divided against itself cannot stand. I believe this government cannot endure, permanently, half slave and half free. I do not expect the Union to be dissolved; I do not expect the house to fall; but I expect it will cease to be divided. It will become all one thing or all the other."

Senator Douglas reached Chicago on July 9th, and. amid the plaudits of his friends, delivered an elaborate speech, which was listened to with great interest by Mr. Lincoln, who was present; on the next evening Mr. Lincoln answered in the presence of a large and enthusiastic audience. Senator Douglas then spoke at Bloomington, and was answered by Mr. Lincoln at Springfield, and the public interest that had been aroused, not only in Illinois but throughout the country, caused the Republican leaders to induce Mr. Lincoln to challenge Senator Douglas to a series of debates on the great question of the hour. Privately Senator Douglas was averse to meeting Mr. Lincoln in this manner, but publicly he promptly accepted the challenge and named seven places in different Congressional Districts in which neither had spoken, as the places where the debates were to be held. These great debates began at Ottawa on August 21, 1858, and were followed by meetings at Freeport, Jonesboro, Charleston, Galesburg, Quincy, and concluded on October 15th at Alton, the entire State having been traversed.

As they read and pondered on the arguments of Mr. Lincoln, it gradually dawned upon the people of the North that a great leader had been found, for it was early seen and felt that Senator Douglas was not holding his own. No greater or clearer exposition of the Northern views of slavery and the questions connected with it had ever been pronounced than Mr. Lincoln's, and the great contest in Illi-

nois was watched with eagerness and interest by the entire
North, and Mr. Lincoln, from a comparatively unknown
State leader, became a great national character.

At Freeport, Mr. Lincoln, contrary to the advice of all
his friends, asked the question which forced Douglas into a
labored attempt to reconcile his doctrine of popular sovereignty with the Dred Scott decision. It was plain that
the question, "Can the people of a United States Territory
in any lawful way, against the wish of any citizen of the
United States, exclude slavery from its limits prior to the
formation of a State Constitution?" could not be answered
without antagonizing either the North or the South. There
was absolutely no middle ground on which Senator Douglas could stand for any length of time.

Mr. Lincoln was willing to lose the Senatorial contest
if Douglas could be defeated for the Presidency, and he
gained his point, although his friends did not immediately
see the strength of it. Senator Douglas, in an artful reply
to this searching question, put forward his doctrine of Popular Sovereignty by asserting that the people could, by "unfriendly legislation," effectually prevent the introduction
of slavery into their midst. When the South read this
declaration, so contrary to the decision of the Supreme
Court, Douglas' fate was sealed as a presidential candidate.
Owing to a totally unfair apportionment of the Senatorial
Districts, which had been made by a Democratic Legislature, Mr. Lincoln lost the contest with Senator Douglas,
who had a majority of eight on the joint ballot in the new

Legislature, but the Republican Ticket won in the popular vote by 4000.

Mr. Lincoln was forty-nine years old and Senator Douglas forty-five when they met in these memorable debates. They had been thrown together for more than twenty years by a most remarkable combination of circumstances. They had both wooed the same woman, Mary Todd, and Lincoln won; both craved for success in politics, and as Douglas belonged to the dominant party in Illinois, he met with early success, and ran the gamut of political honors and was a great national figure before Lincoln was known. Douglas had been Attorney-General, Secretary of State and Judge of the Supreme Court of Illinois; in 1843 he was elected to the National House of Representatives and served until 1847, when he was sent to the Senate, where he served until 1861; his name had been presented for the presidential nomination to the Democratic Conventions of 1852 and 1856. Compared to this series of political successes those of Lincoln were indeed meagre. He had served in the Illinois Legislature; in 1847 was sent to Congress, but served only one term, and from 1849 to 1854 he had devoted himself, with the exception of some canvassing done for Scott in the Campaign of 1852, almost exclusively to his law practice. It was Senator Douglas' Kansas-Nebraska Bill that brought Lincoln again into politics, with emphatic protests and strong arguments against the outrage. When Mr. Douglas returned to Illinois in 1854, he attempted, with much difficulty, to justify his action, and the debates between him and Mr. Lincoln really began in that year. Lin-

coln met his arguments, and after a few speeches Mr. Douglas was ready to quit, and made an agreement with Mr. Lincoln that neither of them should speak again in the campaign. In 1854 Mr. Lincoln was the choice for United
States Senator, but yielded his place to Lyman Trumbull.
He took an active part in the formation of the Republican
Party in Illinois, and at the Bloomington Convention in
1856, which chose delegates to the first Republican National Convention, he made a strong speech that attracted
the attention of the Republicans of Illinois to him and
made him the State leader. He labored earnestly in Illinois for the success of Fremont and Dayton. Throughout
1857 he grew stronger with the party, with the result that
he was the unanimous and only choice in 1858 as the successor to Douglas.

Douglas secured the shadow of a victory, but Mr. Lincoln, and the Republican Party throughout the North, had
the substance, and the fall elections in 1858 were decidedlv
in favor of the Republicans. The Autumn campaigns of
1859 were of the utmost importance, and the Democrats
made great efforts in the North, especially in Ohio. Senator Douglas went personally into that State, and at the
earnest invitation of the Republican Committee, Mr. Lincoln spoke at Columbus on September 16th and at Cincinnati on September 17th. Mr. Dennison, the Republican
candidate in Ohio, was elected, and the Republicans were
successful in Pennsylvania and Iowa.

A few days after the October elections the entire country was thrown into a state of great excitement by John

Brown's invasion of Virginia and his capture of the United States arsenal at Harper's Ferry. He had hoped for a general uprising of the slaves, but it did not occur, and Brown was captured by Robert E. Lee, then a Colonel in the United States Army, and after a trial on a charge of murder and treason against the State of Virginia, was found guilty and hanged December 2, 1859. This affair aroused the Slave Power to a frenzy of excitement, and they immediately demanded an investigation, and strong attempts were made to fix the conspiracy on members of the Republican Party, but it signally failed.

Three days after John Brown's execution, the Thirty-sixth Congress assembled. In the Senate there were thirty-eight Democrats, twenty-five Republicans, and two Americans; the Republicans had gained five Senators. In the House there were one hundred and nine Republicans, eighty-eight administration Democrats, thirteen anti-Lecompton Democrats, and twenty-seven Americans, all of the latter, except four, from the South. The contest for the Speakership developed the deep animosity felt by the South, and threats of disunion and personal violence abounded throughout the session. The Republicans generally remained silent, only taking part in the debates when absolutely necessary. On the first ballots the Republicans divided their votes between Galusha A. Grow, of Pennsylvania, and John Sherman, of Ohio; Mr. Grow having received the fewer number of votes, withdrew, under an agreement, and the contest continued between Mr. Sherman and Mr. Bocock, of Virginia. On January 4, 1860, Sherman was within three votes of an election, but he finally withdrew in favor of William Pennington, a Republican, of New Jersey, who was elected on February 1, 1860, and the House secured a Republican organization. During the debate attendant upon this election, Mr. Crawford, of Georgia, declared, "We will never submit to the inauguration of a black Republican President," and this remark, with others of a like nature, was often repeated. Many of the members of Congress attended the session fully armed, and it often appeared that the Civil War would probably begin in the House of Representatives.

In the decade between 1840 and 1850, the number of slaves in the South increased 800,000; and in the decade between 1850 and 1860, 700,000. The increase of white population in the South was very small compared to that of the North. The census of 1850 showed the population of the country to be 23,191,876, divided as follows:

	White.	Free Black.	Slave.
North	13,269,149	196,262	262
South	6,283,965	238,187	3 204,051

The tremendous increase of slave population and the rapid gain of the North over the South in free population is shown by a comparison of the census of 1850 with that of 1860, when the total population was 31,443,322, divided between the two sections as follows:

	White.	Free Black.	Slave.
North	18,791,159	225,967	64
South	8,182,684	262,003	3,953,696

Owing to the large crops in the South the demand for

slaves exceeded the supply, and the market price of negroes in the decade between 1850 and 1860 was very high. Three results followed the increased demand and the high prices —the Domestic Slave Trade between the States was largely increased; attempts to smuggle in slaves contrary to the Slave Trade Laws were numerous and often successful, and the South began, in Buchanan's administration, to consider the re-establishment of the African slave trade.

During the last years of Buchanan's administration politics were dominated by virtually three parties: the Republicans with their opposition to slavery extension—the leaders being Mr. Lincoln and Mr. Seward; the Northern Democrats, led by Senator Douglas, with his idea of Popular Sovereignty; and the Southern Democrats, with their purpose of slavery extension and protection under the decision of the Supreme Court and the Acts of Congress, their leader being Jefferson Davis, of Mississippi. The schism in the Democratic Party was seen more clearly late in February, 1859, when Senators Douglas and Davis, representing the opposite principles advocated by the Democratic Party, engaged in a bitter debate, which forecasted clearly a division in the Democratic Party in 1860, and the probable election of a Republican President, but who would he be, and what would be the course of the South on his election?

CHAPTER XI.

"Since the November of 1860 his horizon has been black with storms. By day and by night, he trod a way of danger and darkness. On his shoulders rested a government dearer to him than his own life... ....Even he who now sleeps has, by this event, been clothed with new influence. Dead, he speaks to men who now willingly hear what before they refused to listen to.   .Four years ago, O Illinois, we took from your midst an untried man and from among the people. We return him to you a mighty conqueror. Not thine any more, but the nation's; not ours, but the world's."

Henry Ward Beecher, April 16, 1865.

In 1860 the curtain rolled up on the beginning of the last act in the great drama of the struggle between Freedom and Slavery. Because of the events already narrated, a division in the Democratic Party was almost certain if Douglas persisted in being a candidate, and that division would mean the success of the Republican Party. A greater anxiety and fear than perhaps ever before or since in the history of the country pervaded the political situation in the early months of 1860. What would transpire at the Conventions of the great parties? All eyes turned to the first Convention, that of the Democratic Party, which assembled at Charleston, S. C., April 23, 1860. Senator Douglas was a candidate. There was almost an immediate disagreement on the slavery question, and a group of extreme Southern Democrats, unable to agree with their

(112)

Northern brethren who adopted a Douglas platform, withdrew from the Convention. This first group of seceders held a separate meeting, and after adopting a Platform, adjourned to meet at Richmond, Va., on June 11th. In the main Convention opposition to Douglas was still strong, and after fifty-seven ballots, without being able to nominate any candidate, the main Convention adjourned to meet at Baltimore on June 18th. The bolters from the Charleston Convention met in Richmond on June 11th, but immediately adjourned again until June 28th, which was to be ten days after the adjourned meeting of the main Convention. The main Convention duly assembled at Baltimore on June 18th, and as it was apparent that Douglas would be nominated, there was another withdrawal of Southern Democrats accompanied by some of their Northern brethren. Those who remained nominated Stephen A. Douglas for President and Benjamin Fitzpatrick of Alabama for Vice-President. Mr. Fitzpatrick afterwards declined, and the National Democratic Committee named Herschel V. Johnson, of Georgia, for Vice-President. The second group of bolters unanimously nominated John C. Breckinridge, of Kentucky, for President, and Joseph Lane, of Oregon, for Vice-President, and adopted the platform which had been agreed upon by the bolters from the Charleston Convention. The Charleston bolters, when they met again on June 28th, ratified the nominations of Breckinridge and Lane. The Douglas Democratic platform affirmed the Cincinnati platform of 1856, and stated that the party would abide by the decision of the Supreme Court on questions of Constitutional Law, and it denounced the Personal Liberty Laws as revolutionary. The Breckinridge Democratic platform also adopted the Cincinnati platform, but with explanatory resolutions to the effect that neither Congress or any Territorial Legislature had a right to interfere with slavery, pending the formation of a State Constitution, and that it was the duty of the Federal Government to protect slavery at all times. This platform also denounced the Personal Liberty Laws. The Democratic Party had won in 1856 on an ambiguous plank in their platform, relating to slavery in the Territories, that enabled them to secure votes in the North and South by arguments irreconcilable with the political thought of the two sections, and now, in 1860, they were dissipating their strength by disagreeing on an explanation among themselves of that ambiguous plank; it was a just political retribution.

A temporary political party appeared in 1860, known as the Constitutional Union Party; their convention was held at Baltimore on May 9th, and John Bell, of Tennessee, was named for President, and Edward Everett, of Massachusetts, for Vice-President. The Platform of this party declared for "The Constitution of the country, the Union of the States and the enforcement of the Laws." It was an attempt to divert the voters from the geographical and sectional parties, and polled a large popular vote.

The second Republican National Convention convened at Chicago on Wednesday, May 16, 1860, in the "Wigwam," a vast pine board structure specially built for the occasion by the Chicago Republican Club. The split in the

Democratic Party, although the adjourned sessions of that Party had not yet been held, gave increased hope of Republican success this year, and it was felt by a great majority of the delegates and spectators that the Convention would name the next President of the United States. This strong probability added an importance and dignity, not unmingled with awe, to the work of the Convention. Edwin D. Morgan, of New York, called the Convention to order and faced an audience of about ten thousand people, only four hundred and sixty-six of whom were delegates. All of the free States were represented, as well as Delaware, Kentucky, Maryland, Missouri, Texas and Virginia, and the Territories of Kansas and Nebraska and the District of Columbia. Mr. Morgan named David Wilmot for Temporary Chairman, and committees on Permanent Organization, on Credentials, and on Rules were then severally appointed. George Ashmun, of Massachusetts, was reported a Chairman of the Convention, and one Vice-President and one Secretary from each State and Territory were named. A Platform Committee was then appointed, after which the Convention decided, after some debate over the admission of "delegates" from the Slave States, some of whom had never seen their States, to admit all delegates, and this included Horace Greeley, "of Oregon," who had not desired and had not been sent with the New York delegation. A virtual attempt to fasten the two-thirds nominating rule on the Convention was defeated, and it was decided that a majority of the whole number of votes should nominate. Judge William Jessup, of Pennsylvania, reported the platform.

and it was adopted with the utmost enthusiasm. The platform on which Mr. Lincoln was elected should be read by every Republican and every citizen interested in the history and development of the nation.

REPUBLICAN PLATFORM, 1860.

Resolved, That we, the delegated representatives of the Republican electors of the United States, in convention assembled, in discharge of the duty we owe to our constituents and our country, unite in the following declarations:

1.   That the history of the nation during the last four years has fully established the propriety and necessity of the organization and perpetuation of the Republican party, and that the causes which called it into existence are permanent in their nature, and now, more than ever before, demand its peaceful and constitutional triumph.

2.   That the maintenance of the principles promulgated in the Declaration of Independence and embodied in the Federal Constitution, "That all men are created equal; that they are endowed by their Creator with certain inalienable rights; that among these are life, liberty, and the pursuit of happiness; that to secure these rights, governments are instituted among men, deriving their just powers from the consent of the governed," is essential to the preservation of our republican institutions; and that the Federal Constitution, the rights of the states, and the union of the states must and shall be preserved.

3.   That to the union of the states this nation owes its unprecedented increase in population, its surprising development of material resources, its rapid augmentation of wealth, its happiness at home and its honor abroad; and we hold in abhorrence all schemes for disunion, come from whatever source they may; and we congratulate the country that no Republican member of Congress has uttered or countenanced the threats of disunion so often made by Democratic members, without rebuke and with applause from their political associates; and we denounce those threats of disunion, in case of a popular overthrow of their ascendancy, as denying the vital principles of free government, and as an avowal of contemplated treason, which

it is the imperative duty of an indignant people sternly to rebuke and forever silence.

4. That the maintenance inviolate of the rights of the states, and especially the right of each state to order and control its own domestic institutions according to its own judgment exclusively, is essential to that balance of power on which the perfection and endurance of our political fabric depends; and we denounce the lawless invasion by armed force of the soil of any state or territory, no matter under what pretext, as among the gravest of crimes.

5. That the present Democratic administration has far exceeded our worst apprehensions, in its measureless subserviency to the exactions of a sectional interest, as especially evinced in its desperate exertions to force the infamous Lecompton constitution upon the protesting people of Kansas; in construing the personal relations between master and servant to involve an unqualified property in persons; in its attempted enforcement everywhere, on land and sea, through the intervention of Congress and of the federal courts, of the extreme pretensions of a purely local interest; and in its general and unvarying abuse of the power intrusted to it by a confiding people.

6. That the people justly view with alarm the reckless extravagance which pervades every department of the federal government; that a return to rigid economy and accountability is indispensable to arrest the systematic plunder of the public treasury by favored partisans, while the recent startling developments of frauds and corruptions at the federal metropolis show that an entire change of administration is imperatively demanded.

7. That the new dogma—that the Constitution, of its own force, carries slavery into any or all of the territories of the United States —is a dangerous political heresy, at variance with the explicit provisions of that instrument itself, with contemporaneous exposition, and with legislative and judicial precedent; is revolutionary in its tendency and subversive of the peace and harmony of the country.

8. That the normal condition of all the territory of the United States is that of freedom; that, as our republican fathers, when they had abolished slavery in all our national territory, ordained that "no person should be deprived of life, liberty, or property without due process of law," it becomes our duty, by legislation, whenever such legislation is necessary, to maintain this provision of the Constitution against all attempts to violate it; and we deny the authority of Congress, of a territorial legislature, or of any individuals,

to give legal existence to slavery in any territory of the United States.

9. That we brand the recent reopening of the African slave trade, under the cover of our national flag, aided by perversions of judicial power, as a crime against humanity and a burning shame to our country and age; and we call upon Congress to take prompt and efficient measures for the total and final suppression of that execrable traffic.

10. That in the recent vetoes, by their federal governors, of the acts of the legislatures of Kansas and Nebraska, prohibiting slavery in those territories, we find a practical illustration of the boasted Democratic principle of non-intervention and popular sovereignty, embodied in the Kansas-Nebraska bill, and a demonstration of the deception and fraud involved therein.

11. That Kansas should of right be immediately admitted as a state under the constitution recently formed and adopted by her people and accepted by the House of Representatives.

12. That, while providing revenue for the support of the general government by duties upon imports, sound policy requires such an adjustment of these imposts as to encourage the development of the industrial interests of the whole country; and we commend that policy of national exchanges which secures to the workingmen liberal wages, to agriculture remunerative prices, to mechanics and manufacturers an adequate reward for their skill, labor and enterprise, and to the nation commercial prosperity and independence.

13. That we protest against any sale or alienation to others of the public lands held by actual settlers, and against any view of the free-homestead policy which regards the settlers as paupers or suppliants for public bounty; and we demand the passage by Congress of the complete and satisfactory homestead measure which has already passed the House.

14. That the Republican party is opposed to any change in our naturalization laws, or any state legislation by which the rights of citizens hitherto accorded to immigrants from foreign lands shall be abridged or impaired; and in favor of giving a full and efficient protection to the rights of all classes of citizens, whether native or naturalized, both at home and abroad.

15. That appropriations by Congress for river and harbor improvements of a national character, required for the accommodation and security of an existing commerce, are authorized by the Con-

stitution and justified by the obligation of government to protect the lives and property of its citizens.

16. That a railroad to the Pacific Ocean is imperatively demanded by the interests of the whole country; that the federal government ought to render immediate and efficient aid in its construction; and that, as preliminary thereto, a daily overland mail should be promptly established.

17. Finally having set forth our distinctive principles and views, we invite the co-operation of all citizens, however differing on other questions, who substantially agree with us in their affirmance and support.

An exciting incident occurred when Joshua R. Giddings moved to embrace the principles of the Declaration of Independence in the platform, and, when voted down, withdrew from the Convention; but what he proposed was afterwards accomplished by George William Curtis, of New York, and became the second plank of the platform, and Mr. Giddings returned to the Convention.

Two days were consumed in organizing and adopting the platform. The second night of the Convention, that which intervened between Thursday and Friday, was given up to remarkable exertions in behalf of the several candidates. William H. Seward, of New York, was the most prominent candidate before the Convention, and would probably have been named had the nominations been made on the first or second day of the Convention. The other candidates were Abraham Lincoln, of Illinois; Simon Cameron, of Pennsylvania; Salmon P. Chase and John McLean, of Ohio; Edward Bates, of Missouri; William L. Dayton, of New Jersey, and Jacob Collamer, of Vermont. There was a strong opposition to Mr. Seward, based on the ground of his availability, as it was felt by Henry S. Lane, of Indiana, and A. G. Curtin, of Pennsylvania, who were the candidates for Governor in their respective States, that Mr. Seward could not carry those States. Mr. Greeley was also doing his utmost to defeat Mr. Seward, but was advocating the nomination of Edward Bates, of Missouri. The Illinois delegation had been instructed for Mr. Lincoln, and soon added Indiana to his support, and they also obtained promises of a majority vote of the New Hampshire, Virginia and Kentucky delegations on the first ballot, with some scattering votes from other States. Mr. Lincoln's candidacy was very promising, but not entirely certain of success, as, to many, the strength of Mr. Seward appeared invincible; but Mr. Lincoln's supporters were certain that if he could obtain a good vote on the first ballot it would be largely increased on the second ballot by votes from Pennsylvania, Ohio and Vermont. On the third day of the Convention, Friday morning, May 18th, the nominations were made. William M. Evarts presented the name of William H. Seward, and was immediately followed by Norman B. Judd, of Illinois, who nominated Mr. Lincoln. Others were named, and a number of seconding speeches were made, Mr. Lincoln's name being seconded by Caleb B. Smith, of Indiana, and Columbus Delano, of Ohio. The cheers and noisy enthusiasm which attended the various speeches were terrifying in volume, and it was apparent that the Lincoln shouters had the advantage in volume of sound, and the influence of the vast assemblage and the great pressure of environment unquestionably increased Mr. Lincoln's chances for the nomination. The balloting began and proceeded amid intense excitement; two hundred and thirty-three votes were necessary to a choice, and three ballots were taken, with the following result:

	1st Ballot.	2d Ballot.	3d Ballot.
Seward	173½	184½	180
Lincoln	102	181	231½
Cameron	50½	2	
Chase	49	42½	24½
Bates	48	35	22
Dayton	14	10	
McLean .	12	8	5
Collamer	10		

Scattering votes were also cast for Benjamin F. Wade, John M. Reed, Charles Sumner, John C. Fremont, and Cassius M. Clay.

At the completion of the third ballot, Mr. Lincoln lacked one and one-half votes of the nomination. There was a momentary lull, and then David K. Cartter, of Ohio, mounted his seat, caught the attention of the Chairman, and, in the breathless excitement, announced that Ohio changed four votes from Mr. Chase to Mr. Lincoln. There was a moment's silence until it could all be appreciated, and then pandemonium for more than twenty minutes. The immense crowd outside the "Wigwam" was soon apprised of the result and the news spread like wildfire. Mr. Evarts moved the nomination be made unanimous.

There were two prominent candidates for Vice-President, Hannibal Hamlin, of Maine, and Cassius M. Clay, of Kentucky. Others mentioned for this honor were John Hickman and Andrew H. Reeder, of Pennsylvania, and Nathaniel P. Banks, of Massachusetts. Two ballots were taken, and Mr. Hamlin was nominated on the second:

	1st Ballot.	2d Ballot.
Hamlin	194	367
Clay	$101\frac{1}{2}$	86
Hickman	58	13
Reeder	51	
Banks	38	

Others who received complimentary votes on the first ballot were Samuel Houston, William L. Dayton, Henry W. Davis, John M. Reed, Andrew H. Reeder and John Hickman.

During the entire Convention Mr. Lincoln remained at Springfield; there he received the telegraphic news of his nomination, and thither went the Notification Committee, composed of many brilliant men, most of whom had never met him. On May 23d Mr. Lincoln wrote an admirable letter of acceptance, and the campaign was on in earnest, notwithstanding that the Democrats had not yet presented their ticket. In the Western States, where his name and history appealed to the people, Mr. Lincoln's nomination was received with the utmost delight; but in the Eastern States the first feeling over the defeat of Mr. Seward was one of bitter disappointment, but Mr. Seward and the other great leaders promptly and manfully gave their whole support to Mr. Lincoln, and there was never any question that

the party would not be united in his support. The Democratic press vented its snobbishness by constant articles
calling attention to Mr. Lincoln's poverty, and asserting
that he was not a gentleman, and had "never traveled and
had no pedigree."

The Republican Campaign of 1860 consisted of a liberal use of political literature and of a systematic stumping
of the country by the great men of the party, prominent
among whom were Seward, Schurz, Clay, Greeley, Stevens,
and many others, and hundreds of other Republican
speakers of less prominence who traversed the Northern
States. Bands of "Wide-Awakes" were organized everywhere in the North and participated in the parades with
torches and a simple uniform. There were many great
State rallies for the Republican ticket. In the North it
was apparent that the vote would be cast for either Lincoln, Douglas or Bell, and in the slave States for Breckinridge. From the end of May to November the work went
on and the Republicans gained rapidly in strength, notwithstanding the threats of the South to secede if the Federal Government should ever pass into the "treacherous
hands of the Black Republican Party." Mr. Lincoln remained at Springfield during the entire campaign, going
about his usual affairs, and meeting the hundreds of curious
and otherwise who came to see him. He maintained a
strict silence on the great problem of the hour, but watched
the campaign closely, and often gave sound advice to the
managers. On August 8th the greatest State rally held

in the North took place at Springfield, and it was estimated that fully 75,000 people were present.

After some desperate campaigning Senator Douglas gave up all hope of success, and announced that he would go South to urge upon all the duty of submitting to the result of the election, and he steadfastly asserted his intention of standing by the Union.

The only danger was that Mr. Lincoln might not receive a majority of the electoral vote, which would throw the election into the House of Representatives, but this was dispelled when Pennsylvania and Indiana went Republican in October, and the result of the election on November 6th was conceded. Mr. Lincoln received the electoral votes of California, Connecticut, Illinois, Indiana, Iowa, Maine, Massachusetts, Michigan, Minnesota, New Hampshire, New Jersey, New York, Ohio, Oregon, Pennsylvania, Rhode Island, Vermont and Wisconsin, all Northern States, and casting 180 out of 303 electoral votes. Breckinridge carried Alabama, Arkansas, Delaware, Florida, Georgia, Louisiana, Maryland, Mississippi, North Carolina, South Carolina and Texas, all slave States, and casting seventy-two electoral votes. Bell carried Kentucky, Tennessee and Virginia, thirty-nine votes; and Douglas only carried one State, Missouri, with nine votes, but also received three of the seven votes of New Jersey, the remainder going to Mr. Lincoln. The popular vote was as follows:

| Lincoln . | 1,866,352 | Breckinridge . . | 847,514 |
| Douglas . | 1,375,157 | Bell . . . . | 587,830 |

This does not include the popular vote of South Carolina, where the electors were chosen by the Legislature.

The Slave Power lost no time in carrying into effect its threats of disunion. South Carolina seceded on December 20, 1860, and by the end of the year had seized the United States arsenals and other government property in the State, but Fort Sumter was not molested. By February, 1861, Mississippi, Florida, Alabama, Georgia, Louisiana and Texas had also withdrawn. Virginia did not secede until April 17th. On February 4th a Confederate Congress met at Montgomery, Alabama, and on February 9th Jefferson Davis, of Mississippi, became President, and Alexander H. Stephens, of Georgia, became Vice-President of the Confederate States of America.

The breaking up of the Union did not go on without some attempts at compromising the situation, but all such efforts failed. The House and the Senate appointed special committees, who were either unable to agree or whose conclusions were not adopted. On December 18th the Crittenden Compromise Measures were introduced, and after long debate were rejected March 2, 1861. Dramatic withdrawals from Congress were made by the Southern Senators and Representatives, and this enabled Kansas to be admitted, on January 29, 1861, as a free State.

Far from attempting to stop this breaking up of the Union, Buchanan's Administration did everything it could to aid it. Treason ran free in Washington; the Navy was scattered and rendered unavailable; the Army was demoralized, and thousands of stands of arms and other military equipment were removed from the Northern arsenals and sent South; and President Buchanan, through his Cabinet, announced the remarkable doctrine that any State could strike at the Union, appropriate the arms and property of the Government, and that nothing could be done to stop it. It was not treason for South Carolina to act as she did, but it would be treason to attempt to stop her course.

Such was the situation when Mr. Lincoln was inaugurated on March 4, 1861; seven States were out of the Union, a Southern Confederacy had been established with an organized Government, and its President inaugurated; the Army and Navy were crippled, the Treasury drained, and treason and assassination threatened on all sides. From the east portico of the Capitol, with Senator Douglas standing behind holding Mr. Lincoln's hat, the President delivered his first Inaugural Speech. Calm, clear, wise and firm were the words. It concluded, "I am loath to close. We are not enemies, but friends. We must not be enemies. Though passion may have strained, it must not break our bonds of affection. The mystic cords of memory, stretching from every battlefield and patriot grave to every living heart and hearthstone all over this broad land, will yet swell the chorus of the Union when again touched, as surely they will be, by the better angel of our nature."

The bombardment of Ft. Sumter, which began on the morning of April 12, 1861, was the event that unified both the North and the South, and henceforth the issue was to be decided solely by War. In the North, party lines were forgotten, and the President received promises of hearty support on all sides. On April 15th, the President declared the South to be in a state of rebellion, and called for 75,000 troops to recover the Government forts and property, and also called an extraordinary session of Congress, to meet on July 4th. This history is not directly concerned with the trying and bloody events of the Civil War. The tremendous strain on President Lincoln during this period perhaps will never be fully appreciated by the generations which follow it; it was all a horrible nightmare through which the country safely passed under the guidance of President Lincoln and the Republican Party.

On April 16, 1862, Slavery was abolished in the District of Columbia, and on June 19th was forever prohibited in the Territories. On September 22d President Lincoln issued his preliminary Proclamation of Emancipation, declaring all slaves forever free in territory which might still be in rebellion on January 1, 1863. This act, and what was believed to be the failure of the Administration in conducting the War, turned thousands of Democrats in the North away from the President, and in the Fall elections of 1862 large Democratic gains were made. Ohio, Indiana, Pennsylvania, Illinois, New Jersey and Wisconsin went Democratic; New York elected a Democratic Governor, Horatio Seymour; but New England, the Border States and the Western States not mentioned, stood firm for the President, and the Administration was assured of a good working majority in the House.

Before passing to the presidential campaign of 1864, mention must be made of several great legislative acts of

the Republican Party during the first few years of its control of the Government. The Morrill Protective Tariff Bill
was made a law on March 2, 1861, and became the foundation of the Republican Tariff Bills of later years; the Legal
Tender Act of February 25, 1862, was a great turning
point in the financial history of the nation; the Homestead
Act of May 20, 1862, opened up the western country to
actual settlers, and contributed greatly to the development
of the West; the Internal Revenue Act of July 1, 1862,
and a National Banking system, established by the Act of
February 25, 1863, were most important, the latter removing the conflict between the national currency and the currency of the state banks, and marked the beginning of a
sound and stable financial system, the importance of which,
in the remarkable physical development of the country,
cannot be too strongly asserted.

Although throughout 1863 a strong radical element in
the Republican Party worked against the renomination of
President Lincoln in 1864, on the ground of his alleged
timidity in handling the question of the Civil War, this
movement gradually dwindled in strength and had almost
disappeared with the opening of the presidential year of
1864, when an election was to be held with a war in progress and the country divided. Throughout the winter of
1863 and 1864 Mr. Chase made active efforts to secure the
presidential nomination, but the Ohio Legislature demanded Mr. Lincoln's renomination, and Mr. Chase had to
withdraw. State Legislatures throughout the North now
demanded the renomination of the President, and they were

joined in their resolutions by large numbers of clubs and public meetings, and it was apparent to those in the party who were antagonistic to the President that no other candidate would have any chance. But the Copperhead element was still rampant, and the Democrats denounced the President in unmeasured terms, declaring the war to be a failure, and demanding peace.

The radical element of the Republican Party held their Convention first, at Cleveland, Ohio, on May 31, 1864, and nominated John C. Fremont for President and John Cochrane for Vice-President, but these candidates withdrew on September 2d, and no further notice of this meeting is necessary. The regular Republican Convention, or National Union Convention, as it was called, was held at Baltimore on June 7 and 8, 1864, in the Front Street Theater. The Convention was again called to order by Edwin B. Morgan, of New York, who, after a short speech, proposed the name of Robert J. Breckinridge, of Kentucky, for temporary Chairman. Mr. Breckinridge accepted the honor, and said that he did not enter the deliberations of the Convention as a Republican, nor as a Whig or Democrat, but as a Union man. There was some debate over the seating of loyal delegates from the Confederate States, which was settled by admitting them; thirty-one States, including eight of the slave States, were represented. The usual committees on Credentials, Permanent Organization and Resolutions were appointed. The Committee reported the name of William Dennison, of Ohio, for permanent Chairman. The platform was reported by Henry J. Raymond, of New York, and enthusiasticallv adopted. The Republican Platform of 1864, framed while a great Civil War was in progress, is a most interesting document.

REPUBLICAN PLATFORM, 1864.

1. *Resolved*, That it is the highest duty of every American citizen to maintain against all their enemies the integrity of the Union and the paramount authority of the Constitution and laws of the United States; and that, laying aside all differences of political opinion, we pledge ourselves as Union men, animated by a common sentiment and aiming at a common object, to do everything in our power to aid the government in quelling by force of arms the rebellion now raging against its authority, and in bringing to the punishment due to their crimes the rebels and traitors arrayed against it.

2. *Resolved*, That we approve the determination of the government of the United States not to compromise with rebels, or to offer them any terms of peace except such as may be based upon an unconditional surrender of their hostilitv and a return to their just allegiance to the Constitution and laws of the United States; and that we call upon the government to maintain this position and to prosecute the war with the utmost possible vigor, to the complete suppression of the rebellion, in full reliance upon the self-sacrificing patriotism, the heroic valor, and the undying devotion of the American people to the country and its free institutions.

3. *Resolved*, That as slavery was the cause and now constitutes the strength of this rebellion, and as it must be always and everywhere hostile to the principles ot republican government, justice and the national safety demand its utter and complete extirpation from the soil of the republic; and that while we uphold and maintain the acts and proclamations ,by which the government, in its own defense, has aimed a death-blow at this gigantic evil, we are in favor, furthermore, of such an amendment to the Constitution, to be made by the people in conformity with its provisions, as shall terminate and forever prohibit the existence of slavery within the limits of the jurisdiction of the United States.

4. *Resolved*, That the thanks of the American people are due

to the soldiers and sailors of the army and navy who have periled their lives in defense of the country and in vindication of the honor of its flag; that the nation owes to them some permanent recognition of their patriotism and their valor, and ample and permaneut provision for those of their survivors who have received disabling and honorable wounds in the service of the country; and that the memories of those who have fallen in its defense shall be held in grateful and everlasting remembrance.

5. *Resolved*, That we approve and applaud the practical wisdom, the unselfish patriotism, and the unswerving fidelity to the Constitution and the principles of American liberty with which Abraham Lincoln has discharged, under circumstances of unparalleled difficulty, the great duties and responsibilities of the presidential office; that we approve and indorse, as demanded by the emergency and essential to the preservation of the nation, and as within the provisions of the Constitution, the measures and acts which he has adopted to defend the nation against its open and secret foes; that we approve especially the proclamation of emancipation and the employment as Union soldiers of men heretofore held in slavery; and that we have full confidence in his determination to carry these and all other constitutional measures essential to the salvation of the country into full and complete effect.

6. *Resolved*, That we deem it essential to the general welfare that harmony should prevail in the national councils, and we regard as worthy of public confidence and official trust those only who cordially indorse the principles proclaimed in these resolutions, and which should characterize the administration of the government.

7. *Resolved*, That the government owes to all men employed in its armies. without regard to distinction of color, the full protection of the laws of war; and that any violation of these laws, or of the usages of civilized nations in time of war, by the rebels now in arms, should be made the subject of prompt and full redress.

8. *Resolved*, That foreign immigration, which in the past has added so much to the wealth, development of resources, and increase of power to the nation—the asylum of the oppressed of all nations should be fostered and encouraged by a liberal and just policy.

9. *Resolved*, That we are in favor of the speedy construction of the railroad to the Pacific coast.

10. *Resolved*, That the national faith, pledged for the redemp-

tion of the public debt, must be kept inviolate, and that for this purpose we recommend economy and rigid responsibility in the public expenditures, and a vigorous and just system of taxation; and that it is the duty of every loyal state to sustain the credit and promote the use of the national currency.

11. *Resolved*, That we approve the position taken by the government, that the people of the United States can never regard with indifference the attempt of any European power to overthrow by force, or to supplant by fraud, the institutions of any republican government on the western continent; and that they will view with extreme jealousy, as menacing to the peace and independence of their own country the efforts of any such power to obtain new footholds for monarchial governments, sustained by foreign military force, in near proximity to the United States.

After the adoption of the platform, Simon Cameron introduced a resolution declaring for Lincoln and Hamlin as the unanimous choice of the Convention for President and Vice-President; but this resolution was divided so that the Convention could vote separately on the two offices. On the first ballot Mr. Lincoln received the vote of every delegation except Missouri, which voted for Ulysses S. Grant, but changed immediately as soon as the ballot had been announced, and made Mr. Lincoln's nomination unanimous. The interest of the delegation and the spectators through-out the Convention had been centered on the nomination for Vice-President. A number of names were mentioned, the most prominent being Andrew Johnson, of Tennessee, Hannibal Hamlin, of Maine, and Daniel S. Dickinson, of New York. Mr. Johnson was a War Democrat. The sentiment in the Convention was in favor of recognizing this element in the party, and Mr. Johnson was nominated on the first ballot; the vote as cast gave Johnson 200, Ham-

IMPORTANT.

ASSASSINATION

OF

PRESIDENT LINCOLN.

The President Shot at the Theatre Last Evening.

SECRETARY SEWARD

DAGGERED IN HIS BED,

BUT

NOT MORTALLY WOUNDED.

Carence and Frederick Seward Badly Hurt.

ESCAPE OF THE ASSASSINS.

Intense Excitement in Washington.

Scene at the Deathbed of Mr. Lincoln.

J. Wilkes Booth, the Actor, the Alleged s y of the President

THE OFFICIAL DESPATCH.

WAR DEPARTMENT,
WASHINGTON, April 16—1 30 A M

Major General Dix, New York —

This evening at about 9 30 P M, at Ford's Theatre the President, while sitting in his private box with Mr Lincoln, Mrs Harris and Major Rathburn, was shot by an assassin, who sud nenly entered the box and approached behind the President.

The assassin then leaped upon the stage, brandishing a

lin 150, Dickinson 108, and 61 scattering votes, but before the final result was announced many changes were made, and the final vote stood, Johnson 490, Dickinson 17, Hamlin 9.

The Democratic Convention did not meet until August 29th; George B. McClellan, of New Jersey, was nominated for President, and George H. Pendleton, of Ohio, for Vice-President. The platform called Mr. Lincoln's Administration "four years of failure to restore the Union by the experiment of war," and demanded immediate efforts for cessation of hostilities and for peace. Gen. McClellan accepted the nomination, but repudiated the platform, saying, "I could not look in the faces of my gallant comrades of the Army and Navy and tell them that their labors and the sacrifice of so many of our slain and wounded brethren had been in vain." The candidate was nobler than the party.

The President's homely expression, "It is not wise to swap horses while crossing a stream," was the basis of the great trend of political thought in the North, and there was little doubt of the result, although an animated campaign was conducted. The great military victories of the Union forces made the position of the President's opponents absurd. At the election on November 8, 1864, Lincoln and Johnson carried twenty-two States, receiving 212 of the total electoral vote of 233. McClellan and Pendleton carried three States, Delaware, Kentucky and New Jersey. The popular vote, including the Army vote (many States having made provision for taking the vote of the soldiers in the field), was, Lincoln 2,330,552, McClellan 1,835,985. Eleven States did not vote at this election.

The Government was now making rapid strides for the complete abolition of slavery. In June, 1864, the Fugitive Slave Law of 1850 was repealed; in July the Coastwise Slave Trade was forever prohibited, and on January 31, 1865, the Joint Resolution proposing the Thirteenth Amendment to the Constitution, abolishing slavery, passed the House.

On March 4, 1865, President Lincoln was inaugurated for the second time. The beautiful words closing his inaugural will live forever: "With malice toward none; with charity for all; with firmness in the right, as God gives us to see the right, let us strive on to finish the work we are in, to bind up the nation's wounds; to care for him who shall have borne the battle and for his widow, and his orphan— to do all which may achieve and cherish a just and lasting peace among ourselves, and with all Nations."

Gen. Lee surrendered to Gen. Grant at Appomattox Courthouse, Virginia, on April 9, 1865. On April 14th, the Stars and Stripes were again raised over Ft. Sumter, and the glad news swept over the North that the war was over. On the same evening the President was shot in Ford's Theater by John Wilkes Booth, and died the next morning. "Now he belongs to the ages," said Stanton, at the death-bed. The death of the President meant that Andrew Johnson, a War Democrat, would be made President, and from the overwhelming shock of Mr. Lincoln's death the Republicans turned with misgiving and fear to the new Executive.

CHAPTER XII.

RECONSTRUCTION AND THE NATIONAL DEBT.

"By these recent successes, the reinauguration of the national authority, the reconstruction of which has had a large share of thought from the first, is pressed much more closely upon our attention. It is fraught with great difficulty. Nor is it a small additional embarrassment that we, the loyal people, differ among ourselves as to the mode, manner and measure of reconstruction."

A. Lincoln, April 11, 1865. From his last speech before death.

Mr. Lincoln died at 7:22 o'clock a. m. on April 15, 1865; four hours later Vice-President Johnson took the oath of office as President. Before him were two gigantic problems, the solution of which was fraught with the greatest difficulty. In what manner and under what restrictions should the recently rebellious States—eleven in number—be allowed to resume the exercise of their civil functions, and when should their Senators and Representatives be seated in Congress? This was the first problem—Reconstruction. And in what manner should the enormous war debt be handled so that the credit of the Government would be thoroughly re-established and maintained; and how should the enormous paper currency (legal tenders) be managed so that the commercial interests of the country would not be disturbed? These two problems—Reconstruction and the National Debt—were ultimately to be worked out by the party that saved the Union, though now

(135)

a War Democrat was in charge of the Executive Department, and friction and disagreement was almost certain. It was most unfortunate that no definite plan of Reconstruction had been agreed upon by the Legislative and Executive Departments before Mr. Lincoln's death. Such an understanding would have avoided, probably, the bitter conflict that shortly came on between President Johnson and Congress; and the history of the few years following the Rebellion would have presented a record of greater national progress, a quicker welding of the Union, and a prompter re-establishment of national sentiment between the two sections.

While it is true that Mr. Lincoln's plan of Reconstruction did not meet with the approval of Congress, yet it is almost certain that if he had lived there would have been an agreement of some kind; either the party would have followed Mr. Lincoln or Mr. Lincoln would have followed the party. Ultimate harmony between a Republican President and a Republican Congress was certain, although they might temporarily disagree; but harmony between a Republican Congress and a Democratic President once disturbed would scarcely be restored; neither would ever again completely trust the other.

Mr. Lincoln's work of Reconstruction began in 1863 when the Union army had regained Louisiana, Arkansas and Tennessee. His message to Congress in December, 1863, was accompanied by a Proclamation of Amnesty to those who had taken part in the Rebellion in these States, upon their taking an oath to support the Constitution and all federal laws; and upon so doing there was to be a resto ration of property, except slaves. From this pardon were excepted six enumerated classes of persons whose treason had been most offensive. State Governments could be established by those who took the oath, provided their numbers were one-tenth as large as the total number of voters in the State at the presidential election of 1860, and any Government so established would be recognized by the President, but the right of Congress to admit or reject Senators and Representatives was recognized. Louisiana was the first to make preparations to re-enter into the possession of all its State powers under this proclamation, and in the early months of 1864 a State Government was duly completed and an anti-slavery Constitution adopted. Arkansas followed the same course, but when her Senators and Representatives applied to Congress for their seats, they were denied admittance, and it was apparent that there was a distinct disagreement between the President and Congress on the subject of Reconstruction. Congress did not approve of the President's proceeding without asking its advice, and did not approve of his plan, and a Bill was introduced and passed embodying its views on the subject. In this Bill the President was directed to appoint a Provisional Governor for each of the rebellious States, and after military occupation had ceased, the Governor was to enroll the white male citizens who would take an oath to support the Constitution; after a majority had done so an election of delegates to a Constitutional Convention was to follow, and the Constitution was to contain prohibitory clauses on the subject of slavery, the Confederate debt and the right of certain persons to vote. If this Constitution was adopted by a majority of the popular vote, then the President, with the consent of Congress, could recognize the State Government, and it would be permitted to send its Representatives to Congress. This Bill was passed July 2, 1864, on the last day of the session, but it never became a law because the President did not sign it, and did not return it before Congress adjourned. Several days after the adjournment the President issued a Proclamation in which he laid the Congressional plan before the people and declared that he was not in favor of any one scheme of Reconstruction, and that he was also not prepared to set aside the loyal governments which had been formed in Louisiana and Arkansas. By the time Congress met again the President had been re-elected, and it would seem that in some degree there was an endorsement not only of his War Policy but of his plan of Reconstruction. However, the matter was not pressed, and his message to Congress in December, 1864, was silent on the subject. There was no present occasion to bring forward the matter, but the President still adhered to his original plan as far as Louisiana and Arkansas were concerned, and so expressed himself in his last speech before his death.

So the matter of Reconstruction stood when Andrew Johnson became President. There was not much question about the general course he would pursue, because, as War Governor of Tennessee, he had, early in 1865, practically reconstructed that State under Mr. Lincoln's "ten percent"

plan. As Congress was not in session, and would not con-
vene until December, the President had the alternative of
either calling an extra session of Congress or proceeding in
the matter of Reconstruction according to his own ideas
and the suggestions of his Cabinet, he having retained the
Cabinet left by Mr. Lincoln. The latter course was pursued, and after some delay President Johnson began to act.
An Executive Order swept away all laws and decrees of the
Confederacy, raised the blockade and opened the southern
ports to trade.

On May 29, 1865, the President issued a Proclamation of Amnesty and Pardon to all who had participated in
the Rebellion upon their taking a registered oath to support the Constitution and the Union, but the Proclamation
excepted a large number of persons of specified classes,
whose treason was deemed to be too great to allow them to
again participate in the Government. By the middle of
July, Provisional Governors had been appointed by the
President in North Carolina, Mississippi, Texas, Georgia,
Alabama, South Carolina and Florida; the authority of
the United States had already been established in Virginia
early in May, and Louisiana, Arkansas and Tennessee had
been reconstructed under Mr. Lincoln's plan. The President's policy was that as soon as these Governors took
charge, any white person, except the classes specified, could
regain his citizenship by an oath to support the Constitution and the Union. The taking of this oath by a sufficient
number was followed by Reconstruction Conventions,
which were held in the Southern States, and Legislators

and Representatives to Congress were chosen. The work of these Reconstruction Conventions and Legislatures, although they repudiated the debts of the Confederacy and recognized the Thirteenth Amendment, was highly displeasing to the Republicans in the North, who were greatly interested in the fate of the negroes, and who now saw them, by various laws passed by the Southern Legislatures, deprived of all civil rights and reduced to a new form of servitude.

The first session of the Thirty-ninth Congress convened on December 4, 1865, with a large majority of Republicans in both House and Senate, and both bodies in a very angry mood over the action of the President in proceeding with the Reconstruction without their advice or consent, and they were more enraged with the extreme and rash policies adopted by the Southern Legislatures. To add to this bitter feeling came the application of the Southern Senators and Representatives, many of whom less than a year before had been engaged in active rebelloin, to be admitted to their seats. These applicants were refused admission by both branches of Congress. The House and Senate appointed Reconstruction Committees, and the debate immediately began on the great question. It was seen at once that the Republican Party would totally ignore the President's policy and all that had been done under it. The breach widened between the President and Congress, when an Act to enlarge the provisons of the Freedmen's Bureau Bill (passed March 3, 1865) came up. The object of this Bill was to provide for the desti-

ANDREW JOHNSON.

tute and suffering refugees and freedmen and their wives and children. The new Bill was promptly passed, but on February 19, 1866, was vetoed by the President; the Senate failed to pass the Bill over the veto, but later in the year (July, 1866) the measure went through Congress in a slightly altered form, was vetoed by the President and passed over his veto. The Civil Rights Bill, to secure to the freed negroes in the South all of the rights enjoyed bv the white man, except suffrage, was also vetoed by the President on March 27, 1866, and on April 9th was passed over his veto.

The Thirteenth Amendment, abolishing slavery, had been declared a part of the Constitution on December 18, 1865, and the great work of the Emancipation Proclamation was thus completed. The Reconstruction Committee now reported the Fourteenth Amendment to the Constitution, fixing the status of citizens, the basis of representation, etc., and also a Bill declaring that when the Amendment had become part of the Constitution any of the late Confederate States, upon ratifying it, would be allowed representation in Congress, to all of which the President expressed his disapproval. The various presidential vetoes completely broke off any possible chance of harmony between the President and Congress, and in addition to them. the President indulged in a number of rash speeches in which Congress was condemned in no very elegant terms. On February 22, 1866, the President, in a speech at the White House, denounced Congress bitterly for its opposition, and referred in an abusive wav to several prominent

Republican leaders by name, and he followed this up during the late Summer months by several coarse speeches in Western cities while he was on his way to the dedication of a monument to Stephen A. Douglas at Chicago.

During the autumn of 1866 Congressional elections were to be held, and there was naturally an absorbing interest in the result. These elections were of the greatest importance, for if the President's course was approved by the election of a Democratic Congress, almost the entire result of the Civil War would have been undone, and the strife between the North and South might have been renewed and continued in a more serious form. By this time the South, encouraged by the President's opposition, had rejected the Fourteenth Amendment, and were taking a bold stand to maintain their policy. In October, Ohio, Indiana, Iowa and Pennsylvania went Republican, and in November were joined by New York, which went overwhelmingly Republican, and the Republicans in the North were everywhere victorious, and they were thus upheld in their Reconstruction policy by the popular sentiment.

The second session of the Thirty-ninth Congress convened on December 3, 1866. The South, during the recess of Congress, had refused to adopt the Fourteenth Amendment, this having been made, as already stated, a condition precedent to the enjoyment of the full privileges of Statehood, and now nothing remained but for Congress to establish a Government over the Southern States until they should see fit to comply with the conditions laid down by Congress. The ten Southern States (Tennessee had been readmitted by joint resolution July 24, 1866) were divided into five Military Districts, under the supervision of Regular Army Officers, who were to have control over all the people in their Districts, for their peace and protection, until the States recognized the Fourteenth Amendment. This Bill was passed March 2, 1867, over the President's veto, and on the same day, over the President's veto, was passed the Bill "To regulate the tenure of Civil offices." The object of the latter Bill was to prevent the President from removing Republicans from office. No person in civil office who had been appointed with the consent of the Senate was to be removed until his successor was appointed in a like manner.

Efforts to impeach the President were first begun in the House on January 7, 1867, and the Judiciary Committee, to which the matter was referred, reported in March that it was unable to conclude its investigations, and it recommended a continuance of the proceedings. President Johnson now took the step that ultimately brought about his impeachment. In August, 1867, he suspended Mr. Stanton, the Secretary of War; the suspension was not approved by the Senate in January, 1868, but the President, holding that the Tenure of Office Act was unconstitutional, removed (February 21, 1868) Mr. Stanton from office and appointed Adjutant-general Lorenzo Thomas. This act was declared illegal by the Senate and a second impeachment was immediately reported in the House and adopted February 24, 1868. The House selected John A. Bingham, Geo. S. Boutwell, James F. Wilson, Benjamin F.

Butler, Thomas Williams, John A. Logan and Thaddeus Stevens, all Republicans, as managers of the impeachment proceedings. The counsel for the President were no less eminent: Henry Stanbery, Benjamin R. Curtis, William M. Evarts and William S. Groesbeck. On May 11, 1868, the Senate voted thirty-five "guilty" to nineteen "not guilty," and the impeachment failed by one vote. Had the President been impeached, Benjamin F. Wade, of Ohio, would have become President. The result was deeply disappointing to the Republicans, and for many years there was considerable feeling against the seven Republicans who voted with the twelve Democrats against the impeachment, but lapse of time has brought about a view that the interests of the country were best served by the failure of the impeachment, not that President Johnson's policy and the action of the South under it are to be adopted, but because it is believed that the issues caused by the war were more speedily settled by the failure to impeach.

So bitter was the feeling of Congress against the President, and so great was the distrust of him, that when the Thirty-ninth Congress adjourned on March 4, 1867, the Fortieth Congress convened on the same day, and a series of adjourned meetings were held during the months until December, so that the President would not have undisputed sway during the recess which usually came between March and December.

The question of the National Debt, while not arousing the bitter antagonism that marked the attempt to settle the Reconstruction question, was nevertheless of equal, if not greater importance, because it affected the prosperity and business of the entire country. The total debt of the United States on October 31, 1865, was $2,808,549,437.55, of which debt $454,218,038.00 was in United States notes (legal tenders or greenbacks, as they were called) and fractional currency, in active circulation with the National Bank currency. When the Thirty-ninth Congress convened for the first session it had to consider the disposition of this enormous debt, most of which had been incurred at a high war rate of interest; and to decide what, if anything, should be done with this vast volume of fiat currency, and to consider the matter of reducing the Internal Revenue. The greenbacks were, of course, not on a par with coin, as the action of the Government in declaring these notes legal tender had destroyed our credit abroad and had driven all coin out of circulation, and the value of these notes fluctuated almost daily with the market value of coin. The plan of the Secretary of the Treasury, Mr. McCulloch, was to contract the currency so as to lead to a resumption of specie payment and again establish our credit abroad. The situation was without precedent in financial history and there was some excuse for what has since been deemed a wrong step in the beginning. After considerable debate, in which some opposition was shown to the policy of Contraction—this opposition being led by John Sherman, who was, in fact, almost alone in his contention—a Bill was passed (April 12, 1866) allowing the Secretary of the Treasury to redeem a certain amount of legal tenders with Bonds, a course which naturally increased the bonded interest-bearing indebtedness and reduced the volume of circulating medium. The people of the country speedily complained of the contraction of the currency, and attributed the failure of business enterprises and the lack of money to it. This sentiment resulted later in the formation of a new but ephemeral political party, the Greenback Party, which went so far as to advocate the unlimited issue of legal tenders and the payment of all the indebtedness of the United States in United States notes. The public disapproval of contraction showed itself strongly, and this led to a Bill, passed on February 4, 1868, suspending the authority of the Secretary of the Treasury to reduce the currency. The total amount of greenbacks had by this time been reduced to $356,000,000. This practically settled the question of Currency Contraction, although the Greenback Party, created by this agitation, was in existence until the resumption of specie payments in 1879.

As the requirements of the Treasury gradually became less, Congress rapidly amended the Internal Revenue laws, and the Federal taxes on the people, as a result of the war, gradually became less burdensome, and notwithstanding the enormous reduction in the revenue of the Government, the National Debt was reduced nearly three hundred million dollars in the four years following the war. To add to the brightness of this financial history, large sums were paid out toward the construction of the Union and Central Pacific Railroads, and on July 27, 1868, Alaska was purchased from the Russian Government for $7,200,000.

The entire course of this financial history cannot be

claimed to be entirely satisfactory, yet the achievements of the Republican Party during this period, acting in many instances without precedent, were indeed remarkable.

While the exciting scenes connected with the impeachment of the President were going on during the early months of 1868, the South was ratifying the Fourteenth Amendment, and by June, 1868, the long struggle over the Reconstruction question was practically closed by the admission of the Southern States, and in July the Fourteenth Amendment was declared a part of the Constitution. Throughout this long contest the Democrats, North and South, joined in vigorous support of the President because the course of the Republicans was absolutely fatal to their political prospects. The great contest had retarded the progress of the South, and was unfortunate in continuing the bitterness between the two sections of the country. Both sides hailed its conclusion with thanksgiving, and the Republicans now looked forward to the presidential election in the Fall of 1868, which would replace, probably with a Republican, a President whose person and course were so obnoxious to the party.

CHAPTER XIII.

GRANT.

" I endorse their resolutions, and, if elected to the office of President of the United States, it will be my endeavor to administer all the laws in good faith, with economy, and with a view of giving peace, quiet and protection everywhere.......... Peace, and universal prosperity, its sequence, with economy of administration, will lighten the burden of taxation, while it constantly reduces the national debt. Let us have peace."

Ulysses S. Grant's Letter of Acceptance, May 29, 1868.

The impeachment of President Johnson had not been finally disposed of in the Senate when the Fourth Republican National Convention assembled in Crosby's Opera House, Chicago, on May 20, 1868, for the purpose of nominating one whom, it was confidently believed, would succeed President Johnson and thus end the long controversy between the President and Congress, and between the North and the South. There was absolutely no question as to who would be the presidential nominee, for the overwhelming sentiment of the party had long since crystallized in favor of a man whose wonderful career and talents had made him pre-eminently the strongest candidate in the party.

Ulysses S. Grant was born in Ohio in 1822, and had graduated from West Point in 1843. He took part in the Mexican War, and was brevetted Captain for gallant serv-

(148)

ULYSSES S. GRANT.

ices. A few years after the close of that war he resigned his commission and engaged in business until the call to arms in 1861. His great success in the capture of Forts Henry and Donelson brought him the rank of Major General and made him at once one of the most prominent and promising of the Union Generals. His subsequent successes in Tennessee, the capture of Vicksburg and the opening of the Mississippi caused him to be appointed to the revived rank of Lieutenant-General, and taking personal command of the campaign against Richmond, he had, by his dogged persistence, brought success and ended the great conflict. He continued to remain at the head of the Army, and in the bitter contest between the President and Congress during the reconstruction period, though placed in a most trying position, he had displayed rare qualities of tact and judgment, and had gained the confidence of the entire party, and indeed of the American people. Such, briefly, was the career of the man who was now called to accept a presidential nomination.

The assembling at Chicago of a great convention of soldiers and sailors at the same time the Republican Convention met, made the latter even more enthusiastic than the convention of 1860, and the number in attendance was much larger. The Soldiers' Convention met before the Republican Convention, and amid scenes of the wildest enthusiasm, nominated Gen. Grant for the presidency, and condemned the seven Republicans—"traitors" as they were then called—who had voted against the impeachment of President Johnson. At noon, May 20th, the Republican

Convention was called to order by Governor Marcus L. Ward, of New Jersey. He named Carl Schurz, of Wisconsin, as temporary Chairman. The temporary Secretaries were B. R. Cowen, of Ohio, Luther Caldwell, of New York, and Frank S. Richards, of Tennessee. Committees on Credentials, Permanent Organization, Resolutions and Rules were then appointed, each of the committees, with some few exceptions, having on it a representative from each of the States. The name of Joseph R. Hawley was reported for President of the Convention, and the names of one representative from each State as Vice-President, and also thirty-six secretaries. A delegation from the Soldiers' and Sailors' Convention now presented a resolution nominating Gen. Grant for President, and it caused great enthusiasm. Such a procedure was contrary to the rules of the Convention, but the delegates were almost unanimous in desiring the nomination to be made at once, but order was finally restored. After some debate it was decided to give representation in the Convention to the Territories, and to the States not yet reconstructed. The Convention then adjourned until the following morning at ten o'clock, at which time, on assembling, impatient attempts were again made to nominate Gen. Grant contrary to the rules, but the Convention finally quieted down and listened to speeches delivered by F. Hassaurek, John M. Palmer and John W. Forney. The platform, reported by Richard W. Thompson, of Indiana, was adopted with many cheers.

REPUBLICAN PLATFORM, 1868.

The National Republican Party of the United States, assembled in national convention in the City of Chicago on the 21st day of May, 1868, make the following declaration of principles:

1. We congratulate the country on the assured success of the reconstruction policy of Congress, as evinced by the adoption, in the majority of the states lately in rebellion, of Constitutions securing equal civil and political rights to all; and it is the duty of the government to sustain those institutions and to prevent the people of such states from being remitted to a state of anarchy.

2. The guaranty by Congress of equal suffrage to all loyal men at the South was demanded by every consideration of public safety, of gratitude, and of justice, and must be maintained; while the question of suffrage in all the loyal states properly belongs to the people of those states.

3. We denounce all forms of repudiation as a national crime; and the national honor requires the payment of the public indebtedness in the uttermost good faith to all creditors at home and abroad, not only according to the letter, but the spirit of the laws under which it was contracted.

4. It is due to the labor of the nation that taxation should be equalized, and reduced as rapidly as the national faith will permit.

5. The national debt, contracted as it has been for the preservation of the Union for all time to come, should be extended over a fair period for redemption; and it is the duty of Congress to reduce the rate of interest thereon whenever it can be honestly done.

6. That the best policy to diminish our burden of debt is to so improve our credit that capitalists will seek to loan us money at lower rates of interest than we now pay, and must continue to pay, so long as repudiation, partial or total, open or covert, is threatened or suspected.

7. The government of the United States should be administered with the strictest economy; and the corruptions which have been so shamefully nursed and fostered by Andrew Johnson call loudly for radical reform.

8. We profoundly deplore the untimely and tragic death of Abraham Lincoln, and regret the accession of the Presidency of Andrew Johnson, who has acted treacherously to the people who elected him and the cause he was pledged to support; who has usurped high

legislative and judicial functions; who has refused to execute the laws; who has used his high office to induce other officers to ignore and violate the laws; who has employed his executive powers to render insecure the property, the peace, the liberty and life of the citizen; who has abused the pardoning power; who has denounced the national legislature as unconstitutional; who has persistently and corruptly resisted, by every means in his power, every proper attempt at the reconstruction of the states lately in rebellion; who has perverted the public patronage into an engine of wholesale corruption; and who has been justly impeached for high crimes and misdemeanors, and properly pronounced guilty thereof by the vote of thirty-five senators.

9. The doctrine of Great Britain and other European powers, that because a man is once a subject he is always so, must be resisted at every hazard by the United States, as a relic of feudal times, not authorized by the laws of nations, and at war with our national honor and independence. Naturalized citizens are entitled to protection in all their rights of citizenship as though they were native born; and no citizen of the United States, native or naturalized, must be liable to arrest and imprisonment by any foreign power for acts done or words spoken in this country; and, if so arrested and imprisoned, it is the duty of the government to interfere in his behalf.

10. Of all who were faithful in the trials of the late war there were none entitled to more especial honor than the brave soldiers and seamen who endured the hardships of campaign and cruise, and imperilled their lives in the service of the country; the bounties and pensions provided by the laws for these brave defenders of the nation are obligations never to be forgotten; the widows and orphans of the gallant dead are the wards of the people—a sacred legacy bequeathed to the nation's protecting care.

11. Foreign immigration, which in the past has added so much to the wealth, development, and resources, and increase of power to this republic—the asylum of the oppressed of all nations—should be fostered and encouraged by a liberal and just policy.

12. This convention declares itself in sympathy with all oppressed people struggling for their rights.

13. That we highly commend the spirit of magnanimity and forbearance with which men who have served in the rebellion but who now frankly and honestly co-operate with us in restoring the peace of the country and reconstructing the Southern state govern-

ments upon the basis of impartial justice and equal rights, are received back into the communion of the loyal people; and we favor
the removal of the disqualifications and restrictions imposed upon
the late rebels in the same measure as the spirit of disloyalty will
die out, and as may be consistent with the safety of the loyal people.

14. That we recognize the great principles laid down in the
immortal Declaration of Independence as the true foundation of
democratic government; and we hail with gladness every effort
toward making these principles a living reality on every inch of
American soil.

Nominations now being in order, John A. Logan, in
a few words remarkable for their force and beauty, nominated Ulysses S. Grant for President. After the enthusiasm had abated the roll of the States was called, and the
unanimous vote of the delegates, 650 in number, was given
to Gen. Grant, and the audience went wild with delight.
The great contest of the Convention now came over the
nomination for Vice-President. Henry Wilson, Schuyler
Colfax, Benjamin F. Wade, Reuben E. Fenton, James
Speed, Andrew G. Curtin, Hannibal Hamlin, James Harlan, S. C. Pomeroy, J. A. J. Creswell and William D. Kel-
ley were nominated. The leading candidates were Benj.
F. Wade, of Ohio, Mr. Colfax, of Indiana, Mr. Curtin, of
Pennsylvania, Mr. Wilson, of Massachusetts, and Mr. Fenton, of New York, all of whom had rendered the most conspicuous services to the party. Five ballots were taken as
follows:

	1st Ballot	2d Ballot	3d Ballot	4th Ballot	5th Ballot
Wade	...147	170	178	206	38
Wilson	...119	114	101	87	
Colfax	...115	145	165	186	541
Fenton	...126	144	139	144	69
Curtin	... 51	45	40		

Only the votes for the leading candidates are here given. Mr. Colfax was therefore nominated on the fifth ballot, and it was felt that his name added great strength to the ticket. He was then Speaker of the House, to which he had been elected with the organization of the party in 1854, and had served with great ability for six terms.

The Democratic Convention met in New York in Tammany Hall on July 4, 1868. It was a gathering composed principally of Southern leaders and Generals and Northern Copperheads. After a troubled session of six days the Chairman of the Convention, Horatio Seymour, of New York, was nominated for President on the twenty-second ballot, and Francis P. Blair, Jr., of Missouri, was nominated for Vice-President. The platform advocated the payment of the national debt in depreciated currency, the overthrowing of all that had been done under the reconstruction policy of Congress and the taxing of Government bonds. The platform practically doomed the party to defeat before the campaign had really opened. The canvass was exciting, but the October States practically decided the contest, and the election on November 3d registered what had long been conceded. Grant and Colfax received the 214 electoral votes of twenty-six States; Seymour and Blair only carrying eight States, New York among them, with their 80 electoral votes. The popular vote gave Grant and Colfax 3,012,833, and Seymour and Blair 2,703,249.

The third session of the Fortieth Congress assembled on December 7, 1868. One phase of the slavery question still remained unsettled, that of giving the negro the right of suffrage. For several years a strong sentiment had shown itself in the North in favor of granting this right, and Congress had already recognized this sentiment by giving the negro the right to vote in the District of Columbia, which act was passed over President Johnson's veto. The great injustice of freeing the negro and withholding from him the means of protecting his freedom by the right of suffrage was not generally felt, and it remained now for a Republican Congress to crown with a great act of justice the long labors of the party, to remove all the evils of insufferable bondage, and to complete the work of the Emancipation Proclamation and the Thirteenth and Fourteenth Amendments.

On February 27, 1869, Congress proposed, through the Department of State, the Fifteenth Amendment to the Constitution:

"The right of citizens of the United States to vote shall not be denied or abridged by the United States, or by any State, on account of race, color or previous condition of servitude. The Congress shall have power to enforce this article by appropriate legislation."

This Amendment, after submission to the States, was proclaimed a part of the Constitution in 1870.

In his message to Congress in December, 1868, President Johnson said

"The holders of our securities have already received upon their bonds a larger amount than their original investment, measured by the gold standard. Upon this statement of facts it would seem but just and equitable that the

six percent interest now paid by the Government should be
applied to the reduction of the principal in semi-annual in-
stallments, which in sixteen years and eight months would
liquidate the entire national debt."

The policy of repudiation advocated by the Democratic
Party in the campaign of 1868 and the repudiation now
advocated by President Johnson, were promptly rejected
by the Republican Congress, and both branches passed resolutions of condemnation.

General Grant was inaugurated on March, 4, 1869
and the Fortieth Congress adjourned on the same
day. The Forty-first Congress immediately convened
and elected James G. Blaine, of Maine, Speaker by
105 votes to 57 votes for Michael C. Kerr, of Indiana. Mr. Blaine was also elected Speaker of the
Forty-second Congress when it met on March 4, 1871.
On the 18th of March, 1869, Congress decided by the
"Act to strengthen the public credit," to remove as far
as possible the damage done at home and abroad by the repudiation platform of the Democratic Party, and the repudiation message of President Johnson. This Act
pledged the Government at the earliest practicable moment
to pay in coin or its equivalent all obligations, notes and
bonds except those where the law authorizing their issue
stipulated that payment might be made in lawful money.

May 10, 1869, witnessed the opening for traffic of the
Union Pacific Railroad, which had first been advocated by
the Republican Party in its platform in 1856, and which
was now brought to a successful opening by necessary subsidies of money and land given the railroad by Republican

Congresses. The war had resulted in a wonderful development of the physical wealth of the North and West, and the railroad was opened at a most opportune moment to connect the East and West, and make possible the development of all the wonderful resources of the nation. It was unfortunate, however, that unwise management of the bonds and credit of the Western Railroads led to such a disastrous climax in the fall of 1873.

In the decade between 1860 and 1870 the admission of four new States—Kansas in 1861, West Virginia in 1863, Nevada in 1864, and Nebraska in 1867—had raised the total number of States to thirty-seven. In addition, six new Territories had been organized—Colorado and Dakota in 1861, Idaho and Arizona in 1863, Montana in 1864, and Wyoming in 1868. The admission of these new States, the completing of the railroad, the discovery of precious metals, and the general awakening of the North caused a large increase in the population, especially in the West. The total population of the country in 1870 was 38,558,-371, of which 4, 880,009 were negroes, about 4,400,000 of them living in the Southern States.

The second session of the Forty-first Congress met December 6, 1869. The President in his message advocated the refunding of the National Debt, and this was done by the Act of July 14, 1870, which authorized the refunding of the debt at five, four and one-half and four percent, payable in coin and exempt from taxation.

The sentiment in favor of a general amnesty of all persons who had engaged in the rebellion was now growing in the North, and in December, 1869, and March, 1870, Acts were passed removing legal and political disabilities from a large class of persons in the South, but a full pardon was not yet extended to all. The South at this time was most bitter against negro suffrage, and the opposition was shown in a series of most violent outrages and murders perpetrated by the Ku Klux Klans and other similar organizations formed for the purpose of preventing the negro from voting and the "carpet bagger" from living in the community. The outrages and murders done by these organizations became so flagrant that Congress passed a special Act on April 20, 1871 (the Ku Klux Act), to enforce the Fourteenth Amendment.

The other events of Gen. Grant's administration were chiefly of a diplomatic nature, and it is not necessary to dwell upon them in these pages. With the opening of 1872 came the year for another presidential campaign, and the only serious issue was the threatened split in the Republican Party over the question of the treatment of the South. The Democrats were demoralized and had no candidate, and the situation was the most peculiar and abnormal in the history of presidential campaigns. A group of Republicans in Missouri were in favor of a more liberal policy toward the South, and President Grant was roundly condemned for his military rule. This movement became known as the Liberal Republican movement, and a convention was called to meet in Cincinnati on May 1st. This year also witnessed the organization for political action of the Prohibition Party and the Labor Reform Party. The latter held the first of the political conventions and met at Columbus, Ohio, February 22, 1872. Judge David Davis, of Illinois, was nominated for President, and Judge Joel Parker, of New Jersey, for Vice-President; both subsequently withdrew, and in August this party nominated Charles O'Conor for President, who also declined. The platform of the Labor Reform Party demanded lower interest on and taxation of government bonds; the repeal of the law establishing the national banks and withdrawal of the national bank notes; the issue of paper money based on the faith and resources of the nation to be legal tender for all debts; exclusion of the Chinese; no more land grants to corporations, and the organization of a National Labor Reform party. The National Prohibition Convention also met in Columbus, Ohio, on February 22d, and nominated James Black, of Pennsylvania, for President, and Rev. John Russell, of Michigan, for Vice-President.

The National Liberal Republican Convention met at Cincinnati, Ohio, May 1, 1872. It was a mass convention, and Carl Schurz presided as Permanent Chairman. The prominent candidates for the presidency were Judge David Davis, Lyman Trumbull, Chas. Francis Adams, B. Gratz Brown and Horace Greeley, whose name had not been seriously considered until the Convention assembled, and who, on May 3d was nominated on the sixth ballot for President, and B. Gratz Brown, of Missouri, was nominated for Vice-President. The platform demanded universal amnesty and a liberal policy, no more land grants to corporations, and denounced repudiation. The Republicans met in their

Fifth National Convention at Philadelphia, June 5th, in the Academy of Music. There was no question but that President Grant would be renominated, and the only contest was that between Henry Wilson and Schuyler Colfax for the nomination for Vice-President. William Claflin, of Massachusetts, called the meeting to order and named Morton McMichael as temporary Chairman. The usual committees were appointed, and while they were deliberating the convention listened to a number of stirring speeches, several by colored men, who appeared as representatives in a national convention for the first time. Thomas Settle, of North Carolina, was reported as permanent chairman. On the following day, after some preliminary business had been disposed of, Shelby M. Cullom, of Illinois, nominated President Grant for a second term, and the vote, 752, was made unanimous. Henry Wilson, Schuyler Colfax, John F. Lewis, Edmund J. Davis, and Horace Maynard were nominated for Vice-President. One ballot was cast and resulted in the nomination of Henry Wilson, who received 364½ votes to 321½ for Colfax, 26 for Maynard, 16 for Davis, and one each for Jos. R. Hawley and E. F. Noyes. The fifth Republican platform, which was now adopted, read as follows·

REPUBLICAN PLATFORM, 1872.

The Republican Party of the United States, assembled in national convention in the city of Philadelphia on the 5th and 6th days of June, 1872, again declares its faith, appeals to its history, and announces its position upon the questions before the country.

1. During eleven years of supremacy it has accepted with grand courage the solemn duties of the time. It suppressed a gigantic re-

bellion, emancipated four millions of slaves, decreed the equal citizenship of all, and established universal suffrage. Exhibiting unparalleled magnanimity, it criminally punished no man for political offenses, and warmly welcomed all who proved loyalty by obeying the laws and dealing justly with their neighbors. It has steadily decreased with firm hand the resultant disorders of a great war and initiated a wise and humane policy toward the Indians. The Pacific Railroad and similar vast enterprises have been generously aided and successfully conducted, the public lands freely given to actual settlers, immigration protected and encouraged, and a full acknowledgment of the naturalized citizens' rights secured from European powers. A uniform national currency has been provided, repudiation frowned down, the national credit sustained under the most extraordinary burdens, and new bonds negotiated at lower rates. The revenues have been carefully collected and honestly applied. Despite annual large reductions in the rates of taxation, the public debt has been reduced during General Grant's presidency at the rate of a hundred millions a year; great financial crises have been avoided, and peace and plenty prevail throughout the land. Menacing foreign difficulties have been peacefully and honorably composed, and the honor and power of the nation kept in high respect throughout the world. This glorious record of the past is the party's best pledge for the future. We believe the people will not intrust the government to any party or combination of men composed chiefly of those who have resisted every step of this beneficent progress.

2. The recent amendments to the National Constitution should be cordially sustained because they are right, not merely tolerated because they are law, and should be carried out according to their spirit by appropriate legislation, the enforcement of which can safely be entrusted only to the party that secured those amendments.

3. Complete liberty and exact equality in the enjoyment of all civil, political and public rights should be established and effectually maintained throughout the Union, by efficient and appropriate state and federal legislation. Neither the law nor its administration should admit any discrimination in respect of citizens by reason of race, creed, color, or previous condition of servitude.

4. The national government should seek to maintain honorable peace with all nations, protecting its citizens everywhere, and sympathizing with all people who strive for greater liberty.

5. Any system of the civil service under which the subordinate positions of the government are considered rewards for mere party zeal is fatally demoralizing, and we therefore favor a reform of the system by laws which shall abolish the evils of patronage and make honesty, efficiency and fidelity the essential qualifications for public positions, without practically creating a life-tenure of office.

6. We are opposed to further grants of the public lands to corporations and monopolies, and demand that the national domain be set apart for free homes for the people.

7. The annual revenue, after paying current expenditures, pensions, and the interest on the public debt, should furnish a moderate balance for the reduction of the principal, and that revenue, except so much as may be derived from a tax on tobacco and liquors, should be raised by duties upon importations, the details of which should be so adjusted as to aid in securing remunerative wages to labor, and promote the industries, prosperity, and growth of the whole country.

8. We hold in undying honor the soldiers and sailors whose valor saved the Union. Their pensions are a sacred debt of the nation, and the widows and orphans of those who died for their country are entitled to the care of a generous and grateful people. We favor such additional legislation as will extend the bounty of the government to all our soldiers and sailors who were honorably discharged, and who in the line of duty became disabled, without regard to the length of service or the cause of such discharge.

9. The doctrine of Great Britain and other European powers concerning allegiance—"Once a subject always a subject"—having at last, through the efforts of the Republican party, been abandoned, and the American idea of the individual's right to transfer allegiance having been accepted by European nations, it is the duty of our government to guard with jealous care the rights of adopted citizens against the assumption of unauthorized claims by their former governments, and we urge continued careful encouragement and protection of voluntary immigration.

10. The franking privilege ought to be abolished and the way prepared for a speedy reduction in the rates of postage.

11. Among the questions which press the attention is that which concerns the relations of capital and labor, and the Republican party recognizes the duty of so shaping legislation as to secure full protection and the amplest field for capital, and for labor, the creator

of capital, the largest opportunities and a just share of the mutual profits of these two great servants of civilization.

12. We hold that Congress and the President have only fulfilled an imperative duty in their measures for suppression of violent and treasonable organizations in certain lately rebellious regions, and for the protection of the ballot-box; and therefore they are entitled to the thanks of the nation.

13. We denounce repudiation of the public debt, in any form or disguise, as a national crime. We witness with pride the reduction of the principal of the debt, and of the rates of interest upon the balance, and confidently expect that our excellent national currency will be perfected by a speedy resumption of specie payment.

14. The Republican party is mindful of its obligations to the loyal women of America for their noble devotion to the cause of freedom. Their admission to wider fields of usefulness is viewed with satisfaction; and the honest demand of any class of citizens for additional rights should be treated with respectful consideration.

15. We heartily approve the action of Congress in extending amnesty to those lately in rebellion, and rejoice in the growth of peace and fraternal feeling throughout the land.

16. The Republican party proposes to respect the rights reserved by the people to themselves as carefully as the powers delegated by them to the state and to the federal government. It disapproves of the resort to unconstitutional laws for the purpose of removing evils by interference with rights not surrendered by the people to either the state or national government.

17. It is the duty of the general government to adopt such measures as may tend to encourage and restore American commerce and ship-building.

18. We believe that the modest patriotism, the earnest purpose, the sound judgment, the practical wisdom, the incorruptible integrity, and the illustrious services of Ulysses S. Grant have commended him to the heart of the American people, and with him at our head we start to-day upon a new march to victory.

19. Henry Wilson, nominated for the Vice-Presidency, known to the whole land from the early days of the great struggle for liberty as an indefatigable laborer in all campaigns, an incorruptible legislator, and representative man of American institutions, is worthy to associate with our great leader and share the honors which we pledge our best efforts to bestow upon them.

It is important also to note that Grant and Wilson had already been nominated by the Workingmen's National Convention in New York on May 23d.

The Democratic National Convention met at Baltimore on July 9th and endorsed the Liberal Republican nominees, Greeley and Brown, and the Liberal Republican platform. A convention of "straight-out" Democrats met at Louisville, Kentucky, September 3d to 5th, and repudiated the Baltimore convention, nominating ʲCharles O'Conor, of New York, for President, and John Q. Adams, of Massachusetts, for Vice-President, who both declined, but the convention, unable to secure other candidates, left the ticket as named. A Colored Liberal Republican Convention at Louisville on September 25th also nominated Greeley and Brown. In addition to these various conventions, the Liberal Republican Revenue Reformers' Convention met in New York June 25th, and nominated William S. Groesbeck, of Ohio, for President, and F. L. Olmstead, of New York, for Vice-President.

The contest between Grant and Greeley was a remarkable one, and at its opening there was considerable doubt as to the outcome; but as the summer months went by it was seen that the coalition between the Liberal Republicans and the Democrats was working out unsatisfactorily. The October States went Republican, and indicated clearly what could be expected in November. The election on November 5th was an overwhelming victory for the Republicans; Grant and Wilson carried 29 States with their 286 electoral votes out of a total electoral vote of 366, Arkansas and

Louisiana not being counted for either side. The popular vote gave Grant 3,597,132, Greeley 2,834,125, O'Conor 29,489, Black 5,608. The election was followed in a few weeks by the death of Mr. Greeley; broken-hearted by the death of his wife a few days before the election, and exhansted by the tremendous strains of the campaign, and disappointed by the result, the great editor closed one of the most remarkable careers in American history.

The hostility of England to the North during the Civil War led to the filing of the Alabama Claims, which were adjusted by the Geneva Tribunal, and the United States, on September 14, 1872, was awarded $15,500,000 in gold in full payment of these claims.

The third session of the Forty-second Congress began December 2, 1872, and immediately, on motion of Mr. Blaine, a committee was appointed to investigate the Democratic charges made during the preceding presidential campaign, that the Vice-President, the Secretary of the Treasury, Speaker of the House, and other prominent Republicans, had accepted, in return for political influence, stock in the Credit Mobilier, a company originally engaged in the construction of the Union Pacific. The result of this committee's investigation was the clearing of the prominent men charged, but a vote of censure was passed on Representatives Oakes Ames and James Brooks for connection with the scandal.

An Act went into effect on February 12, 1873, the provisions of which, it was afterwards argued, caused the "demonetization" of silver. This demonetization had alreadv occurred in 1853, when nothing was said in the Act of that year as to the silver dollar piece which had for some years entirely disappeared from circulation. The Act of 1873 simply recognized a condition which had been present for more than twenty years when it provided for the coinage of ten, twenty-five and fifty-cent silver pieces and omitted the dollar. The Act of 1873 was passed because all coin had been driven out of circulation by the United States notes and fractional currency issued during the War, and the Treasury Department, deeming the time appropriate for the issuance of subsidiary silver coins and revision of the coinage laws, suggested, after consultation with experts, the Act of 1873. The Act was, in fact, an important step toward specie resumption. This law also provided for a trade dollar for use in trade with China and Japan. This dollar was to weigh 420 grains, so as to give it the advantage over the Mexican dollar of 416 grains. It was made legal tender for a limited amount only, and several years afterwards was withdrawn from circulation.

President Grant was reinaugurated on March 4, 1873, and the Republican Party seemingly had a prospect of a long lease of power, for the strength of all opposition seemed to have been dissipated by the campaign of 1872; but before the year of the reinauguration had passed, circumstances occurred absolutely beyond the control of the party, the result of which caused a complete change of the political aspect of the country. In September, 1873, while business affairs were in a good condition and labor well employed, a sudden financial panic engulfed the country and

brought demoralization to almost all industries. The direct
cause of this panic was the abuse of credit in the enormous
building of railroads which had been going on for several
years prior to 1873. The market had been flooded with
railroad bonds, and as the old portions of the Western railroads did not earn enough to pay for new construction, the
railroads gradually began to default in the payment of interest on their bonds, and the New York bankers became
overburdened with them; the natural result was that
they were compelled to call in their loans, money became tight, and the storm broke in September, 1873,
when the great financial house of Jay Cooke & Co. closed
its doors. By the end of October the panic was over, but
the effects were felt long afterwards in thousands of ruined
enterprises. It gave new arguments to the champions of
fiat currency, and the whole situation told against the success of the Republican Party. When the first session of
the Forty-third Congress opened on December 1, 1873
(James G. Blaine elected Speaker), arguments for currency inflation were advanced on all sides, and resulted in
the passage of a bill on April 14, 1874, to inflate the currency $44,000,000. President Grant wisely vetoed the
measure and it failed of passage over his veto. The Congressional elections in the fall of 1874 showed the influence
of the disastrous industrial conditions upon politics, for the
Democrats obtained control of the House for the first time
in fifteen years. That a great political revulsion was in
progress was apparent when Ohio in 1873 and New York
in 1874 elected Democratic Governors. When the Forty-

fourth Congress convened on December 6, 1875, Michael C. Kerr, Democrat, of Indiana, was chosen Speaker by 173 votes over James G. Blaine, who received 106. This practically showed the party strength in the House.

The most important Act of President Grant's second term was the Resumption of specie payment, which was provided for in the bill reported to the Senate December 21, 1874, by John Sherman. By this Act there was to be a coinage of ten, twenty-five and fifty-cent silver pieces, which were to be exchanged for fractional currency until it was all redeemed. There was to be an issue of bonds, and the surplus revenue was to be used to buy coin. So much of the Act of 1870 which limited the amount of national bank notes to $350,000,000 was repealed, and these banks were now authorized to issue more bills; but for every $100.00 issued the Secretary of the Treasury must call in $80.00 of the greenbacks until but $300,000,000 of them remained. The total amount of paper currency in the United States at this time was $780,000,000, divided into $382,000,000 U. S. notes, $44,000,000 fractional currency and $354,000,000 national bank notes, and each dollar of this paper currency was worth about eighty-nine cents in coin. The Act further provided that after January 1, 1879, the Secretary of the Treasury was to redeem in coin all United States legal tender notes then outstanding, on presentation. President Grant approved this bill January 14, 1875, with a special message to Congress.

The spring of 1876 witnessed the opening of the Centennial Exposition at Fairmount Park, Philadelphia, by

President Grant and Emperor Dom Pedro II. of Brazil. In this year a successor was to be chosen to President Grant, and for the first time in the history of the party since 1860 there was to be a contest over the presidential nomination. The long continuance in power of the party had its natural effect of creating factions, and this, together with the recent Democratic successes, made necessary a most careful selection of a candidate and of a platform for this campaign.

CHAPTER XIV

HAYES.

"   and to put forth my best efforts in behalf of a civil policy which will forever wipe out in our political affairs the color line and the distinction between North and South, to the end that we may have, not merely a united North or a united South, but a united country."

Rutherford B. Hayes, Inaugural Address, March 5, 1877.

The Sixth Republican National Convention met at Cincinnati, Ohio, June 14, 1876, and, as already noted, for the first time since 1860 there was to be a contest for the presidential nomination. James G. Blaine was most prominently mentioned during the months preceding the Convention, and was unquestionably the favorite of a majority of the delegates when they met. His friends were united and enthusiastic, but there was a factional opposition, led by Mr. Conkling, of New York, that united on the seventh ballot and resulted in the nomination of a candidate who had received comparatively little attention before the Convention met. The next strongest candidates after Mr. Blaine seemed to be Oliver P. Morton, of Indiana, and Benjamin H. Bristow, of Kentucky, both of whom had rendered conspicuous services to the party and to the country. Other candidates were Roscoe Conkling, of New York, Rutherford B. Hayes, of Ohio, and John F. Hartranft, of

(170)

Pennsylvania. The Convention was called to order by Edwin D. Morgan who named Theodore M. Pomeroy, of New York, temporary Chairman. The usual committees were appointed and Edward McPherson, of Pennsylvania, was reported as permanent Chairman. Gen. Joseph R. Hawley, of Connecticut, reported the following platform:

Republican Platform, 1876.

When in the economy of Providence, this land was to be purged of human slavery, and when the strength of government of the people, by the people, and for the people was to be demonstrated, the Republican party came into power. Its deeds have passed into history, and we look back to them with pride. Incited by their memories to high aims for the good of our country and mankind, and looking to the future with unfaltering courage, hope and purpose, we, the representatives of the party, in national convention assembled, make the following declaration of principles:

1. The United States of America is a nation, not a league. By the combined workings of the national and state governments, under their respective constitutions, the rights of every citizen are secured, at home and abroad, and the common welfare promoted.

2. The Republican party has preserved these governments to the hundredth anniversary of the nation's birth, and they are now embodiments of the great truth spoken at its cradle: "That all men are created equal; that they are endowed by their Creator with certain inalienable rights, among which are life, liberty, and the pursuit of happiness; that for the attainment of these ends governments have been instituted among men, deriving their just powers from the consent of the governed." Until these truths are cheerfuly obeyed, or, if need be, vigorously enforced, the work of the Republican party is unfinished.

3. The permanent pacification of the southern section of the Union and the complete protection of all its citizens in the free enjoyment of all their rights, is a duty to which the Republican party stands sacredly pledged. The power to provide for the enforcement

of the principles embodied in the recent constitutional amendments is vested by those amendments in the Congress of the United States, and we declare it to be the solemn obligation of the legislative and executive departments of the government to put into immediate and vigorous exercise all their constitutional powers for removing any just causes of discontent on the part of any class, and for securing to every American citizen complete liberty and exact equality in the exercise of all civil, political, and public rights. To this end we imperatively demand a Congress and a Chief Executive whose courage and fidelity to these duties shall not falter until these results are placed beyond dispute or recall.

4. In the first act of Congress signed by President Grant the national government assumed to remove any doubts of its purpose to discharge all just obligations to the public creditors, and "solemnly pledged its faith to make provisions, at the earliest practicable period, for the redemption of the United States notes in coin." Commercial prosperity, public morals, and the national credit demand that this promise be fulfilled by a continuous and steady progress to specie payment.

5. Under the Constitution the President and heads of departments are to make nominations for office; the Senate is to advise and consent to appointments, and the House of Representatives is to accuse and prosecute faithless officers. The best interest of the public service demands that these distinctions be respected; that Senators and representatives who may be judges and accusers should not dictate appointments to office. The invariable rule in appointments should have reference to the honesty, fidelity and capacity of the appointees, giving to the party in power those places where harmony and vigor of administration require its policy to be represented, but permitting all others to be filled by persons selected with sole reference to the efficiency of the public service, and the right of all citizens to share in the honor of rendering faithful service to the country.

6. We rejoice in the quickening conscience of the people concerning political affairs, and will hold all public officers to a rigid responsibility, and engage that the prosecution and punishment of all who betray official trusts shall be swift, thorough and unsparing.

7. The public-school system of the several states is the bulwark of the American Republic, and with a view to its security and permanence we recommend an amendment to the Constitution of the United

States, forbidding the application of any public funds or property for the benefit of any schools or institutions under sectarian control.

8. The revenue necessary for current expenditures and the obligations of the public debt must be largely derived from duties upon importations, which, so far as possible, should be adjusted to promote interests of American labor and advance the prosperity of the whole country.

9. We reaffirm our opposition to further grants of the public lands to corporations and monopolies, and demand that the national domain be devoted to free homes for the people.

10. It is the imperative duty of the government so to modify existing treaties with European governments that the same protection shall be afforded to the adopted American citizen that is given to the native born; and that all necessary laws should be passed to protect immigrants, in the absence of power in the states for that purpose.

11. It is the immediate duty of Congress to fully investigate the effect of the immigration and importation of Mongolians upon the moral and material interests of the country.

12. The Republican party recognizes with approval the substantial advances recently made toward the establishment of equal rights for women, by the many important amendments effected by Republican legislatures, in the laws which concern the personal and property relations of wives, mothers and widows, and by the appointment and election of women to the superintendence of education, charities, and other public trusts. The honest demands of this class of citizens for additional rights, privileges, and immunities should be treated with respectful consideration.

13. The Constitution confers upon Congress sovereign power over the territories of the United States for their government, and in the exercise of this power it is the right and duty of Congress to prohibit and extirpate, in the territories, that relic of barbarism, polygamy; and we demand such legislation as shall secure this end and the supremacy of American institutions in all the territories.

14. The pledges which the nation has given to her soldiers and sailors must be fulfilled, and a grateful people will always hold those who imperilled their lives for the country's preservation in the kindest rememberance.

15. We sincerely deprecate all sectional feeling and tendencies. We therefore note with deep solicitude that the Democratic party counts, as its chief hope of success, upon the electoral vote of a

united South, secured through the efforts of those who were recently arrayed against the nation; and we invoke the earnest attention of the country to the grave truth that a success thus achieved would reopen sectional strife and imperil national honor and human rights.

16. We charge the Democratic party with being the same in character and spirit as when it sympathized with treason with making its control of the House of Representatives the triumph and opportunity of the nation's recent foes; with reasserting and applauding in the National Capitol the sentiments of unrepentant rebellion; with sending Union soldiers to the rear and promoting Confederate soldiers to the front; with deliberately proposing to repudiate the plighted faith of the government; with being equally false and imbecile upon the overshadowing financial question; with thwarting the ends of justice by its partisan mismanagements and obstruction; with proving itself, through the period of its ascendancy in the Lower House of Congress utterly incompetent to administer the government; and we warn the country against trusting a party thus alike unworthy, recreant and incapable.

17. The national administration merits commendation for its honorable work in the management of domestic and foreign affairs, and President Grant deserves the continued hearty gratitude of the American people for his patriotism and his eminent services, in war and in peace.

18.   We present as our candidates for President and Vice-President of the United States two distinguished statesmen, of eminent ability and character, and conspicuously fitted for those high offices, and we confidently appeal to the American people to intrust the administration of their public affairs to Rutherford B. Hayes and William A. Wheeler.

On the second day the nominations were made of the above-named candidates, with stirring speeches, the most remarkable of which were the three delivered for Mr. Blaine. Robert G. Ingersoll, in presenting Mr. Blaine's name, uttered the eloquent words which caused his celebrated effort to become known as the "Plumed Knight Speech"; near its conclusion he said, "Like an armed warrior, like a plumed knight, James G. Blaine marched down the halls of the American Congress and threw his shining lance full and fair against the brazen foreheads of the defamers of his country and the maligners of his honor. For the Republicans to desert this gallant leader now is as though an army should desert their General upon the field of battle." This nomination was seconded by Henry M. Turner, colored, and William P. Frye, of Maine. Gov. Hayes was nominated by Edwin F. Noyes, seconded by Benjamin F. Wade. The various nominating speeches concluded the second day's business and the balloting began on the opening of the third day of the Convention. The number of votes necessary for a choice was 378, and seven ballots were taken, with the following result for the leading candidates:

	1st.	2d.	3d.	4th.	5th.	6th.	7th.
Blaine	285	290	293	292	286	308	351
Morton .	125	120	113	108	95	85	
Bristow .	113	114	121	126	114	111	21
Conkling	99	93	90	84	82	81	
Hayes	61	64	67	68	104	113	384
Hartranft	58	63	68	71	69	50	

Scattering votes were also cast for Messrs. Wheeler, Jewell and Washburne. At the close of the seventh ballot, Mr. Hayes', nomination was made unanimous on motion of William P. Frye. During the sixth ballot the unit rule was decided against and each delegate allowed to vote as he pleased, and this became the rule of all subsequent conventions of the party, although in the convention of 1880 the supporters of Gen. Grant made a strong effort to fasten the unit rule on that convention. The candidates for the vice-presidential nomination were Wm. A. Wheeler, Marshall Jewell, Stewart L. Woodford, Jos. R. Hawley and F. T. Frelinghuysen, but after the first ballot had proceeded as far as South Carolina the nomination of Mr. Wheeler was made unanimous.

The nomination of Mr. Hayes was a great surprise to the country and consequently, at first, created little enthusiasm in the party, but it was shortly seen that he was in fact a strong candidate, and the party united solidly behind him and took up the canvass with considerable enthusiasm. Rutherford B. Hayes was born at Delaware, Ohio, October 4, 1822, and graduated at Kenyon College in 1842. He studied law, and practiced for a short time at Fremont, Ohio, afterwards moving to Cincinnati, where he became the City Solicitor. He volunteered in the Civil War, distinguished himself in many important engagements, and rose from the rank of Major to brevet Major-General. The War over, he entered Congress (1865), and at the close of his term was twice elected Governor, serving from 1868 to 1872; was defeated for Congress in 1872, but his election in 1875 to the Governorship, over the Democratic Governor, William Allen, in a remarkable honest-money campaign, brought him into greater national prominence, and now resulted in his nomination for the Presidency. His nomination was a bitter disappointment to the many friends of Mr. Blaine, but they promptly ratified it.

The Republican Platform of 1876, already given, was strong in expression and lofty in its sentiments, which were in keeping with those engendered by the Centennial Year.

The Democratic Convention assembled at St. Louis, Mo., June 27th. The nomination of Samuel J. Tilden, of New York, was almost a foregone conclusion before the Convention met, and he was nominated on the second ballot. Thomas A. Hendricks, of Indiana, who was the strongest opponent of Tilden for the presidential nomination, was named for Vice-President by a unanimous vote. The Democratic platform of 1876 was a lengthy and remarkable one, containing "the sustended arguments of a stump speech." Its planks, with few exceptions, began with "we denounce" or "reform is necessary," and it was a general arraignment of the entire course of the Republican Party while in power, and stated near its conclusion, "reform can only be had by peaceful, civic revolution. We demand a change of system, a change of administration, and a change of parties, that we may have a change of measures and men."

The other political conventions of this year were the Prohibition Convention held at Cleveland, Ohio, on May 17th, at which Green Clay Smith, of Kentucky, was nominated for President, and G. T. Stewart, of Ohio, for Vice-President. The Independent National or Greenback Party met at Indianapolis May 18th, and nominated Peter Cooper, of New York, for President, and U. S. Senator Newton Booth, of California, for Vice-President, who declined and was replaced by Samuel F. Cary, of Ohio. Its platform demanded the immediate repeal of the Specie Resumption Act of January 14, 1875, and the issuance of United States notes, convertible on demand into United

States obligations, bearing a rate of interest not exceeding one cent a day on each $100.00, and exchangeable for United States notes at par, as being the best circulating medium that could be devised. It insisted that bank paper must be suppressed, and it protested against the further issuance of gold bonds for sale in foreign markets, and against the sale of government bonds for the purpose of purchasing silver to be used as a substitute for fractional currency. At the election in November the Greenback Party polled a total of 81,737 votes, not influencing the electoral vote of any State, with the possible exception of Indiana, which Tilden carried with 213,526 votes to 208,011 for Hayes, Cooper receiving 17,233 in this State. The total Prohibition vote this year was 9,522. The Democrats, throughout the campaign, had high hopes of success the hard times which had followed the panic of 1873, the factional disturbances in the Republican Party, charges of official dishonesty, and dissatisfaction of some Republicans with the financial policy of the party, and the success of the Democrats in several of the Northern States all indicated an exceedingly close election. The Republican campaign was largely in the hands of Zachariah Chandler, of Michigan, Chairman of the Republican National Committee, as Mr. Hayes took little part in the details or organization of the canvass. Colorado, admitted in August of this year, raised the number of States to thirty-eight, with a total electoral vote of 369, making 185 votes necessary for an election. The October States did not indicate anything decisive for either side; Ohio going Republican and Indiana Democratic by small majorities. The election was held on Nevember 7th, and a few hours after the polls were closed it was found that Tilden and Hendricks had carried Connecticut, New York, New Jersey and Indiana, and if they had received the vote of the solid South it would give them 203 of the electoral votes and consequently the election. But Mr. Chandler, on information received, sent out a telegram from headquarters in Washington saying that the Republicans had been successful in South Carolina, Louisiana and Florida, and that Hayes and Wheeler were elected by a majority of one. A general outline of the remarkable contest that now followed, and its decision, must suffice for these pages. Each party sent a number of its prominent members to the capitals of the disputed States to witness the count. The legal canvassing boards in all of these States decided in favor of Hayes and Wheeler. Then followed, as it was afterwards discovered, many attempts to bribe an elector in the disputed States to vote for Mr. Tilden, but when the electors met in the various States on December 6th, the vote was 185 for Hayes and Wheeler and 184 for Tilden and Hendricks. As hostile sets of electors were present in four States—Florida, South Carolina, Louisiana and Oregon— it was therefore of the highest importance to know who would count the votes when Congress jointly assembled for that purpose. The Senate and its presiding officer were Republicans, the House was Democratic, and it was apparent that with so much at stake neither would make any concession to the other. This was a state of affairs unprovided for in the Constitution or in any laws that had been passed, and the result was that for four months after the election nobody knew who would be inaugurated as President in March, 1877. The difficulty was temporarilv solved by the Electoral Commission Law, which became effective January 29, 1877. It provided that any electoral votes from any State from which but one return had been received should not be rejected except by the affirmative vote of the two Houses, but if more than one return was received from any State it should be referred to a Commission, to be composed of five members of the Senate, five members of the House and five Supreme Court Justices, and the decision of a majority of this Commission was to decide unless otherwise ordered bv a concurrent vote of both Houses. Senators Oliver P. Morton, George F. Edmunds, F. T. Frelinghuysen, Republicans, and Allan G. Thurman and Thomas F. Bayard, Democrats, were chosen to represent the Senate; Josiah G. Abbott, Eppa Hunton and H. B. Payne, Democrats, and James A. Garfield and George F. Hoar, Republicans, represented the House; four Justices of the Supreme Court had been designated by the law to act, and these were Nathan Clifford and Stephen J. Field, Democrats, and William Strong and Samuel F. Miller, Republicans; they were to choose the fifth Justice and Joseph P. Bradley, Republican, was selected. By a strict party vote the Commission decided, 8 to 7, all questions in favor of the Republicans. These decisons, as already noted, could not be set aside without the concurrent vote of both Houses, which manifestly could not be ob-

RUTHERFORD B. HAYES.

tained, and at 4:10 a. m. March 2, 1877, it was declared
by Mr. Ferry, President pro tem. of the Senate, that Hayes
and Wheeler had been elected by 185 votes to 184 for Tilden and Hendricks. The popular vote at the November
election was Tilden 4,285,992 and Hayes 4,033,768.

Before passing to the events of President Hayes' administration, it is interesting to note that when the second
session of the Forty-fourth Congress met on December 4,
1876, an election was held to fill the position of Speaker,
left vacant by the death of Mr. Kerr. Samuel J. Randall,
Democrat, was elected by 162 votes to 82 votes for James
A. Garfield, and it is therefore seen that President Hayes
would enter upon his term with one branch of Congress
Democratic.

Mr. Hayes was publicly inaugurated March 5, 1877,
the 4th falling upon Sunday. The striking declaration of
his inaugural address was the paragraph setting forth the
policy that he would pursue in the Southern question, and
this policy was exactly the reverse of that of his predecessor. He withdrew the military protection to the colored voter and entered upon a policy of pacification by
putting the whites of the South on their honor. This was
practically turning over the entire South to the Democrats, and they were not slow to seize the advantage, and
they immediately began to work for a "solid South," which
became an assured fact when the results of the election of
1880 were known. This policy was extremely unsatisfactory to most of the members of the Republican Party, and
considerable antagonism to the President was shown.

Lapse of time, however, has vindicated President Hayes, and it is now felt that while his administration was not brilliant, still it was safe, progressive and satisfactory. The President also had his ideas on the subject of Civil Service Reform, and on June 22, 1877, he issued an order that no officer of the Government should be required or permitted to take part in the management of political organizations or election campaigns.

The first session (extra) of the Forty-fifth Congress opened October 15, 1877. The most important business of this session, and indeed of President Hayes' administration, was the legislation on the silver question, which came up before the House suddenly on November 5, 1877, on motion of Mr. Richard P. Bland, of Missouri, that the rules be suspended so as to permit the introduction of a bill for the free coinage of the standard silver dollar. The motion was carried, and had the effect of cutting off all debate and amendment. The bill, as passed in the House, provided for the coinage of the standard silver dollar ($412\frac{1}{2}$ grains), to be legal tender at face value for all debts public and private, and any owner of silver bullion might deposit it in any United States mint and have it coined into dollars for his own benefit. The Bland bill was thus a remonetization of silver on absolutely a free coinage basis, and if passed by the Senate and approved by the President in its original form it would unquestionably have had a serious effect upon the credit of the Government. Its introduction and passage in the House caused a flurry in the money market, and distinctly affected the refunding of the public debt, but fortunately it was amended in the Senate so as to deprive it largely of its destructive effect on the national credit. Mr. Allison (Republican), of the Committee on Finance in the Senate, reported an amendment, striking out the free coinage provision, and providing that the Secretary of the Treasury should purchase at the market price not less than $2,000,000 nor more than $4,000,000 per month of silver bullion to be coined into dollars, any gain to be for the benefit of the Treasury. The House accepted the Allison amendment, but President Hayes vetoed the bill and it was passed over his veto February 28, 1878.

A strong but unsuccessful attempt had been made to repeal the specie resumption act, but now, after seventeen years of suspension of specie payment, which had seriously affected the public credit during all these years, the time approached for resumption. John Sherman was Secretary of the Treasury under President Hayes, and the great act of resumption took place quietly under his direction on January 1, 1879. Mr. Sherman had fought for resumption in both Houses of Congress, and was now permitted, by his official position, to bring about the execution of the law. Its effect on the public credit had been marked for several months before the statutory time of resumption by a better feeling throughout the country in financial circles. The manner in which the entire subject had been treated reflected the greatest credit on the ability of Mr. Sherman, and ranked him with Alexander Hamilton as a great financier.

The Chinese Immigration question had been growing in prominence for several years, and it resulted in a bill to restrict this immigration. The bill passed the House and the Senate, but was vetoed by President Hayes, and its supporters were unable to obtain the necessary vote to pass it over the veto. As the Forty-fifth Congress had adjourned without making the necessary appropriations for the legislative, executive and judicial departments, President Hayes was forced to call an extra session of the Forty-sixth Congress, which met March 18, 1879. In the House Mr. Randall was re-elected Speaker by 143 votes to 125 for James A. Garfield, and for the first time since 1857 the Democratic Party was in complete control of both branches of Congress.

As the time approached for another national campaign the merits of several possible candidates were thoroughly discussed. President Hayes was not a candidate, and the contest for the nomination was seemingly between General Grant and James G. Blaine, with John Sherman as a possible compromise candidate. Several interesting elements entered into the situation and made it extremely doubtful who would be successful, and the result was, the most remarkable contest the party had had in any of its previous conventions, and was solved by the selection, on the thirty-sixth ballot, of one whose name had not even been placed in nomination.

CHAPTER XV.

"The doctrines announced by the Chicago Convention are not the temporary devices of a party to attract votes and carry an election; they are deliberate convictions, resulting from a careful study of the spirit of our institutions, the events of our history, and the best impulses of our people...... If elected, it will be my purpose to enforce strict obedience to the Constitution and the laws, and to promote, as best I may, the interest and honor of the whole country, relying for support upon the wisdom of Congress, the intelligence and patriotism of the people, and the favor of God."

James A. Garfield, Letter of Acceptance. Mentor, Ohio, July 10, 1880.

General Grant arrived at San Francisco in December. 1879, from his triumphal tour of the world, and his journey eastward was made the occasion of a great popular welcome and ovation. This wide-spread enthusiasm lent encouragement to those who were intent upon his nomination for a third term, and they proceeded to strengthen his prospects. Senators Conkling, of New York, Cameron, of Pennsylvania, and Logan, of Illinois, formed a powerful combination in favor of General Grant, and they were successful in their preliminary work of forcing the adoption of the unit rule on the delegations of their States, but it soon became apparent that many of the delegates would vote as they saw fit, and would appeal, if necessary, to the convention to sustain them. James G. Blaine was the

(185)

next strongest candidate, and to his standard rallied a strong host of supporters, many of whom were opposed to a third term for any person. As near as the preliminary figuring could be done it showed the strength of Grant and Blaine to be nearly the same, and this gave hope to the friends of John Sherman that he might be decided on as a compromise candidate, if it became impossible to nominate either Grant or Blaine.

The Seventh Republican National Convention met in the Exposition Hall at Chicago, Ill., on Wednesday, June 2, 1880, and was called to order by Senator J. Donald Cameron, of Pennsylvania, Chairman of the National Committee. George F. Hoar, of Massachusetts, was chosen temporary Chairman, the various committees were then appointed, but owing to contests among the delegates from several States, nothing further could be done, and the convention adjourned early in the afternoon. On the following morning Mr. Hoar was reported as permanent president, and the usual number of vice-presidents and secretaries were also reported. Owing to the delay in the report of the Committee on Credentials nothing further of any moment was done on this day, and the convention adjourned about 7:30 p. m., after an unsuccessful attempt, on motion of Mr. Henderson, of Iowa, to force the Committee on Rules to report. In the vote on a substitute to this motion a most important ruling was made—the vote of Alabama was reported in full for the substitute, but one of the delegates protested and asked the right to cast his vote against it. This was permitted by the president, and the ruling was allowed to stand by the convention, and was thus a condemnation of the unit system of voting. Upon the opening of the third day of the convention (Friday), Mr. Conkling offered a resolution that as the sense of the convention every member of it was bound in honor to support its nominee, no matter who was nominated, and that no man should hold a seat who was not ready to so agree. Out of a total of 719 votes, three (all from West Virginia) were cast against the resolution, whereupon Mr. Conkling offered a second resolution that these delegates did not deserve and had forfeited their votes. The delegates explained that they did not wish it understood that they would not support the nominee, but they simply desired to register their disapproval of the expediency of the resolution. This incident is of the greatest importance in the history of this convention, because it brought Mr. Garfield to his feet in a brief but weighty speech, in which he defended those who had voted in the negative, and finally induced Mr. Conkling to withdraw his second resolution. This speech attracted the attention of the entire convention, and Mr. Garfield from that moment became one of the great leaders in the convention. Mr. Garfield then reported the rules which were adopted, with one amendment, after considerable debate. The great contest of the convention next to the presidental nomination was the report of the Committee on Credentials, in which it was attempted by the friends of Gen. Grant to force the unit rule on the convention. The majority report of this committee favored district representation, and at last this was decided on after a long and remarkable debate extending through Friday until 2 o'clock in the morning and all of the Saturday session until 5 p. m.

Edwards Pierrepont, of New York, reported the platform, which was adopted after one amendment inserting a civil service reform plank.

REPUBLICAN PLATFORM, 1880.

The Republican Party, in national convention assembled, at the end of twenty years since the federal government was first committed to its charge, submits to the people of the United States this brief report of its administration:

It suppressed a rebellion which had armed nearly a million of men to subvert the national authority; it reconstructed the union of the states with freedom instead of slavery as its corner stone; it transformed 4,000,000 human beings from the likeness of things to the rank of citizens; it relieved Congress of the infamous work of hunting fugitive slaves, and charged it to see that slavery does not exist.

It has raised the value of our paper currency from thirty-eight per cent to the par of gold; it has restored, upon a solid basis, payment in coin of all national obligations, and has given us a currency absolutely good and equal in every part of our extended country; it has lifted the credit of the nation from the point of where six percent bonds sold at eighty-six to that where a percent bonds are eagerly sought at a premium.

Under its administration railways have increased from 31,000 miles in 1860 to more than 82,000 miles in 1879.

Our foreign trade increased from $700,000,000 to $1,150,000,000 in the same time, and our exports, which were $20,000,000 less than our imports in 1860, were $265,000,000 more than our imports in 1879.

Without resorting to loans, it has, since the war closed, defrayed the ordinary expenses of government, besides the accruing interest on the public debt, and has disbursed annually more than $30,000,000 for soldiers' and sailors' pensions. It has paid $880,000,000 of the public debt, and, by refunding the balance at lower rates, has reduced the annual interest charge from nearly $150,000,000 to less than $89,000,000.

All the industries of the country have revived, labor is in demand, wages have increased, and throughout the entire country there is evidence of a coming prosperity greater than we have ever enjoyed.

Upon this record the Republican Party asks for the continued confidence and support of the people, and the convention submits for their approval the following statement of the principles and purposes which will continue to guide and inspire its efforts.

1. We affirm that the work of the Republican Party for the last twenty years has been such as to commend it to the favor of the nation; that the fruits of the costly victories which we have achieved through immense difficulties should be preserved; that the peace regained should be cherished; that the Union should be perpetuated, and that the liberty secured to this generation should be transmitted undiminished to other generations; that the order established and the credit acquired should never be impaired; that the pensions promised should be paid; that the debt, so much reduced, should be extinguished by the full payment of every dollar thereof; that the reviving industries should be further promoted, and that the commerce, already increasing, should be steadily encouraged.

2. The Constitution of the United States is a supreme law, and not a mere contract. Out of confederated states it made a sovereign nation. Some powers are denied to the nation, while others are denied to the states; but the boundary between the powers delegated and those reserved is to be determined by the national, and not by the state tribunal.

3. The work of popular education is one left to the care of the several states, but it is the duty of the national government to aid that work to the extent of its constitutional ability. The intelligence of the nation is but the aggregate of the intelligence in the several states, and the destiny of the nation must be guided, not by the genius of any one state, but by the average genius of all.

4. The Constitution wisely forbids Congress to make any law respecting the establishment of religion, but it is idle to hope that the nation can be protected against the influence of secret sectarian-ism which each state is exposed to its domination. We therefore recommend that the Constitution be so amended as to lay the same

prohibition upon the legislature of each state, and to forbid the appropriation of public funds for the support of sectarian schools.

5. We reaffirm the belief avowed in 1876, that the duties levied for the purpose of revenue should so discriminate as to favor American labor; that no further grants of the public domain should be made to any railway or other corporation; that slavery having perished in the states, its twin barbarity—polygamy—must die in the territories; that everywhere the protection accorded to a citizen of American birth must be secured to citizens by American adoption; that we deem it the duty of Congress to develop and improve our seacoast and harbors, but insist that further subsidies to private persons or corporations must cease; that the obligations of the Republic to the men who preserved its integrity in the day of battle are undiminished by the lapse of fifteen years since their final victory—to do them honor is and shall forever be the grateful privilege and sacred duty of the American people.

6. Since the authority to regulate immigration and intercourse between the United States and foreign nations rests with the Congress of the United States and the treaty-making power, the Republican Party, regarding the unrestricted immigration of Chinese as a matter of grave concernment under the exercise of both these powers, would limit and restrict that immigration by the enactment of such just, humane and reasonable laws and treaties as will produce that result.

7. That the purity and patriotism which characterized the earlier career of Rutherford B. Hayes in peace and war, and which guided the thoughts of our immediate predecessors to him for a presidential candidate, have continued to inspire him in his career as Chief Executive; and that history will accord to his administration the honors which are due to an efficient, just and courteous discharge of the public business, and will honor his vetoes interposed between the people and attempted partisan laws.

8. We charge upon the Democratic Party the habitual sacrifice of patriotism and justice to a supreme and insatiable lust for office and patronage; that to obtain possession of the national government and control of the place, they have obstructed all efforts to promote the purity and to conserve the freedom of the suffrage, and have devised fraudulent ballots and invented fraudulent certification of returns; have labored to unseat lawfully elected members of Congress, to secure at all hazards the vote of a majority of the states in the House of Representatives; have endeavored to

occupy by force and fraud the places of trust given to others by the people of Maine, rescued by the courage and action of Maine's patriotic sons; have, by methods vicious in principle and tyrannical in practice, attached partisan legislation to appropriation bills upon whose passage the very movement of the government depended; have crushed the rights of the individual; have advocated the principles and sought the favor of the rebellion against the nation, and have endeavored to obliterate the sacred memories and to overcome its inestimably valuable results of nationality, personal freedom, and individual equality.

The equal, steady, and complete enforcement of the laws and the protection of all our citizens in the enjoyment of all the privileges and immunities guaranteed by the Constitution, are the first duties of the nation.

The dangers of a "Solid South" can only be averted by a faithful performance of every promise which the nation has made to the citizen. The execution of the laws, and the punishment of all those who violate them, are the only safe methods by which an enduring peace can be secured and genuine prosperity established throughout the South. Whatever promises the nation makes the nation must perform. A nation cannot with safety relegate this duty to the states. The "Solid South" must be divided by the peaceful agencies of the ballot, and all honest opinions must there find free expression. To this end the honest voter must be protected against terrorism, violence or fraud.

And we affirm it to be the duty and the purpose of the Republican Party to use all legitimate means to restore all the states of this Union to the most perfect harmony which may be possible, and we submit to the practical, sensible people of these United States to say whether it would not be dangerous to the dearest interests of our country at this time to surrender the administration of the national government to a party which seeks to overthrow the existing policy under which we are now so prosperous, and thus bring distrust and confusion where there is now order, confidence and hope.

9. The Republican Party, adhering to the principles affirmed by its last national convention of respect for the constitutional rules governing appointments to office, adopts the declaration of President Hayes that the reform of the civil service should be thorough, radical and complete. To this end it demands the co-

operation of the legislative with the executive departments of the government, and that Congress shall so legislate that fitness, ascertained by proper practical tests, shall admit to the public service.

The opening words of the fifth plank became the deciding issue of the campaign. The nominations for President were made at the evening session Saturday. James G. Blaine was first placed in nomination by Thomas F. Joy, and seconded by F. M. Pixley and Wm. P. Frye; Ulysses S. Grant was nominated by Roscoe Conkling and seconded by Wm. O. Bradley; John Sherman was nominated by James A. Garfield and seconded by F. C. Winkler and R. B. Elliott; William Windom was nominated by E. F. Drake; George F. Edmunds by Frederick Billings, and Elihu B. Washburn by J. E. Cassady. The nominating speeches concluded near midnight, and aroused the utmost enthusiasm among the 15,000 men and women who were packed in the great hall. The convention adjourned at midnight to meet and begin balloting on Monday morning. The first ballot on Monday morning resulted as follows, 756 delegates being present:

Grant 304	Edmunds .		34
Blaine 284	Washburne		30
Sherman 93	Windom		10

Twenty-eight ballots were taken on Monday with very little material change. Mr. Garfield received one vote on the second ballot, and afterwards received not more than two votes on any ballot until the thirty-fourth, taken on Tuesday, when Wisconsin broke and gave sixteen votes for Garfield, and this was the beginning of the movement by the

Blaine and Sherman forces to combine and nominate Mr. Garfield, who was named on the thirty-sixth ballot. The vote for General Grant was solid until the end, never falling below that of the first ballot, 304. The concluding ballots are here given:

	34th Ballot.	35th Ballot.	36th Ballot.
Grant	312	313	306
Blaine	275	257	42
Sherman	107	99	3
Edmunds	11	11	
Washburne	30	23	5
Windom	4	3	
Garfield	17	50	399

Mr. Garfield was nominated and the convention gave way to almost twenty minutes of cheering and enthusiasm, at the conclusion of which Roscoe Conkling moved that the nomination be made unanimous. As a concession to the disappointed Grant forces, Chester A. Arthur, of New York, was nominated for Vice-President on the first ballot over Elihu B. Washburne, Marshall Jewell, Thomas Settle, Horace Maynard and Edmund J. Davis, the ballot standing 468 for Arthur and 193 for Washburne, his nearest competitor, with scattering votes for the rest.

Although the nomination of Mr. Garfield, like that of Mr. Hayes, was totally unexpected, he was not unknown, and had already, by his services and career, earned for himself an enviable place in the nation's history. Born in Cuyahoga county, Ohio, in 1831, he had risen from an

honorable poverty to the presidency of a College at the age
of 26. He served one term in the Ohio Senate, and at the
opening of the Civil War he was commissioned a Lieuten-
ant-Colonel·of Volunteers, and without any military expe-
ricuce and with a small force he routed a large body of
Confederates at Middle Creek, Ky., in January, 1862, for
which he received the highest praise from his superiors and
the rank of Brigadier-General from President Lincoln.
The rest of his military career was equally satisfactory and
prominent, and he reached the rank of Major-General after
Chickamauga. Resigning his commission, he took his seat
in the House of Representatives in December, 1863, and
immediately became a leader of the Republican forces, and
his legislative work had been most conspicuous. He served
from the Thirty-eighth to the Forty-Sixth Congresses in-
clusive, was on the Electoral Commission of 1877, and at
the time of his nomination had been elected from Ohio to
the United States Senate, but had not yet taken his seat.

The Greenback-Labor Convention met at Chicago, June
9th, and nominated James B. Weaver, of Iowa, for President, and B. F. Chambers, of Texas, for Vice-President,
declaring in its platform that all money should be issued
and its volume controlled by the Government; that the public domain should be kept for settlers, and that Congress
should regulate commerce between the States. The Prohibition Convention at Cleveland, June 17th, nominated
Neal Dow, of Maine, for President, and A. M. Thompson,
of Ohio, for Vice-President. The last of the great party
conventions, that of the Democrats, met at Cincinnati.

June 22d, and nominated General Winfield S. Hancock, of Pennsylvania, for President, on the second ballot, and William H. English, of Indiana, for Vice-President by acclamation. The Democratic platform was concise, and in sharp contrast to the verbose platform of 1876; it demanded an honest money of gold and silver, and paper convertible into coin on demand; tariff for revenue only; and that the public land be given to none but actual settlers.

For the first time since 1844 there was no agitation in any of the party platforms of the slave or southern questions, and all parties agreed on the Chinese question. The campaign opened with defeat for the Republicans in Maine, but this led to greater efforts in the West. Late in the canvass the tariff issue became the most prominent one, and the declaration of the Democratic party for a tariff for revenue only was used against them with tremendous effect by the Republicans. Special efforts were made to gain the October States, and the Republican cause was greatly strengthened and perhaps won in them by several speeches delivered by General Grant and Senator Conkling. In desperation the Democrats, near the end of the canvass (October 20th), published broadcast a letter purporting to come from Mr. Garfield and addressed to "H. L. Morey." The letter stated opinions on the Chinese question which, if true, would have cost many votes, but the letter was promptly shown to be a contemptible forgery, and so plain was the evidence that the letter was disavowed by most Democrats. The election on November 2d was a victory

for Garfield and Arthur, who received 214 electoral votes
to 155 for Hancock and English. The popular vote was:

Garfield	4,454,416	Weaver	308,578
Hancock	4,444,952	Dow .	10,305

An analysis of the popular and electoral vote disclosed the
fact that every former slave State was carried by the Democratic Party, and the "Solid South" for the Democrats
again became a factor in national politics.

Mr. Garfield was inaugurated March 4, 1881, and almost immediately was involved in the controversy between
the "Stalwart" and the "Half Breed" Republicans in New
York, the former being led by Senators Roscoe Conkling
and Thomas C. Platt, and the latter being those who were
opposed to the machine-like politics of the State. The
"Stalwarts" had gained great strength during Gen. Grant's
administration, but had been checked by President Hayes;
they were the strongest advocates of Gen. Grant for a third
term, and were greatly disappointed over his defeat in the
convention, but had loyally supported the nominee, and
had now made up their minds to control the Federal
patronage in New York. President Garfield was drawn
into the muddle by his appointment of William H. Rob-
ertson, a "Half Breed," to the Collectorship of New York.
This called forth a protest signed by Postmaster-General
James, Vice-President Arthur and Senators Conkling and
Platt, the Senators announcing that they would oppose the
confirmation in the Senate. This caused the President to
withdraw all New York appointments until the matter
should be settled, and as it was seen that the nomination

CHESTER A. ARTHUR.

would be confirmed, Senators Conkling and Platt resigned (May 16th), and appealed to the New York Legislature for re-election, but they were defeated, Elbridge 'C'. Lapham and Warren Miller being elected in their places. The controversy excited the whole country, and it was believed by many to have influenced the deplorable tragedy which took place July 2, 1881. About 9:30 a. m., on that day, the President and Mr. Blaine entered the Baltimore & Potomac station in Washington to join a party which would leave that morning for Long Branch, where the President was to join his wife. The President and Mr. Blaine entered the Ladies' Waiting Room, and shortly afterward two shots, fired by Charles Jules Guiteau, were heard, and the President fell mortally wounded. He lingered in great suffering until September 19th, when he died at Elberon, New Jersey, whither he had been removed from Washington.

Vice-President Arthur was at his home in New York City at the time of President Garfield's death, and there took the oath of office as President in the early morning hours of September 20th, and took the formal oath in Washington on September 22d. It is of interest to know something of the man who was called, by these distressing circumstances, to the presidential chair.

President Arthur was born at Fairfield, Vermont, October 5, 1830; after teaching school, he studied law and was admitted to practice in New York City; he served honorably and notably during the Civil War, most of the time as a staff officer, and at its conclusion became active in

local politics in New York City, and was Collector of the
Port of New York from 1871 to 1878, being removed in
the latter year by President Hayes.   His nomination was
made to satisfy the "Stalwarts," and he took an active part
in the controversy between President Garfield and the New
York Senators, and now came to the office of President,
with the popular mind, agitated by the murder of the
President and the factional fight in New York, greatly incensed and antagonized against any one connected with the
"Stalwarts." President Arthur soon gained the confidence
of the people by the conservatism and dignity of his administration, and his term was a satisfactory and pros-
perons one.

The Forty-seventh Congress opened its first session on
December 5, 1881, with David Davis presiding in the
Senate; in the House, Joseph Warren Keifer, Republican,
of Ohio, was elected Speaker by 148 votes to 129 for Samuel J. Randall, and the Republicans were again in control
of both branches of Congress.   The legislation of this Congress was marked by the redemption of the party pledges of
the preceding campaign.   The Edmunds law (March,
1882) was directed at polygamy in Utah and the territories.   Immigration of Chinese laborers to the United
States was suspended for ten years (May 6, 1882), a pre-
vions bill making the time twenty years having been vetoed
by President Arthur.   A bill was also approved (May 15,
1882) appointing a Tariff Commission.   The Commission
met in Washington in July.   It was constituted from both
political parties, and was composed of men of high stand-

ing. When the second session of the Forty-seventh Congress convened on December 4, 1882, it listened to the second annual message from President Arthur, in which the main subject to receive attention was the rapid reduction of the national debt by the large annual surplus revenue. The Tariff Commission at the same time submitted an exhaustive report, containing a schedule of duties recommended by it; after considerable debate and many changes in the schedule, a tariff bill was passed and approved by the President, March 3, 1883, the Democrats steadily opposing it.

Civil Service Reform was taken up and provided for in the Pendleton Civil Service Reform bill (January, 1883), which provided for a non-partisan commission and defined their duties; the effect of this bill was to withdraw from politics the employes of the Government.

The strong prejudices which accompanied Mr. Arthur into office never fully disappeared; during 1882 and 1883 there was considerable public unrest which had its natural influence on political action; it was caused by dissatisfaction among the laboring classes against combinations of capital, which were now resulting from the extraordinary development of the nation's resources, and also because many producers were dissatisfied with the provisions of the new tariff schedule. Although the country was enjoying great prosperity and business confidence, there was a feeling for a change of politics and men. These various causes, and the fact that the strong slavery and sectional issues had disappeared from politics, were demoralizing to the Republican strength in many of the pivotal States, and portended an exceedingly close election in the campaign of 1884. Ohio elected a Democratic Secretary of State in 1882, and followed it the next year by electing Mr. Hoadley, Democrat, over Mr. Foraker, Republican, for Governor. Many other important Democratic victories were gained in 1882—Pennsylvania electing a Democratic Governor and New York electing Grover Cleveland by the enormous majority of 192,000, a victory which secured him the Democratic presidential nomination in 1884. President Arthur was a candidate for the presidential nomination in 1884, and his strength came mainly from the South, but the overwhelming Republican sentiment in the northern and western States demanded the nomination of one whose distinguished services and magnetic personality would unquestionably, with a united party behind him, bring another victory to the party in its eighth national contest.

CHAPTER XVI.

BLAINE.

"We seek the conquests of peace. We desire to extend our commerce and in a special degree with our friends and neighbors on this continent. We have not improved our relations with Spanish America as wisely and as persistently as we might have done. For more than a generation the sympathy of these countries has been allowed to drift away from us. We should now make every effort to gain their friendship."

James G. Blaine, 1884.

When the eighth Republican National Convention assembled at Chicago on Tuesday, June 3, 1884, it was to consider a situation that had never before been presented to a Republican convention. A Republican President, who had gained the office because of the assassination of his predecessor, was before the convention asking for the strongest endorsement of his administration. Only two Republican Presidents had up to this time been candidates for a second term. In the convention of 1864 Mr. Lincoln had no opposition for his second term, and the same was true of General Grant in the convention of 1872. Mr. Hayes was not a candidate for re-election in 1880, and the result, as we have seen, was the Garfield "miracle" in that convention, and now Mr. Garfield's successor was before this convention with a strongly organized backing, mainly from the South, seeking the nomination. But opposed to

(201)

him was an overwhelming sentiment in favor of Mr.
Blaine, whose nomination had been prevented in 1880 by
the opposition of the Grant leaders. A dangerous element
in this convention was present in the Independent Republicans, who had united on George F. Edmunds as their
candidate for President. The convention was called to
order by Dwight M. Sabin, of Minnesota, Chairman of the
National Committee. Mr. Lodge moved to substitute John
R. Lynch, colored, of Mississippi, as temporary Chairman
in place of Powell Clayton, who had been selected by the
National Committee, and after considerable debate, in
which Theodore Roosevelt, of New York, spoke in favor of
the motion to substitute, Mr. Lynch was elected temporary
Chairman by 431 votes to 387 for Mr. Clayton. The remainder of the day was consumed in the appointment of
vice-presidents and secretaries and the various committees.
Wednesday morning a resolution was introduced similar
to that of 1880, that every member of the convention was
bound in honor to support the nominee, but this resolution
was subsequently withdrawn. John B. Henderson, of Missouri, was reported as permanent Chairman, miscellaneous
business consumed some time, and the convention adjourned to meet at 7:30 p. m. The Committee on Credentials not being ready to report, the evening was given over
to speech making. On Thursday morning the convention
heard the report of the Committee on Credentials, and con-
curred in it, and also on the report of the Committee on
Rules. William McKinley, of Ohio, Chairman of the
Committee on Resolutions, reported the platform, and it
was adopted without amendment.

Republican Platform, 1884.

The Republicans of the United States, in national convention assembled, renew their allegiance to the principles upon which they have triumphed in six successive presidential elections, and congratulate the American people on the attainment of so many results in legislation and administration, by which the Republican party has, after saving the Union, done so much to render its institutions just, equal, and beneficent, the safe-guard of liberty and the embodiment of the best thought and highest purpose of our citizens.

The Republican Party has gained its strength by quick and faithful response to the demands of the people for the freedom and equality of all men; for a united nation, assuring the rights of all citizens; for the elevation of labor; for an honest currency; for purity in legislation, and for integrity and accountability in all departments of the government, and it accepts anew the duty of leading in the work of progress and reform.

We lament the death of President Garfield, whose sound statesmanship, long conspicuous in Congress, gave promise of a strong and successful administration—a promise fully realized during the short period of his office as President of the United States. His distinguished services in war and peace have endeared him to the hearts of the American people.

In the administration of President Arthur we recognize a wise, conservative, and patriotic policy, under which the country has been blessed with remarkable prosperity, and we believe his eminent services are entitled to and will receive the hearty approval of every citizen.

It is the first duty of a good government to protect the rights and promote the interests of its own people.

The largest diversity of industry is most productive of general prosperity, and of the comfort and independence of the people.

We therefore demand that the imposition of duties on foreign imports shall be made, "not for revenue only," but that in raising the requisite revenues for the government such duties shall be so levied as to afford security to our diversified industries and protection to the rights and wages of the laborer, to the end that active and intelligent labor, as well as capital, may have its just reward, and the laboring man his full share in the national prosperity.

Against the so-called economic system of the Democratic party, which would degrade our labor to the foreign standard, we enter our earnest protest.

The Democratic Party has failed completely to relieve the people of the burden of unnecessary taxation, by a wise reduction of the surplus.

The Republican Party pledges itself to correct the inequalities of the tariff and to reduce the surplus, not by the vicious and indiscriminate process of horizontal reduction, but by such methods as will relieve the tax-payer without injuring the laborer or the great productive interests of the country.

We recognize the importance of sheep husbandry in the United States, the serious depression which it is now experiencing, and the danger threatening its future prosperity; and we therefore respect the demands of the representatives of this important agricultural interest for a readjustment of duties upon foreign wool, in order that such industry shall have full and adequate protection.

We have always recommended the best money known to the civilized world; and we urge that efforts should be made to unite all commercial nations in the establishment of an international standard, which shall fix for all the relative value of gold and silver coinage.

The regulation of commerce with foreign nations and between the states is one of the most important prerogatives of the general government; and the Republican Party distinctly announces its purpose to support such legislation as will fully and efficiently carry out the constitutional power of Congress over interstate commerce.

The principle of public regulation of railway corporations is a wise and salutary one for the protection of all classes of the people; and we favor legislation that shall prevent unjust discrimination and excessive charges for transportation, and that shall secure to the people and the railways alike the fair and equal protection of the laws.

We favor the establishment of a national bureau of labor; the enforcement of the eight-hour law; a wise and judicious system

JAMES G. BLAINE.

of general legislation by adequate appropriation from the national revenues, wherever the same is needed. We believe that everywhere the protection to a citizen of American birth must be secured to citizens by American adoption; and we favor the settlement of national differences by international arbitration.

The Republican Party having its birth in a hatred of slave labor and a desire that all men may be true and equal, is unalterably opposed to placing our workingmen in competition with any form of servile labor, whether at home or abroad. In this spirit spirit we denounce the importation of contract labor, whether from Europe or Asia, as an offense against the spirit of American institutions; and we pledge ourselves to sustain the present law restricting Chinese immigration, and to provide such further legislation as is necessary to carry out its purposes.

Reform of the civil service, auspiciously begun under Republican administration, should be completed by the further extension of the reform system, already established by law, to all the grades of the service to which it is applicable. The spirit and purpose of the reform should be observed in all executive appointments, and all laws at variance with the objects of existing reform legislation should be repealed, to the end that the dangers of free institutions which lurk in the power of official patronage may be wisely and effectively avoided.

The public lands are a heritage of the people of the United States, and should be reserved as far as possible for small holdings by actual settlers. We are opposed to the acquisition of large tracts of these lands by corporations or individuals, especially where such holdings are in the hands of non-residents or aliens, and we will endeavor to obtain such legislation as will tend to correct this evil. We demand of Congress the speedy forfeiture of all land grants which have lapsed by reason of non-compliance with acts of incorporation, in all cases where there has been no attempt in good faith to perform the conditions of such grants.

The grateful thanks of the American people are due to the Union soldiers and sailors of the late war; and the Republican Party stands pledged to suitable pensions for all who were disabled, and for the widows and orphans of those who died in the war. The Republican Party also pledges itself to the repeal of the limitations contained in the Arrears Act of 1879, so that all invalid soldiers shall share alike, and their pensions begin with the date of disability or discharge, and not with the date of application.

The Republican Party favors a policy which shall keep us from entangling alliances with foreign nations, and which gives us the right to expect that foreign nations shall refrain from meddling in American affairs—a policy which seeks peace and trade with all powers, but especially with those of the Western Hemisphere.

We demand the restoration of our navy to its old-time strength and efficiency, that it may in any sea protect the rights of American citizens and the interests of American commerce; and we call upon Congress to remove the burdens under which American shipping has been depressed; so that it may again be true that we have a commerce which leaves no sea unexplored, and a navy which takes no law from superior force.

Resolved, That appointments by the President to offices in the territories should be made from the bona fide citizens and residents of the territories wherein they are to serve.

Resolved, That it is the duty of Congress to enact such laws as shall promptly and effectually suppress the system of polygamy within our territories, and divorce the political from the ecclesiastical power of the so-called Mormon Church; and that the laws so enacted should be rigidly enforced by the civil authorities, if possible, and by the military, if need be.

The people of the United States, in their organized capacity, constitute a nation, and not an American federacy of states. The national government is supreme within the sphere of its national duties; but the states have reserved rights which should be faithfully maintained. Each should be guarded with jealous care, so that the harmony of our system of government may be preserved and the Union kept inviolate.

The perpetuity of our institutions rests upon the maintenance of a free ballot, an honest count and correct returns. We denounce the fraud and violence practiced by the Democracy in Southern States, by which the will of a voter is defeated, as dangerous to the preservation of free institutions; and we solemnly arraign the Democratic party as being the guilty recipient of the fruits of such fraud and violence.

We extend to the Republicans of the South, regardless of their former party affiliations, our cordial sympathy, and pledge to them our most earnest efforts to promote the passage of such legislation as will secure to every citizen, of whatever race and color, the full and complete recognition, possession, and exercise of all civil and political rights.

The candidates were presented on Thursday evening. A. H. Brandagee presented Jos. R. Hawley, of 'Connecticut; Shelby M. Cullom presented the name of John A. Logan, of Illinois; Judge Wm. H. West, the blind orator of Ohio, nominated James G. Blaine amid scenes of great enthusiasm, and the nomination was seconded by Cushman K. Davis, William C. Goodloe, Thomas C. Platt and Galusha A. Grow; Martin I. Townsend placed Chester A. Arthur in nomination and was seconded by H. H. Bingham, John R. Lynch, Patrick H. Winston and P. B. S. Pinchback; J. B. Foraker nominated John Sherman, of Ohio, and John D. Long presented the name of George F. Edmunds, of Vermont. This closed the list of nominations. The convention adjourned about two o'clock Friday morning. On assembling about 11:30 a. m. the convention proceeded at once to balloting. Four ballots were taken and Mr. Blaine gained steadily on each ballot. At the end of the third ballot the opposition forces endeavored to secure an adjournment without success, and then J. B. Foraker, of Ohio, moved to suspend the rules and nominate Mr. Blaine by acclamation, but to save time the motion was withdrawn and the balloting proceeded. Shelby M. Cullom attempted to read a telegram from John A. Logan, withdrawing in favor of Mr. Blaine, but was prevented by the administration party. The ballots were as follows, with 820 delegates present:

	1st Ballot.	2d Ballot.	3d Ballot.	4th Ballot.
Blaine	334½	349	375	541
Arthur	278	276	274	207
Edmunds	93	85	69	41
Logan	63½	61	53	7
Sherman	30	28	25	
Hawley	13	13	13	15
Lincoln	4	4	8	2
W. T. Sherman	2	2	2	

After the tumult had subsided H. G. Burleigh, of New York, moved, in behalf of President Arthur, and at his request, that the nomination be made unanimous, which was done with tremendous cheers. At the evening session Preston B. Plumb, of Kansas, nominated John A. Logan for Vice-President. An effort was made to make it unanimous, but as there were a few dissenting voices to this, a ballot was taken, showing 779 votes for Logan, six for Gresham, and six for Foraker. Blaine, "The Plumed Knight" of Maine, and Logan, "The Black Eagle" of Illinois, made a ticket well calculated to create tremendous enthusiasm throughout the country.

James G. Blaine was born at West Brownsville, Pa., January 31, 1830, and after graduating from college became a teacher, and in 1854 settled at Augusta, Maine, and took the editorship of a newspaper and soon became prominent. He was elected to the State Legislature in 1858, and became Chairman of the Republican State Committee; he entered Congress in 1863 from Maine, made a brilliant reputation and became the party leader in the House; was

Speaker of the House three terms, from 1869 to 1875; served in the United States Senate from 1876 to 1881. In 1876 he was a prominent candidate for the nomination, as also in 1880. After the election of Mr. Garfield he was Secretary of State, but resigned shortly after President Arthur's accession.

The National Anti-Monopoly Convention was held at Chicago on May 14th, and nominated Benjamin F. Butler, of Massachusetts, for President, and left the office of Vice-President to be filled by a committee, Gen. A. M. West, of Mississippi, being subsequently chosen. The National Greenback-Labor Convention at Indianapolis, on May 28th, endorsed the nomination of Butler and West. The Democratic National Convention met at Chicago on July 8, 1884, and nominated Grover Cleveland, of New York, for President, on the second ballot, and Thomas A. Hendricks, of Indiana, for Vice-President, by acclamation. These selections were made to secure, if possible, the electoral vote of the two doubtful and pivotal States. The Democratic platform demanded a change of parties; it declared that the will of the people had been defeated by fraud in 1876; that the Republican Party was extravagant, and had failed to keep its pledges; denounced the existing tariff and pledged the party to its regulation. The Prohibition National Convention at Pittsburg, on July 12th, named John P. St. John, of Kansas, for President, and William Daniels, of Maryland, for Vice-President.

The campaign of 1884 was one of the most remarkable ever fought by the Republican Party. An unusual feature was that for the first time in its history a strong wing of the Republican Party openly refused to support the nominee. These Independent Republicans became known as "Mugwumps," an Indian name meaning a great or wise person. It was first applied derisively, but afterwards accepted by the Independents as a party name. They were not strong in numbers, but as the campaign drew near its close and it was seen that the election would be very close, the seriousness of the Republican revolt was felt. The entire campaign was marked with great personal bitterness, and charges of corruption and dishonesty were made against both candidates; against Mr. Blaine because of his alleged connection with the Little Rock Railroad matter in 1876. This accusation was brought to the people by the publication of the Mulligan letters September 16, 1884, but the charge was without foundation. The defection of the Mugwumps and the bitter personal attacks had the effect of making Mr. Blaine's friends more enthusiastic in their work for him, and he probably would have won the contest had it not been for the unfortunate utterance of Dr. Burchard in New York City, six days before the election, at a reception by Mr. Blaine to a delegation of clergymen, in which the Democratic Party was referred to as one whose antecedents have been "Rum, Romanism and Rebellion" This remark was dishonestly attributed to Mr. Blaine, and unquestionably lost thousands of votes, because the accusation could not be refuted satisfactorily in the few days remaining before the election. New York, with its thirty-six electoral votes, was lost by the narrow margin of 1149 popular votes, and the election went to the Democrats. A Democratic House was also elected. The electoral vote gave Cleveland and Hendricks 219 and Blaine and Logan 182. The popular vote was: Cleveland 4,874,986, Blaine 4,851,981, Butler 175,370, St. John 150,369.

Mr. Cleveland was inaugurated March 4, 1885, and the country had a Democratic President for the first time since Mr. Buchanan was inaugurated in 1857, counting the administration of Mr. Johnson as Republican. Mr. Cleveland's first term of office reached from March, 1885, to March, 1889, and was marked by no legislation or events seriously affecting the condition of the great parties. There was a liberal use of the veto power, and the Democratic Party was split into two factions over the tariff question, one wing demanding free trade and the other tariff for revenue only, with incidental protection. The first session of the Forty-ninth Congress met December 7, 1885, and owing to the death of Vice-President Hendricks, John Sherman was elected President pro tem. of the Senate. John G. Carlisle, Democrat, was elected Speaker of the House. Owing to the fact that the House and the Senate were controlled by different parties there was no party legislation during the sessions of the Forty-ninth Congress, and the same may be said of the Fiftieth Congress, which opened its first session on December 5, 1887. The third annual message of President Cleveland, read at the opening of this Congress, declared for free trade, and this became the slogan of the Democratic Party, the House

passing the Mills Tariff Bill, which was rejected by the
Senate. As Mr. Cleveland's term drew to a close it was
announced that he would be a candidate for re-nomination.
In the Republican Party there was no certainty as to who
would receive the nomination. Mr. Blaine announced that
he would not be a candidate, and it was felt that the nomination would probably go to John Sherman. The declaration of Mr. Cleveland in favor of free trade afforded a
direct issue in 1888, and the Republicans accepted it
promptly by declaring for a protective tariff.

BENJAMIN HARRISON.

CHAPTER XVII.

"No other people have a government more worthy of their respect and love, or a land so magnificent in extent, so pleasant to look upon, and so full of generous suggestion to enterprise and labor. God has placed upon our head a diadem, and has laid at our feet power and wealth beyond definition or calculation. But we must not forget that we take these gifts upon the condition that justice and mercy shall hold the reins of power, and that the upward avenues of hope shall be free to all the people."

Benjamin Harrison's Inaugural Address, March 4, 1889.

Three National Conventions met on May 15, 1888. The Union Labor Convention at Cincnnati nominated Alson J. Streeter, of Illinois, for President, and Samuel Evans, of Texas, for Vice-President; the United Labor Convention, at the same place, nominated Robert H. Cowdrey, of Illinois, and W. H. T. Wakefield, of Kansas; and the Equal Rights Convention, at Des Moines, Iowa, nominated Mrs. Belva A. Lockwood, of the District of Columbia, for President, and Alfred H. Love, of Pennsylvania, for Vice-President. The popular vote for these tickets in the various States was small and did not influence the result. The Prohibition Convention met at Indianapolis May 20, 1888, and nominated Clinton B. Fisk, of New Jersey, and John A. Brooks, of Missouri; the total Pro-

(213)

hibition vote was 249,506, a gain of 100,000 over the total vote of 1884.

In this year, for the first time since 1860, the Democratic National Convention was held before the Republican National Convention. The Democrats assembled at St. Louis, Missouri, on June 5, 1888, and nominated Grover Cleveland without any opposition, something which had not occurred in a Democratic Convention for forty-eight years; Allen G. Thurman, of Ohio, was nominated for Vice-President on the first ballot. The Democratic platform of 1888 reaffirmed that of 1884, and endorsed the "views expressed by President Cleveland in his last earnest message to Congress as a correct interpretation of that platform upon the question of tariff reduction;" it welcomed a scrutiny of its four years of executive power; advocated homesteads for the people, and civil service and tariff reform. When the Republicans met at Chicago it appeared that John Sherman, of Ohio, was the strongest candidate, and that he might receive the nomination on the third or fourth ballot, but there was a large number of "favorite sons," and no one could exactly determine what might happen before the balloting was concluded. Mr. Blaine, in the closing months of 1887, was unquestionably the unanimous choice of the party, and he would probably have been nominated by acclamation had he not in a letter from Florence, Italy, dated January 25, 1888, declined absolutely to be a candidate. So earnest, however, was the desire for his nomination, that many of his friends refused to be silenced by his emphatic declaration, and it became

necessary for him to write a second letter from Paris on
May 17th, in which he reiterated his former declaration,
and refused to allow his name to be considered, but he predicted that the tariff question would be the issue, and that
an overwhelming success for the Republican Party would
be the result of the campaign. The confusion caused by
his withdrawal led to the large number of candidates, but
gradually the sentiment of the party began to look for a
man who would not only be able to carry the States won by
the Republicans in 1884, but who would also make the best
showing in the doubtful States, principal among which
were New York and Indiana.

On Tuesday, June 19, 1888, at 12:30 p. m., the Re-
publican National Convention was called to order by
Chairman B. F. Jones, of the National Committee. After
an eloquent prayer by Dr. Gunsaulus, of the Plymouth
Church, Chicago, the call for the convention was read by
Secretary Fessenden. The name of John M. Thurston, of
Nebraska, for temporary Chairman, was reported by the
National Committee; the roll-call of States was then made,
at which the delegates announced the names of the persons
selected to serve on the Permanent Organization, Rules and
Order of Business, Credentials and Resolutions Committees. Considerable time was consumed in a preliminary
hearing of the factional fight in Virginia between the Mahone and Wise Republicans. A notable feature of this
session of the convention was the speech by John C. Fremont, the first candidate of the party for President. The
convention adjourned at 3:30 p. m. until the following day

at noon. On convening, the Committee on Permanent Organization reported the name of M. M. Estee, of California. for permanent President, and also the usual number of vice-presidents and honorary secretaries. The Committee on Rules and Order of Business reported and the report was adopted. One important rule was that no change of votes could be made after the vote had been announced, until after the result of the ballot had been announced; this tended to prevent a stampede, and added materially to the deliberateness of the convention. The Committee on Credentials not being ready to report, the convention adjourned at 2:15 p. m. to meet again at 8 p. m.; at the opening of the evening session neither of the Committees on Credentials or Resolutions were ready to report, and the convention listened to stirring speeches by William O. Bradley, of Kentucky, and Governor J. B. Foraker, of Ohio. The Committee on Credentials then reported, and on the Virginia contest seated the Mahone delegates-at-large and the Wise District delegates from all but one district. The convention adjourned at 11:25 p. m. to meet at 10 a. m. Thursday. On Thursday morning, after the roll had been called for names and members of the National Committee, the platform was reported by William McKinley, of Ohio, who received a remarkable ovation as he moved forward to take the stand. It was adopted unanimously by a rising vote, and was the longest ever presented by a Republican Convention.

REPUBLICAN PLATFORM, 1888.

The Republicans of the United States, assembled by their delegates in national convention, pause on the threshold of their proceedings to honor the memory of their first great leader, the immortal champion of liberty and the rights of the people—Abraham Lincoln; and to cover also with wreaths of imperishable remembrance and gratitude the heroic names of our later leaders, who have more recently been called away from our councils—Grant, Garfield, Arthur, Logan, Conkling. May their memories be faithfully cherished. We also recall, with our greetings and with prayer for his recovery, the name of one of our living heroes, whose memory will be treasured in the history both of Republicans and of the Republic—the name of that noble soldier and favorite child of victory, Phillip H. Sheridan.

In the spirit of those great leaders, and of our own devotion to human liberty, and with that hostility to all forms of despotism and oppression which is the fundamental idea of the Republican Party, we send fraternal congratulations to our fellow-Americans of Brazil upon their great act of emancipation, which completed the abolition of slavery throughout the two American continents. We earnestly hope that we may soon congratulate our fellow-citizens of Irish birth upon the peaceful recovery of home rule for Ireland.

FREE SUFFRAGE.

We reaffirm our unswerving devotion to the national Constitution and to the indissoluble union of the states; to the autonomy reserved to the states under the Constitution; to the personal rights and liberties of citizens in all the states and territories in the Union, and especially to the supreme and sovereign right of every lawful citizen, rich or poor, native or foreign born, white or black, to cast one free ballot in public elections and to have that ballot duly counted. We hold the free and honest popular ballot and the just and equal representation of all the people to be the foundation of our republican government, and demand effective legislation to secure the integrity and purity of elections, which are the foundations of all public authority. We charge that the

present administration and Democratic majority in Congress owe
their existence to the suppression of the ballot by a criminal nullification of the Constitution and laws of the United States.

PROTECTION TO AMERICAN INDUSTRIES.

We are uncompromisingly in favor of the American system of
protection; we protest against its destruction as proposed by the
President and his party. They serve the interests of Europe; we
will support the interests of America. We accept the issue and
confidently appeal to the people for their judgment. The protective system must be maintained. Its abandonment has always
been followed by general disaster to all interests, except those of
the usurer and the sheriff. We denounce the Mills bill as destructive to the general business, the labor, and the farming interests of
the country, and we heartily indorse the consistent and patriotic
action of the Republican representatives in Congress in opposing its
passage.

DUTIES ON WOOL.

We condemn the proposition of the Democratic Party to place
wool on the free list, and we insist that the duties thereon shall be
adjusted and maintained so as to furnish full and adequate protection to that industry.

THE INTERNAL REVENUE.

The Republican Party would effect all needed reduction of the
national revenue by repealing the taxes upon tobacco, which are
an annoyance and burden to agriculture, and the tax upon spirits
used in the arts and for mechanical purposes, and by such revision
of the tariff laws as will tend to check imports of such articles as
are produced by our people, the production of which gives employment to our labor, and release from import duties those articles of
foreign production (except luxuries) the like of which cannot be
produced at home. If there shall still remain a larger revenue
than is requisite for the wants of the government, we favor the entire repeal of internal taxes rather than the surrender of any part
of our protective system, at the joint behests of the whisky trusts
and the agents of foreign manufacturers.

FOREIGN CONTRACT LABOR.

We declare our hostility to the introduction into this country of foreign contract labor and of Chinese labor, alien to our civilization and our Constitution, and we demand the rigid enforcement of the existing laws against it, and favor such immediate legislation as will exclude such labor from our shores.

COMBINATIONS OF CAPITAL.

We declare our opposition to all combinations of capital, organized in trusts or otherwise, to control arbitrarily the condition of trade among our citizens; and we recommend to Congress and the state legislatures, in their respective jurisdictions, such legislation as will prevent the execution of all schemes to oppress the people by undue charges on their supplies or by unjust rates for the transportation of their products to market. We approve the legislation by Congress to prevent alike unjust burdens and unfair discrimination between the states.

HOMES FOR THE PEOPLE.

We reaffirm the policy of appropriating the public lands of the United States to be homesteads for American citizens and settlers, not aliens, which the Republican Party established in 1862, against the persistent opposition of the Democrats in Congress, and which has brought our great Western domain into such magnificent development. The restoration of unearned railroad land-grants to the public domain for the use of actual settlers, which was begun under the administration of President Arthur, should be continued. We deny that the Democratic Party has ever restored one acre to the people, but declare that by the joint action of the Republicans and Democrats about 50,000,000 acres of unearned lands originally granted for the construction of railroads have been restored to the public domain, in pursuance of the conditions inserted by the Republican Party in the original grants. We charge the Democratic administration with failure to execute the laws securing to settlers title to their homesteads, and with using appropriations made for that purpose to harass innocent settlers with spies and prosecutions, under the false pretense of exposing frauds and vindicating the law.

HOME RULE IN TERRITORIES.

The government by Congress of the territories is based upon necessity only, to the end that they may become states in the Union; therefore, whenever the conditions of population, material resources, public intelligence and morality are such as to insure a stable local government therein, the people of such territories should be permitted, as a right inherent in them, the right to form for themselves constitutions and state governments, and be admitted to the Union. pending the preparation for statehood, all officers thereof should be selected from the bona fide residents and citizens of the territory wherein they are to serve.

ADMITTANCE OF SOUTH DAKOTA.

South Dakota should of right be immediately admitted as a state in the Union, under the constitution framed and adopted by her people, and we heartily indorse the action of the Republican Senate in twice passing bills for her admission. The refusal of the Democratic House of Representatives, for partisan purposes, to favorably consider these bills, is a willful violation of the sacred American principle of local self-government, and merits the condemnation of all just men. The pending bills in the Senate for acts to enable the people of Washington, North Dakota, and Montana Territories to form constitutions and establish state governments should be passed without unnecessary delay. The Republican Party pledges itself to do all in its power to facilitate the admission of the Territories of New Mexico, Wyoming, Idaho and Arizona to the enjoyment of self-government as states—such of them as are now qualified as soon as possible, and the others as soon as they may become so.

MORMONISM.

The political power of the Mormon Church in the territories as exercised in the past is a menace to free institutions, a danger no longer to be suffered. Therefore we pledge the Republican Party to appropriate legislation asserting the sovereignty of the nation in all territories where the same is questioned, and in furtherance of that end to a place upon the statute books legislation stringent enough to divorce the political from the ecclesiastical power, and thus stamp out the attendant wickedness of polygamy.

JOHN SHERMAN.

BIMETALISM.

The Republican Party is in favor of the use of both gold and silver as money, and condemns the policy of the Democratic administration in its efforts to demonetize silver.

REDUCTION OF LETTER POSTAGE.

We demand the reduction of letter postage to one cent per ounce.

FREE SCHOOLS.

In a Republic like ours, where the citizen is the sovereign and the official the servant, where no power is exercised except by the will of the people, it is important that the sovereign—the people—should possess intelligence. The free school is the promoter of that intelligence which is to preserve us a free nation; therefore the state or nation, or both combined, should support free institutions of learning sufficient to afford to every child growing up in the land the opportunity of a good common school education.

ARMY AND NAVY FORTIFICATIONS.

We earnestly recommend that prompt action be taken by Congress in the enactment of such legislation as will best secure the rehabilitation of our American merchant marine, and we protest against the passage by Congress of a free-ship bill, as calculated to work injustice to labor by lessening the wages of those engaged in preparing materials as well as those directly employed in our shipyards. We demand appropriations for the early rebuilding of our navy; for the construction of coast fortifications and modern ordnance, and other approved modern means of defense for the protection of our defenseless harbors and cities; for the payment of just pensions to our soldiers; for the necessary works of national importance in the improvement of harbors and the channels of internal, coastwise, and foreign commerce; for the encouragement of the shipping interests of the Atlantic, Gulf and Pacific States, as well as for the payment of the maturing public debt. This policy will give employment to our labor, activity to our various industries, increase the security of our country, promote trade, open new and direct markets for our produce, and cheapen the cost of transportation. We affirm this to be far better for our country than the Democratic policy of loaning the government's money, without interest, to "pet banks."

THE MONROE DOCTRINE.

The conduct of foreign affairs by the present administration has been distinguished by its inefficiency and its cowardice. Having withdrawn from the Senate all pending treaties effected by Republican administrations for the removal of foreign burdens and restrictions upon our commerce and for its extension into better markets, it has neither effected nor proposed any others in their stead. Professing adherence to the Monroe doctrine, it has seen, with idle complacency, the extension of foreign influence in Central America and of foreign trade everywhere among our neighbors. It has refused to charter, sanction, or encourage any American organization for constructing the Nicaraguan Canal, a work of vital importance to the maintenance of the Monroe doctrine, and of our national influence in Central and South America, and necessary for the development of trade with our Pacific territory, with South America, and with the islands and farther coasts of the Pacific Ocean.

PROTECTION OF OUR FISHERIES.

We arraign the Democratic administration for its weak and unpatriotic treatment of the fisheries question, and its pusillanimous surrender of the essential privileges to which our fishing vessels are entitled in Canadian ports under the treaty of 1818, the reciprocal maritime legislation of 1830, and the comity of nations, and which Canadian vessels receive in the ports of the United States. We condemn the policy of the present administration and the Democratic majority in Congress toward our fisheries as unfriendly and conspicuously unpatriotic, and as tending to destroy a valuable national industry and an indispensable resource of defense against a foreign enemy. The name of American applies alike to all citizens of the republic, and imposes upon all alike the same obligation of obedience to the laws. At the same time that citizenship is and must be the panoply and safeguard of him who wears it, and protect him, whether high or low, rich or poor, in all his civil rights. It should and must afford him protection at home and follow and protect him abroad, in whatever land he may be, on a lawful errand.

CIVIL-SERVICE REFORM.

The men who abandoned the Republican Party in 1884, and continue to adhere to the Democratic Party have deserted not only the cause of honest government, of sound finance, of freedom, of purity of the ballot, but especially have deserted the cause of reform in the civil service. We will not fail to keep our pledges because they have broken theirs, or because their candidate has broken his. We therefore repeat our declaration of 1884, to wit: "The reform of the civil service, auspiciously begun under the Republican administration, should be completed by the further extension of the reform system, already established by law, to all the grades of the service to which it is applicable. The spirit and purpose of the reform should be observed in all executive appointments, and all laws at variance with the object of existing reform legislation should be repealed, to the end that the dangers to free institutions which lurk in the power of official patronage may be wisely and effectively avoided.

PENSIONS FOR THE SOLDIERS.

The gratitude of the nation to the defenders of the Union cannot be measured by laws. The legislation of Congress should conform to the pledge made by a loyal people, and be so enlarged and extended as to provide against the possibility that any man who honorably wore the Federal uniform should become the inmate of an almshouse, or dependent upon private charity. In the presence of an overflowing treasury, it would be a public scandal to do less for those whose valorous service preserved the government. We denounce the hostile spirit of President Cleveland in his numerous vetoes of measures for pension relief, and the action of the Democratic House of Representatives in refusing even a consideration of general pension legislation.

In support of the principles herewith enunciated, we invite the co-operation of patriotic men of all parties, and especially of all workingmen, whose prosperity is seriously threatened by the free-trade policy of the present administration.

Next in order of business was the presentation of candidates for President. Mr. Warner presented the name of Jos. R. Hawley, of Connecticut; Leonard Sweet nominated Walter Q. Gresham, of Illinois; Albert G. Porter nominated Benjamin Harrison, of Indiana, and at the close of this speech the convention recessed until 3 p. m., at which time Mr. Harrison's nomination was seconded by Mr. Terrill, of Texas, and Mr. Gallinger, of New Hampshire; Mr. Hepburn, of Iowa, nominated Wm. B. Allison; Robert E. Frazer nominated Russel A. Alger; Senator Hiscock nominated Chauncey M. Depew; Daniel B. Hastings nominated John Sherman; Mr. Smith nominated E. H. Fitler, and Governor Rush nominated Jeremiah M. Rusk, and the convention adjourned at 7:26 p. m., until the morning, when the balloting would begin.

On Friday, June 22d, the convention met about 11 a. m., and, after taking three ballots without any result or indication of the nomination of any person, adjourned to meet at an evening session. At the evening session Mr. Depew withdrew his name, and after some miscellaneous business the session adjourned without taking a ballot. On Saturday, June 23d, two ballots were taken without any final result, but they showed a decided increase for Mr. Harrison and indicated his nomination. A recess was taken until 4 p. m., and on meeting at that hour the convention adjourned without taking any further ballots, until Monday morning. On Monday, the sixth, seventh and eighth ballots were taken, resulting in the nomination of Mr. Harrison on the eighth, the nomination being made unanimous on motion of Governor Foraker, of Ohio. The votes for the principal candidates on the different ballots were as follows:

	1st	2d	3d	4th	5th	6th	7th	8th
Sherman	229	249	244	235	224	244	231	118
Gresham	111	108	123	98	87	91	91	59
Depew	99	99	91	...	...	...	...	...
Alger	84	116	122	135	142	137	120	100
Harrison	80	91	94	217	213	231	278	544
Allison	72	75	88	88	99	73	76	
Blaine	35	33	35	42	48	40	15	5

Others who received votes on the various ballots were John J. Ingalls, Jeremiah M. Rusk, W. W. Phelps, E. H. Fitler, Joseph R. Hawley, Robert T. Lincoln, William McKinley, Jr. (who received votes on every ballot, two on the first ballot, his highest, sixteen, on the seventh), Samuel F. Miller, Frederick Douglas, Joseph B. Foraker, Frederick D. Grant and Creed Haymond.

The man who was thus honored by the Republican Party over all of the other eminent men before the convention was by no means an unknown quantity. Mr. Harrison was born at North Bend, Ohio, August 20, 1833. He was a grandson of President William Henry Harrison, and his great-great-grandfather was one of the signers of the Declaration of Independence. After graduating from college he was admitted to the bar and practiced law in Indianapolis; he was elected Reporter of the Indiana Supreme Court in 1860, and left the position to become a volunteer in the Federal army in 1862, and was made Colonel of an Indiana regiment; his army record was good, and he left the service with the brevet rank of Brigadier-General. Resuming his law practice he became very suc-

cessful, and his public speaking made him prominent. In
1876 he was defeated by a small majority for Governor of
Indiana, and in 1880 his name had been presented to the
Republican National Convention. He had served in the
United States Senate from 1881 to 1887.

Levi P. Morton, of New York, was nominated for
Vice-President on the first ballot, receiving 591 votes to
119 for Wm. W. Phelps and 103 for Wm. O· Bradley, of
Kentucky. Blanch K. Bruce, of Mississippi, and Walter
F. Thomas, of Texas, also received votes.

The campaign of 1888 was fought with earnestness and
vigor on both sides. The tariff question overshadowed all
others at this period and was made the great issue of the
canvass. Like those of 1880 and 1884, this campaign was
not without a striking incident that had its influence on the
vote. On October 25, 1888, occurred the publication of
the Murchison correspondence, in which the British Minister, Lord Sackville-West, in a letter dated September
13th, indiscreetly answered a letter purporting to come
from one Charles F. Murchison, of Pomona, Cal., a naturalized Englishman, asking advice how to vote. Lord Sackville-West's reply, while not direct, was that a vote for the
Democratic Party would be more friendly to England than
one for the Republican Party, a declaration which was immediately seized upon by the Republicans and made much
of to influence the votes of those who were undecided on the
tariff issue.

At the election on November 6th Harrison and Morton
carried twenty States, with their 233 electoral votes, and

Cleveland and Thurman carried eighteen States, with 123 electoral votes. The popular vote was ·

Harrison	5,439,853	Cleveland	...5,540,329
Fisk	249,505	Streeter	146,935

The Republicans also gained control of both branches of Congress.

President Harrison's term, reaching from March, 1889, to March, 1893, was one of political turmoil. The first session of the Fifty-first Congress convened on December 2, 1889, and Thomas B. Reed, of Maine, was elected Speaker of the House. The majority of the Republicans being so small, he soon announced his intention of ignoring the usual rule of not counting a member as present unless he voted, and stated a new rule, of counting those who were present as present, even though they did not vote. This and other rulings were adopted by a party vote, and Mr. Reed was called the "Czar" by the Democrats.

The most important work of this Congress and the great political event of Harrison's administration was the enactment of the McKinley Tariff Bill, which was reported to the House of Representatives on April 16, 1890, by William McKinley, Chairman of the Committee on Ways and Means. After considerable debate, it was passed by the House on May 21st, and by the Senate in September, and became a law October 1, 1890. The continued efforts of the Democrats brought the McKinley Tariff law into much public disfavor, and resulted in overwhelming Democratic victories in the Congressional elections in November, 1890, by which the Democrats regained control of the House, and their minority of 18 in the Fifty-first Congress was changed to a majority of 129 in the Fifty-second.

A new party, the People's Party, which will be considered later, appeared in politics with success for the first time at the elections in 1890. Other important measures advocated and adopted by the Republicans in the Fifty-first Congress were more liberal Pension Laws (June 27, 1890), and the Sherman Anti-Trust Bill (June 26, 1890). The so-called Sherman Silver Act of July 14, 1890, was in reality a concession to the strong silver element which was appearing in both the great parties at this time, and which was to have so momentous an influence on political history in later presidential campaigns. This Act provided for the purchase of 4,500,000 ounces of silver bullion each month, to be paid for in paper money called Treasury Notes, redeemable on demand in gold or silver, and for the coinage of 2,000,000 ounces per month in dollars; after July 1, 1891, the silver was not to be coined, but might be stored in the Treasury and silver certificates issued. The purchasing clause of the Bland-Allison Act of 1878 was repealed.

As the time approached for the presidential campaign of 1892 the political situation was peculiar. President Harrison was openly a candidate for re-election, but he was unpopular with many of the strong Republican leaders, who, as a matter of course, turned to Mr. Blaine, then Secretary of State. Mr. Blaine, however, on February 6, 1892, wrote Mr. Clarkson, Chairman of the National Republican Committee, declining to be a candidate, but his friends, notwithstanding, persisted in booming him. The country was astonished on June 4th, three days before the Convention, to learn that Mr. Blaine had resigned from the Cabinet. Did it mean that he was desirous of returning to private life, or of withdrawing his declination and entering actively into the fight for the nomination? Mr. Blaine did not explain, and the uncertainty was perplexing as the day for the Convention approached.

In the Democratic Party the situation at first was equally uncertain as to who might be the nominee, but as the State Delegations were chosen, it was seen that Mr. Cleveland would again be nominated in spite of the opposition of Gov. Hill and the New York delegation. Public attention centered, in June, 1892, on Minneapolis and Chicago, where the Republican and Democratic Conventions were to be held.

CHAPTER XVIII.

CLEVELAND'S SECOND TERM.

"Cleveland's (second) election created the disturbances that followed it. The fear of radical changes in the Tariff Law was the basis of them. That law caused the falling of prices, the stagnation of some industries, and the suspension of others. No doubt the fall in the value of silver and the increased demand for gold largely precipitated and added to the other evils."

John Sherman's Recollections.

The delegates for the Tenth Republican National Convention assembled at Minneapolis, Minn., in the opening days of June, 1892. The friends of Mr. Blaine were booming his candidacy, although no direct expression had come from him as to whether or not he actively desired the nomination. His sudden and unexpected resignation from President Harrison's Cabinet had created a situation difficult to analyze, but the general opinion was that he had hurt his prospects by his action. The anti-Harrison sentiment was strong, however, and there was much talk of the possible nomination of a "dark horse," and the name of William McKinley, of Ohio, "the Napoleon of Tariff," was most spoken of in this respect. As the day of the Convention drew near both the Blaine and Harrison men expressed the utmost confidence in their certain success, and the first occasion in the Convention that would call for a test of strength was looked for with great interest.

(230)

About 12:24 p. m., Tuesday, June 7, 1892, Chairman James S. Clarkson, of the Republican National Committee, called the Tenth Convention to order, and announced the selection, by the National Committee, of J. Sloat Fassett, of New York, as temporary Chairman. At the close of Mr. Fassett's speech of acceptance the Convention called for Thomas B. Reed, who reluctantly came forward and addressed the Convention briefly. The roll-call of States for the selection of members of the various committees consumed the time until almost two o'clock, when the convention adjourned to meet the next morning. On reassembling the Committee on Credentials was granted further time; the Committee on Permanent Organization reported the name of William McKinley, of Ohio, for Permanent President of the Convention, who took the gavel amid great applause and enthusiasm, and delivered a short, pithy speech. The Committee on Rules reported, and further time was granted the Committee on Resolutions. After calling the roll of States for names of the new National Committeemen, the Convention adjourned for the day. On Thursday morning, June 9th, the Committee on Credentials was still not ready to report, and as nothing could be done until they did report, the Convention took a recess at 11:45 a. m. to 8 p. m. At the opening of the evening session Mr. Depew, of New York, congratulated Col. Dick Thompson, of Indiana, who had voted for every President of the United States for the past sixty years, on reaching on that day his eighty-third birthday, and the Convention listened to a short speech of thanks from Col. Thompson.

The Committee on Credentials now reported, and the majority were in favor of the seating of enough administration delegates to make a net gain of 12 votes for Harrison, and the first contest of strength between the Blaine and the Harrison forces came on a motion to substitute the minority report in favor of seating the Blaine delegates. The vote on this motion was taken amid intense excitement, and resulted in a victory for the Harrison forces by a close vote of 462½ to 423. Joseph B. Foraker, of Ohio, Chairman of the Committee on Resolutions, now reported the platform, which was in the following words:

REPUBLICAN PLATFORM, 1892.

The representatives of the Republicans of the United States, assembled in general convention on the shores of the Mississippi River, the everlasting bond of an indestructible republic, whose most glorious chapter of history is the record of the Republican Party, congratulate their countrymen on the majestic march of the nation under the banners inscribed with the principles of our platform of 1888, vindicated by victory at the polls and prosperity in our fields, workshops and mines, and make the following declaration of principles:

THE PRINCIPLE OF PROTECTION.

We reaffirm the American doctrine of protection. We call attention to its growth abroad. We maintain that the prosperous condition of our country is largely due to the wise revenue legislation of the last Republican Congress. We believe that all articles which cannot be produced in the United States, except luxuries, should be admitted free of duty, and that on all imports coming into competition with the products of American labor there should be levied duties equal to the difference between wages abroad and at home.

We assert that the prices of manufactured articles of general consumption have been reduced under the operations of the Tariff Act of 1890.

We denounce the efforts of the Democratic majority of the House of Representatives to destroy our tariff laws piecemeal, as manifested by their attacks upon wool, lead, and lead ores, the chief products of a number of states, and we ask the people for their judgment thereon.

TRIUMPH OF RECIPROCITY.

We point to the success of the Republican policy of reciprocity, under which our export trade has vastly increased and new and enlarged markets have been opened for the products of our farms and workshops. We remind the people of the bitter opposition of the Democratic Party to this practical business measure, and claim that, executed by a Republican administration, our present laws will eventually give us control of the trade of the world.

FREE AND SAFE COINAGE OF GOLD AND SILVER.

The American people, from tradition and interest, favor bimetalism, and the Republican party demands the use of both gold and silver as standard money, with such restrictions and under such provisions, to be determined by legislation, as will secure the maintenance of the parity of values of the two metals, so that the purchasing and debt-paying power of the dollar, whether of silver, gold, or paper, shall be at all times equal. The interests of the producers of the country, its farmers and its workingmen, demand that every dollar, paper, or coin, issued by the government shall be as good as any other. We commend the wise and patriotic steps already taken by our government to secure an international conference to adopt such measures as will insure a parity of value between gold and silver for use as money throughout the world.

FREEDOM OF THE BALLOT.

We demand that every citizen of the United States shall be allowed to cast one free and unrestricted ballot in all public elections, and that such ballot shall be counted and returned as cast; that such laws shall be enacted and enforced as will secure to every citizen, be he rich or poor, native or foreign born, white or black, this sovereign right, guaranteed by the Constitution. The free and honest popular ballot, the just and equal representation of all the people, as well as their just and equal protection under the laws, are the foundation of our republican institutions, and the party will never relax its efforts until the integrity of the ballot and the purity of elections shall be fully guaranteed and protected in every state.

OUTRAGES IN THE SOUTH.

We denounce the continued inhuman outrages perpetrated upon American citizens for political reasons in certain Southern States of the Union.

EXTENSION OF FOREIGN COMMERCE.

We favor the extension of our foreign commerce, the restoration of our mercantile marine by home-built ships, and the creation of a navy for the protection of our national interests and the honor of our flag; the maintenance of the most friendly relations with all foreign powers, entangling alliance with none, and the protection of the rights of our fishermen.

MONROE DOCTRINE.

We reaffirm our approval of the Monroe doctrine, and believe in the achievement of the manifest destiny of the Republic in its broadest sense.

RESTRICTION OF IMMIGRATION.

We favor the enactment of more stringent laws and regulations for the restriction of criminal, pauper, and contract immigration.

EMPLOYEES OF RAILROADS.

We favor the efficient legislation by Congress to protect the life and limbs of employees of transportation companies engaged in carrying on interstate commerce, and recommend legislation by the respective states that will protect employees engaged in state commerce, in mining and manufacturing.

CHAMPIONING THE OPPRESSED.

The Republican Party has always been the champion of the oppressed and recognizes the dignity of manhood, irrespective of faith, color or nationality. It sympathizes with the cause of home rule in Ireland, and protests against the persecution of the Jews in Russia.

FREEDOM OF THOUGHT AND SPEECH.

The ultimate reliance of free popular government is the intelligence of the people and the maintenance of freedom among all men. We therefore declare anew our devotion to liberty of thought and conscience, of speech and press, and approve all agencies and instrumentalities which contribute to the education of the children of the land; but while insisting upon the fullest measure of religious liberty, we are opposed to any union of church and state.

TRUSTS CONDEMNED.

We reaffirm our opposition, declared in the Republican platform of 1888, to all combinations of capital, organized in trusts or otherwise to control arbitrarily the condition of trade among our citizens. We heartily indorse the action already taken upon this subject, and ask for such further legislation as may be required to remedy any defects in existing laws and to render their enforcement more complete and effective.

FREE DELIVERY SERVICE.

We approve the policy of extending to town, villages, and rural communities the advantages of the free-delivery service now enjoyed by the larger cities of the country, and reaffirm the declaration contained in the Republican platform of 1888, pledging the reduction of letter postage to one cent at the earliest possible moment consistent with the maintenance of the Postoffice Department and the highest class of postal service.

SPIRIT OF CIVIL-SERVICE REFORM.

We commend the spirit and evidence of reform in the civil service, and the wise and consistent enforcement by the Republican Party of the laws regulating the same.

THE NICARAGUA CANAL.

The construction of the Nicaragua Canal is of the highest importance to the American people, both as a measure of defense and to build up and maintain American commerce, and it should be controlled by the United States Government.

TERRITORIES.

We favor the admission of the remaining territories at the earliest practicable day, having due regard to the interests of the people of the territories and of the United States.

FEDERAL TERRITORIAL OFFICERS.

All the federal officers appointed for the territories should be selected from bona fide residents thereof, and the right of self government should be accorded as far as practicable.

ARID LANDS.

We favor cession, subject to the homestead laws, of the arid public lands to the states and territories in which they lie, under such congressional restrictions as to disposition, reclamation, and occupancy by settlers as will secure the maximum benefits to the people.

THE COLUMBIAN EXPOSITION.

The World's Columbian Exposition is a great national undertaking, and Congress should promptly enact such reasonable legislation in aid thereof as will insure a discharging of the expense and obligations incident thereto and the attainment of results commensurate with the dignity and progress of the nation.

SYMPATHY FOR TEMPERANCE.

We sympathize with all wise and legitimate efforts to lessen and prevent the evils of intemperance and promote morality.

PLEDGES TO THE VETERANS.

Ever mindful of the services and sacrifices of the men who saved the life of the nation, we pledge anew to the veteran soldiers of the Republic a watchful care and a just recognition of their claims upon a grateful people.

HARRISON'S ADMINISTRATION COMMENDED.

We commend the able, patriotic, and thoroughly American administration of President Harrison. Under it the country has enjoyed remarkable prosperity, and the dignity and honor of the nation, at home and abroad, have been faithfully maintained, and we offer the record of pledges kept as a guarantee of faithful performance in the future.

After the adoption of the platform the Convention adjourned for the day.

At the opening of the session on June 10th, Mrs. J. Ellen Foster, Chairman of the Woman's Republican Association of the United States, was heard, and next in order was the nomination of candidates for President. Senator Wolcott nominated James G. Blaine in an eloquent speech; W. H. Eustis seconded this nomination, and at the conclusion of his splendid speech there was twenty-seven minutes of the wildest enthusiasm for Blaine; W. E. Mollison and G. B. Boyd also seconded Mr. Blaine's nomination. Richard W. Thompson, ex-Secretary of the Navy, nominated Benjamin Harrison, and was seconded by Chauncey M. Depew, Warner Miller, Senator Spooner and B. E. Finck. The total number of votes was 905, making 453 necessary to a choice. Only one ballot was taken as follows:

Benjamin Harrison .535 1-6   Thomas B. Reed 4
James G. Blaine   182 5-6   Robert T. Lincoln......1
William McKinley ..182

Mr. Harrison was thus nominated on the first ballot, and on motion of Mr. McKinley the nomination was made unanimous. Whitelaw Reid of New York was nominated for Vice-President by acclamation, and the Convention adjourned.

The Democratic National Convention assembled at Chicago, Ill., June 21, 1892. Grover Cleveland, of New York, was nominated for the third time by a vote of 617 1-3 to 114 for David B. Hill, his nearest opponent. Adlai E. Stevenson, of Illinois, was named for Vice-President. The Democratic platform of 1892 denounced Republican protection as a fraud and a robbery of the great majority of the American people for the benefit of the few, and said that the McKinley Tariff Law was the "culminating atrocity" of class legislation, and promised its repeal; the platform declared for a tariff for purposes of revenue only, and advocated the speedy repeal of the Sherman Act of 1890.

The Prohibition Convention met at Cincinnati, Ohio, June 24, and nominated John Bidwell, of California, and J. B. Cranfill, of Texas. A new party had been organizing quietly for some time, and was destined to exercise a momentous effect upon the campaign of this year and also of 1896. A Farmers' Alliance Convention had met at St. Louis in December, 1889, and formed a confederation with the Knights of Labor, Greenback and Single Tax Parties.

In December, 1890, they met at Ocala, Florida, and adopted what is known as the "Ocala Platform," practically all of the ideas of which were embodied in the platform of the first National Convention of the People's Party, which met at Omaha, Neb., July 2, 1892. At this Convention James B. Weaver, of Iowa, was nominated for President, and James G. Field, of Virginia, for Vice-President. The platform of the People's Party in 1892 stated that corruption dominated everything, and that the country generally was on the verge of "moral, political and material ruin," and stated that in the last twenty-five years' struggle of the two great parties "grievous wrongs have been inflicted upon the suffering people;" and declared that the union of the labor forces shall be permanent, and demanded the free and unlimited coinage of silver and gold at 16 to 1; for an income tax; for Postal Savings Bank; for Government ownership of railroads, telegraphs and telephones. The Socialist-Labor Convention met at New York August 28, 1892, and nominated Simon Wing, of Massachusetts, and Charles H. Matchett, of New York, and adopted a series of social and political demands.

The campaign of 1892 was somewhat uninteresting as compared to those of previous years; the political land slide of 1890 was still felt by the Republicans, but notwithstanding it, the situation seemed hopeful. The main encouragement for the Republicans was that the disturbances in the Democratic party in New York might result so seriously as to lose that State for the Democrats, but the hope was futile, and at the election on November 8, 1892, Cleveland

and Stevenson received 277 electoral votes, to 145 for Harrison and ~~Morton~~, and 22 for the People's candidates, Weaver and Field. The popular vote was: Cleveland, 5,556,928; Harrison, 5,176,106; Weaver, 1,041,021; Bidwell, 262,034; Wing, 21,164.

The great surprise of this election, to the members of both of the old parties, was the unexpected strength shown by the candidates of the People's Party. By fusing with the Democrats they received the electoral votes of Colorado, Idaho, Nevada and Kansas, and split the vote in North Dakota and Oregon. This fusion of the People's Party and the Democrats in the West portended serious effects on the destiny of the Democratic Party in subsequent campaigns.

President Cleveland was inaugurated March 4, 1893, and begun his second term of four years, which was marked by the worst financial and industrial disasters, affecting thousands upon thousands of the American people, ever known in the history of the country. Before he was inaugurated, a Treaty of Annexation of Hawaii had been signed (February 14, 1893), and was being considered by the Senate, but almost his first act of importance was to withdraw the Treaty from the consideration of the Senate on March 9, 1893.

Fear of Democratic tinkering with the tariff began almost immediately with Cleveland's inauguration, and manifested itself in a lack of confidence and general business uncertainty; in addition, the currency was in bad shape, and the business interests feared strongly that the Silver Act of 1890 might result in the adoption of the silver standard for the United States. The evils of the Greenback system were now felt with full force; they could be redeemed in specie, but were not cancelled, and were put in circulation again, thus causing a continuous drain on the gold reserve of the country. The amount of greenbacks in circulation was about $350,000,000, and the Treasury notes issued under the Silver Act of 1890, exchangeable in gold, made a total gold obligation close to $500,000,000. The threatening state of affairs now resulted in a general withdrawal and hoarding of gold, and foreign capital, beginning to lose its confidence in the stability of American affairs, withdrew investments, resulting in a heavy drain on the gold reserve, which now, for the first time, fell below $100,000,000 in April, 1893. The general climax of all of these conditions reached its height in the Summer and Fall of 1893, and a panic of fearful proportions set in, resulting in the collapse of hundreds of banks and involving and ruining business enterprises all over the country. Never before had a panic reached so far or affected so many people as that of this year.

With the hope of benefiting the situation by the repeal of the Silver Act of 1890, President Cleveland called an extraordinary session of the Fifty-third Congress, which met August 7, 1893. In the Senate were 44 Democrats and 38 Republicans, one Independent and two Farmers' Alliance; the House was composed of 220 Democrats and 128 Republicans and eight Populists, and organized by electing Chas. F. Crisp, of Georgia, Speaker. On November 1, 1893, a Bill was passed repealing the Silver purchase law of 1890, but in both branches of Congress there was a majority in favor of free coinage, and this fact, notwithstanding that nothing was or could be done in the way of legislation, on this subject, although it was attempted several times, continued to disturb the nation's financial and commercial interests. Business conditions gradually continued to grow worse, and this situation confronted the second session of the Fifty-third Congress, which met on December 3, 1893. The Democratic Party in the House immediately took up the proposition of repealing the McKinley tariff law, and on December 19th, Mr. Wm. L. Wilson, Chairman of the Committee on Ways and Means, presented the Wilson Tariff Bill to the House, and it was passed by that body February 1, 1894. In the Senate it met with Democratic opposition, which joined with the Republicans in amending the bill so as to protect certain industries. A compromise was effected with the House, and the mutilated and unsatisfactory bill became a law on August 27, 1894, without President Cleveland's signature.

One alarming feature of the panic of 1893 was that, as the industrial conditions continued to grow worse, a lawless and frenzied element made itself felt in alarming strikes in many parts of the country, in some instances making necessary the calling out of the Regular Army. Another manifestation of alarming and revolutionary tendency was the marching on Washington of two armies of men to demand action from the Government, relieving their distress; their number and character, however, did not represent the best spirit of the American people, but that conditions were so alarming as to cause such a movement is indeed a matter for serious reflection.

Two years of Democratic failure in the management of the affairs of the country had its effect on the Congressional elections in 1894, and the Democrats experienced an overwhelming and crushing defeat, and the Fifty-fourth Congress to meet in December, 1895, would be composed of 39 Democrats, 44 Republicans and six Alliance Senators; and 104 Democrats, 245 Republicans, one Silverite and seven Populists in the House. The continued drain on the gold reserve made necessary the issuance of bonds to obtain gold, and the bonded debt of the country was increased during Cleveland's term $262,000,000. The Wilson tariff bill, it was felt, would be insufficient to produce enough revenue to meet the expenditures of the Government, and an attempt was made to meet the deficit by imposing a tax of two percent on all incomes over $4,000, but this was subsequently declared unconstitutional by the Supreme Court. Only one bright spot seems to appear in all this disastrous period, and it was the vigorous policy of interference by the President in the dispute between Great Britain and Venezuela. A bold and decided stand was taken for the Monroe Doctrine, but even this had its evil effect, for the business interests were agitated by the fear of war with Great Britain.

Such was the disastrous story of four years of Democratic control of the Government, and the Republicans, in the early months of 1896, looked forward with the utmost confidence to the elections of their candidates, who would be named in a convention to be held at St. Louis, Mo., in June.

CHAPTER XIX.

M'KINLEY.

"We have been moving in untried paths, but our steps have been guided by honor and duty. There will be no turning aside, no wavering, no retreating. No blow has been struck except for liberty and humanity, and none will be. We will perform without fear every national and international obligation. The Republican Party was dedicated to freedom forty-four years ago. It has been the party of liberty and emancipation from that hour, not of profession, but of performance. It broke the shackles of 4,000,000 of slaves and made them free, and to the party of Lincoln has come another supreme opportunity which it has bravely met in the liberation of 10,000,000 of the human family from the yoke of imperialism.

William McKinley, Canton, Ohio, July 12, 1900.

The opening months of 1896 were marked by a great struggle in both of the old political parties; in the Democratic Party the struggle was one of principle; in the Republican—of men. The silver question, which had been a disturbing and unsettled factor in the politics of both of the great parties for many years, dominated the Democratic Party in 1896 entirely, notwithstanding the strenuous efforts of the Cleveland administration and the Eastern Democrats to have the party declare against it. The instruction of the Democratic State delegations was overwhelmingly in favor of the free coinage of silver at the ratio of 16 to 1, and the matter was decided long before the Democratic Convention met. But how would the Gold

INAUGURATION OF WILLIAM McKINLEY, MARCH 4, 1897.

Democrats be treated in the Convention; and what action would they take when it declared for silver? Who would carry the banner of the Democratic Party under the new issue? In the Republican Party there was little fear that the Convention would be stampeded in favor of free silver, as the instructions of the Republican delegates were as emphatic for a sound money platform as those of the Democratic Party had been for free silver. When the sentiment of the Republican Party became known there was very little discussion of the silver question, notwithstanding that it was apparent that the silver element of the party would assert itself in the Convention, and would probably secede on the adoption of the gold plank in the platform. The great contest in the Republican Party in 1896 was between the two leading candidates for the presidential nomination. Wm. McKinley, of Ohio, and Thomas B. Reed, of Maine, were these candidates, and by reason of their great services to the party there was at first almost an equal division of sentiment for their nomination. Joseph H. Manley was Mr. Reed's campaign manager, and the political destinies of Mr. McKinley were in the hands of Marcus A. Hanna, of Ohio, who proved himself in this canvass to be the greatest political manager in the nation's history. The months preceding the Convention were occupied by a great struggle for the State delegations, and although the managers for Mr. Reed did not give up the fight until a few days before the Convention, it was early seen that the strong trend of favor was toward Mr. McKinley, and the indications were that he would be nominated on the first ballot.

The excitement caused by the unusual contest in both parties was intense as the time for the national conventions
approached.

The Eleventh Republican National Convention met at
St. Louis, Mo., on Tuesday, June 16, 1896, and was called
to order about 12:20 p. m. by Senator Thomas H. Carter,
of Montana, Chairman of the National Committee, and a
pronounced advocate of free silver.   After a prayer by
Rabbi Samuel Sale, Chairman Carter announced the selection by the National Committee of Charles W. Fairbanks, of Indiana, as temporary Chairman, who accepted
the honor in an eloquent speech.   After selecting the
various committees the Convention adjourned for the day.
On Wednesday morning, June 17th, the Committee on
Permanent Organization announced the name of John M.
Thurston, of Nebraska, as President of the Convention.
He took the gavel and delivered a short, strong speech,
arousing the Convention to great enthusiasm.   At the opening of the afternoon session, Chairman J. Franklin Fort,
of the Committee on Credentials, reported, and, after a
long debate concerning the contest between rival delegations from Texas and Delaware, the majority report was
adopted, and after adopting the report of the Committee on
Rules, presented by Gen. Harry Bingham, the Convention
adjourned.   On the morning of the third day of the convention the platform was reported by Senator-elect Joseph
B. Foraker of Ohio.

REPUBLICAN PLATFORM, 1896.

The Republicans of the United States, assembled by their representatives in national convention, appealing for the popular and historical justification of their claims to the matchless achievements of the thirty years of Republican rule, earnestly and confidently address themselves to the awakened intelligence, experience, and conscience of their countrymen in the following declaration of facts and principles:

For the first time since the civil war the people have witnessed the calamitous consequences of full and unrestricted Democratic control of the government. It has been a record of unparalleled incapacity, dishonor, and disaster. In administrative management it has ruthlessly sacrificed indispensable revenue, entailed an unceasing deficit, eked out ordinary current expenses with borrowed money, piled up the public debt by $262,000,000 in time of peace, forced an adverse balance of trade, kept a perpetual menace hanging over the redemption fund, pawned American credit to alien syndicates and reversed all the measures and results of successful Republican rule.

In the broad effect of its policy it has precipitated panic, blighted industry and trade with prolonged depression, closed factories, reduced work and wages, halted enterprise, and crippled American production while stimulating foreign production for the American market. Every consideration of public safety and individual interest demands that the government shall be rescued from the hands of those who have shown themselves incapable to conduct it without disaster at home and dishonor abroad, and shall be restored to the party which for thirty years administered it with unequaled success and prosperity, and in this connection we heartily indorse the wisdom, the patriotism, and the success of the administration of President Harrison.

TARIFF.

We renew and emphasize our allegiance to the policy of protection as the bulwark of American industrial independence and the foundation of American development and prosperity. This true American policy taxes foreign products and encourages home industry; it puts the burden of revenue on foreign goods; it secures the American market for the American producer; it upholds the American standard of wages for the American workingman; it puts the factory by the side of the farm, and makes the American farmer less dependent on foreign demand and price; it diffuses general thrift, and founds the strength of all on the strength of each. In its reasonable application it is just, fair and impartial; equally opposed to foreign control and domestic monopoly, to sectional discrimination and individual favoritism.

We denounce the present Democratic tariff as sectional, injurious to the public credit, and destructive to business enterprise. We demand such an equitable tariff on foreign imports which come into competition with American products as will not only furnish adequate revenue for the necessary expenses of the government, but will protect American labor from degradation to the wage level of other lands. We are not pledged to any particular schedules. The question of rates is a practical question to be governed by the conditions of time and of production; the ruling and uncompromising principle is the protection and development of American labor and industry. The country demands a right settlement, and then it wants rest.

RECIPROCITY.

We believe the repeal of the reciprocity arrangements negotiated by the last Republican administration was a national calamity, and we demand their renewal and extension on such terms as will equalize our trade with other nations, remove the restrictions which now obstruct the sale of American products in the ports of other countries, and secure enlarged markets for the products of our farms, forests and factories.

Protection and reciprocity are both twin measures of Republican policy and go hand in hand. Democratic rule has recklessly struck down both, and both must be re-established. Protection for what we produce; free admission for the necessaries of life which we do not produce; reciprocity agreements of mutual interests which gain open markets for us in return for our open market to others. Protection builds up domestic industry and trade, and secures our own market for ourselves; reciprocity builds up foreign trade, and finds an outlet for our surplus.

SUGAR.

We condemn the present administration for not keeping faith
with the sugar-producers of this country. The Republican party favors such protection as will lead to the production on American soil
of all the sugar which the American people use, and for which they
pay other countries more than $100,000,000 annually.

WOOL AND WOOLENS.

To all our products—to those of the mine and the fields as well
as to those of the shop and the factory; to hemp, to wool, the product of the great industry of sheep husbandry, as well as to the finished woolens of the mills—we promise the most ample protection.

MERCHANT MARINE.

We favor restoring the American policy of discriminating duties
for the upbuilding of our merchant marine and the protection of our
shipping in the foreign carrying trade, so that American ships—the
product of American labor, employed in American shipyards, sail-
ing under the Stars and Stripes, and manned, officered, and owned by
Americans—may regain the carrying of our foreign commerce.

FINANCE.

The Republican Party is unreservedly for sound money. It
caused the enactment of the law providing for the resumption of
specie payments in 1879; since then every dollar has been as good as
gold.

We are unalterably opposed to every measure calculated to de-
base our currency or impair the credit of our country. We are, therefore, opposed to the free coinage of silver except by international
agreement with the leading commercial nations of the world, which
we pledge ourselves to promote, and until such agreement can be obtained, the existing gold standard must be preserved. All our silver
and paper currency must be maintained at parity with gold, and we
favor all measures designed to maintain inviolably the obligations
of the United States and all our money, whether coin or paper, at
the present standard, the standard of the most enlightened nations
of the earth.

PENSIONS.

The veterans of the Union army deserve and should receive fair treatment and generous recognition. Whenever practicable, they should be given the preference in the matter of employment, and they are entitled to the enactment of such laws as are best calculated to secure the fulfillment of the pledges made them in the dark days of the country's peril. We denounce the practice in the Pension Bureau, so recklessly and unjustly carried on by the present administration, of reducing pensions and arbitrarily dropping names from the rolls, as deserving the severest condemnation of the American people.

FOREIGN RELATIONS.

Our foreign policy should be at all times firm, vigorous, and dignified, and all our interests in the western hemisphere carefully watched and guarded. The Hawaiian Islands should be controlled by the United States, and no foreign power should be permitted to interfere with them; the Nicaragua Canal should be built, owned, and operated by the United States; and by the purchase of the Danish Islands we should secure a proper and much needed naval station in the West Indies.

ARMENIAN MASSACRES.

The massacres in Armenia have aroused the deep sympathy and just indignation of the American people, and we believe that the United States should exercise all the influence it can properly exert to bring these atrocities to an end. In Turkey, American residents have been exposed to the gravest dangers and American property destroyed. There and everywhere American citizens and American property must be absolutely protected at all hazards and at any cost.

MONROE DOCTRINE.

We reassert the Monroe doctrine in its full extent, and we reaffirm the right of the United States to give the doctrine effect by responding to the appeal of any American State for friendly intervention in case of European encroachment. We have not interfered and shall not interfere with the existing possessions of any European power in this hemisphere, but these possessions must not on any extent be extended. We hopefully look forward to the eventual withdrawal of the European powers from this. hemisphere, and to the ultimate union of all English-speaking parts of the continent by the free consent of its inhabitants.

CUBA.

From the hour of achieving their own independence, the people of the United States have regarded with sympathy the struggles of other American peoples to free themselves from European dominion. We watch with deep and abiding interest the heroic battle of the Cuban patriots against cruelty and oppression, and our best hopes go out for the full success of their determined contest for liberty.

The Government of Spain having lost control of Cuba and being unable to protect the property or lives of resident American citizens or to comply with its treaty obligations, we believe that the Government of the United States should actively use its influence and good offices to restore peace and give independence to the island.

THE NAVY.

The peace and security of the Republic and the maintenance of its rightful influence among the nations of the earth demand a naval power commensurate with its position and responsibility. We therefore favor the continued enlargement of the navy and a complete system of harbor and seacoast defenses.

FOREIGN IMMIGRATION.

For the protection of the quality of our American citizenship and of the wages of our workingmen against the fatal competition of low priced labor, we demand that the immigration laws be thoroughly enforced, and so extended as to exclude from entrance to the United States those who can neither read nor write.

CIVIL SERVICE.

The civil-service law was placed on the statute-book by the Republican party, which has always sustained it, and we renew our repeated declarations that it shall be thoroughly and honestly enforced, and extended wherever practicable.

FREE BALLOT.

We demand that every citizen of the United States shall be allowed to cast one free and unrestricted ballot, and that such ballot shall be counted and returned as cast.

LYNCHINGS.

We proclaim our unqualified condemnation of the uncivilized and barbarous practice well known as lynching or killing of human beings suspected or charged with crime, without process of law.

NATIONAL ARBITRATION.

We favor the creation of a national board of arbitration to settle and adjust differences which may arise between employers and employes engaged in interstate commerce.

HOMESTEADS.

We believe in an immediate return to the free-homestead policy of the Republican Party, and urge the passage by Congress of a satisfactory free-homestead measure such as has already passed the House and is now pending in the Senate.

TERRITORIES.

We favor the admission of the remaining territories at the earliest practicable date, having due regard to the interests of the people of the territories and of the United States. All the federal officers appointed for the territories should be selected from bona fide residents thereof, and the right of self-government should be accorded as far as practicable.

ALASKA.

We believe the citizens of Alaska should have representation in the Congress of the United States, to the end that needful legislation may be intelligently enacted.

THOMAS B. REED.

TEMPERANCE.

We sympathize with all wise and legitimate efforts to lessen and prevent the evils of intemperance and promote morality.

RIGHTS OF WOMEN.

The Republican Party is mindful of the rights and interests of women. Protection of American industries includes equal opportunities, equal pay for equal work, and protection to the home. We favor the admission of women to wider spheres of usefulness, and welcome their co-operation in rescuing the country from Democratic and Populist mismanagement and misrule.

Such are the principles and policies of the Republican Party. By these principles we will abide and these policies we will put into execution. We ask for them the considerate judgment of the American people. Confident alike in the history of our great party and in the justice of our cause, we present our platform and our candidates in the full assurance that the election will bring victory to the Republican Party and prosperity to the people of the United States.

There had been a strong effort in the Committee on Resolutions by the silver men urging the adoption of a free silver plank, and Senator Henry M. Teller, of Colorado, had made an affecting appeal but without avail.

At the conclusion of the reading of the platform by Senator Foraker, one of the most dramatic incidents in any Republican convention took place, when Senator Teller arose, and in behalf of the silver men submitted the following substitute for the financial plank as read:

"The Republican Party authorizes the use of both gold and silver as equal standard money, and pledges its power to secure the free and unlimited coinage of gold and silver at our mints at the ratio of sixteen parts of silver to one of gold."

After presenting this substitute Senator Teller delivered his farewell address to the Convention, at the conclusion of which Senator Foraker moved that the substitute be laid on the table, thus cutting off any debate. On a roll-call of the States the motion was carried by a vote of 818½ to 105½. The financial plank was then voted on separately, and the one reported was adopted by a vote of 812½ to 110½. The entire platform was then adopted by an overwhelming viva voce vote. The crucial moment of the Convention was at hand. Senator Cameron, of Utah, was now permitted to read a statement which had been prepared by the silver men to be read in the event of the adoption of the gold plank. The silver manifesto was signed by Senator Henry M. Teller, of Colorado, Senator F. T. Dubois, of Idaho, Senator Frank J. Cameron, of Utah, Representative Chas. S. Hartman, of Montana, and A. C. Cleveland, of Nevada, the members of the Committee on Resolutions for their States. Senators Cameron and Teller then shook hands with Messrs. Thurston and Foraker, descended from the stage, and, passing slowly down the aisle, left the hall, followed by about thirty-two other silver delegates. The scene was most impressive, the remaining delegates and spectators standing on their chairs, shouting and singing national airs. After listening to explanations by the silver delegates who remained in the convention, the roll-call of States was had for the National Committeemen. Marcus A. Hanna, of Ohio, whose brilliant management of McKinley's interests had made his name a household word, was selected unanimously as Chairman of the National

Committee. Candidates for the presidential nomination were now presented. John M. Baldwin nominated Senator Wm. B. Allison, of Iowa; Senator Henry Cabot Lodge presented the name of Thomas B. Reed in a scholarly and masterful appeal; with his usual eloquence Chauncey M. Depew nominated Levi P. Morton, of New York; then came the great enthusiasm of the Convention when Senator Joseph B. Foraker stepped to the stage and began his speech, a remarkable effort, naming William McKinley, of Ohio. After he had spoken a short time he was interrupted by fully twenty-eight minutes of the wildest enthusiasm when the name of William McKinley was first mentioned by him. John M. Thurston seconded the nomination of McKinley, as did J. Madison Vance. Senator Matthew S. Quay was nominated by Governor Daniel H. Hastings, after which the balloting commenced. There were 924 delegates, and only one ballot was taken, with the following result:

McKinley .	661½	Reed	84½
Morton	58	Quay	61½
Allison	35½	Cameron	1

The nomination was then made unanimous, Messrs. Depew, Platt, Lodge, Hastings and others joining in the motion. Nominations for Vice-President being now in order, Samuel Fessenden named William G. Bulkeley, of Connecticut; J. Franklin Fort nominated Garret A. Hobart, of New Jersey; Wm. M. Randolph named H. Clay Evans, of Tennessee; S. W. K. Allen nominated Chas. W. Lippitt, of Rhode Island, and D. F. Bailey named James A. Walker,

of Virginia. The nomination went to Mr. Hobart on the
first ballot.

Hobart	533½	Walker	24
Evans	277½	Lippitt	8
Bulkeley	39.		

A few scattering votes were also given for Thomas B. Reed,
Chauncey M. Depew, John M. Thurston, Frederick D.
Grant, and Levi P. Morton. After selecting the notifica-
tion committees, the Convention adjourned *sine die*.

The Republican nominee in 1896, William McKinley,
was born at Niles, Ohio, in 1843, and was therefore only
18 years of age at the opening of the Civil War, for which
he enlisted in the ranks of a company of volunteers. After
the battle of Antietam he was promoted to Second Lieuten-
ant, and was subsequently advanced to Major, his commission being signed by President Lincoln. The war over, Mr.
McKinley studied law and was admitted to the bar and
practiced with much success, and soon became prominent in
Ohio politics. He was a member of the National House of
Representatives from 1877 to 1891, during which time he
had steadily increased in the esteem of his colleagues and
the people. His framing of the tariff law of 1890 had
brought him into great prominence. He was defeated for
re-election in the political revolution of 1890, but was
elected Governor of Ohio in 1892, and served as such until
January, 1896, a few months before the Convention.

The Democratic National Convention met at Chicago,
Ills., Tuesday, July 7, 1896, and the silver forces immediately took control of the Convention by unseating David

B. Hill, of New York, who had been chosen by the National Committee as temporary Chairman, and substituting John B. Daniel of Virginia. The Democratic platform of 1896, adopted on the third day of the Convention, contained the following plank, which, with the opposite declaration in the Republican platform, became the controlling issue of the campaign:

> "We demand the free and unlimited coinage of both gold and silver at the present legal ratio of 16 to 1, without waiting for the aid or consent of any nation."

A minority report was presented by Senator David B. Hill, but was rejected by a vote of 626 to 303. It was during the debate on the motion to substitute this minority report that William J. Bryan delivered his remarkable speech for free silver, an effort that created remarkable scenes of enthusiasm in the Convention and made him immediately the idol of the free silver forces. The speech concluded:

> "If they dare to come out in the open field and defend the gold standard as a good thing, we will fight them to the uttermost. Having behind us the producing masses of this nation and the world, supported by the commercial interests, the laboring interests and the toilers everywhere, we will answer their demand for a gold standard by saying to them: 'You shall not press down upon the brow of labor this crown of thorns; you shall not crucify mankind upon a cross of gold.'"

This Democratic Convention nominated William J. Bryan

for President on the fifth ballot, and named Arthur Sewall, of Maine, for Vice-President on the fifth ballot.

The People's Party Convention met at St. Louis, Mo., July 22, 1896, and ratified the nomination of William J. Bryan for President, but the Middle-of-the-Road members named Thomas E. Watson, of Georgia, for Vice-President, the Vice-President being named first in this Convention; the money plank in the People's Party platform in 1896 was the same in effect as that of the Democratic platform, and its other demands were in general the same as those of 1892. The Silver Party Convention met on the same day (July 22d) in St. Louis and endorsed Bryan and Sewall by acclamation. There were a large number of Democrats in 1896 who were unwilling to endorse the Chicago platform and the candidates, and at the same time they were not willing to vote for the Republican nominees, so they held a convention at Indianapolis September 2, 1896, and nominated John M. Palmer, of Illinois, for President, and Simon B. Buckner, of Kentucky, for Vice-President, and adopted a sound money platform and the name of the "National Democratic Party." Three other conventions had been held; the Prohibition Convention at Philadelphia on May 27, 1896, which nominated Joshua Levering, of Maryland, and Hale Johnson, of Illinois, but a contest had arisen in this convention over the silver question, and it resulted in the secession of a number of delegates who met on the next day and styled themselves "The National Party." They nominated Rev. Chas. E. Bentley, of Nebraska, and James H. Southgate, of North Carolina, and adopted a bi-metallic platform. The Socialist-Labor Convention met at New York on July 6, 1896, and nominated Charles H. Matchett, of New York, and Matthew Maguire of New Jersey.

The campaign of 1896 was not only remarkable in its inception, but continued throughout to be one of the most spectacular in our political history. At first there was general shifting of the old party lines and a "bolting" from all of the party candidates, but the Republican Party suffered the least in this respect. Mr. Bryan conducted a remarkable personal canvass of the entire country, and was greeted by large crowds to see him and hear his arguments. Mr. McKinley remained throughout the canvass at his home in Canton, Ohio, receiving hundreds of visiting delegations and delivering a large number of earnest speeches which were telegraphed over the country and carefully read. Monster street parades were held in the large cities and thousands of badges and lithographs adorned the persons and homes of the enthusiastic partisans, and, as the campaign drew to a close, the people were wrought up to a high pitch of excitement. One striking feature of the canvass was that the ruin and disaster of the four years of Cleveland's second term which, late in 1895, indicated an easy victory for the Republicans, was largely forgotten by the people in the new, exciting and novel issues raised and argued by Mr. Bryan, but those who carefully analyzed the returns of the States which voted in the elections held in August and September, and the trend of public opinion, saw that a Republican victory was almost certain, and this

proved true on November 6, 1896, when the popular vote
in the several States secured to McKinley and Hobart 271
electoral votes to 176 for Bryan and Sewall. The total
popular vote at the election of 1896 was as follows:

McKinley . . .7,111,607	Bryan 6,509,052
Palmer 134,645	Levering 131,312
Matchett. 36,373	Bentley 13,968

William McKinley was inaugurated for his first term
on March 4, 1897, and immediately called a special session
of Congress to take action on the tariff. The Wilson Tariff
Law, as already noted, had totally failed to provide sufficient revenue to meet the expenses of the Government, and
the result was a steady and growing deficit in the Treasury.
On March 18, 1897, Nelson Dingley, Jr., of Maine, introduced his Tariff Bill in the House, and it became a law
with the President's signature on July 24, 1897.

The Cuban question now came to the front and occupied public attention more seriously than ever before. The
United States had always taken a lively interest in Cuban
affairs, and when the Cubans revolted in 1895 for the sixth
time against the cruel domination of the Spaniards there
was deep sympathy for them in this country, that continued to grow as the months went by. In 1896 the Cubans
were accorded the rights of belligerents by the United
States. Throughout the Summer of 1897 the country was
horrified by the reports from the "reconcentrado" camps
established by General Weyler, and sent aid and relief to
the suffering Cubans. The climax of hostility toward
Spain came with the terrible news on February 15, 1898,

SECOND INAUGURATION OF WILLIAM McKINLEY, MARCH 4, 1901

that the Battleship "Maine" had been blown up in Havana
Harbor and 260 American sailors killed. War was declared in April, 1898, and the glorious achievements of
American arms are too fresh in memory to require an extended review of them in these pages. Peace came with the
Protocol signed at Washington, August 12, 1898, and the
formal Treaty of Peace was signed at Paris, December 10,
1898. Spain released her title to Cuba, and the United
States acquired Puerto Rico, Guam and the Philippine
Islands, paying Spain the sum of $20,000,000 for the lat-
ter, and taking control of the islands for the suppression of
civil war and to avoid foreign complications. While the
Spanish-American war was in progress the country ex-
panded territorially by the annexation of Hawaii, which
was accomplished bv joint resolution, signed by the President July 7, 1898.

The Fifty-sixth Congress organized with the election of
David B. Henderson, of Iowa, as Speaker of the House,
and the most important legislation was the Gold Standard
Act of 1900, which effectually settled the money question,
as far as the gold or silver standard was concerned, by providing for the coinage of a dollar consisting of 25 8-10
grains of gold, nine-tenths fine, as the standard of value,
and that all forms of money issued in coin were to be maintained at a parity of value with this gold standard. The
Act further provided that all United States notes and
Treasury notes shall be redeemed in gold coin, and a redemption fund of $150,000,000 was established. Presi-
dent McKinley signed this most important Act, and it be-

came a law on March 14, 1900. In March, 1900, President McKinley, taking up the question of governing the Philippine Islands, appointed a Civil Commission composed of William H. Taft, of Ohio, President; Prof. Dean C. Worcester, of Michigan; Luke E. Wright, of Tennessee; Henry C. Ide, of Vermont, and Prof. Bernard Moses, of California, to continue and perfect the work of organizing and establishing civil government in the Philippines, which had already been commenced by the military authorities. The Commission proceeded to the Philippines in the following April, and their work was one of the most remarkable in the history of the nation, bringing order out of chaos, to the complete satisfaction not only of the people of this country but also the Filipinos, with very few exceptions. Education and enlightenment followed the broad-minded policy of this government, and through the splendid work of Governor William H. Taft military control was gradually made unnecessary and the Filipinos were rapidly prepared for self-government.

Great prosperity marked the business conditions of the country during President McKinley's administration, and the balance in the U. S. Treasury at the end of his term was nearly $495,000,000, which was a strong contrast to the penury and borrowing during Cleveland's second term. This splendid record, the successful conduct of the Spanish-American war, the success in governing the new territories of the United States, the courageous and dignified action in regard to foreign affairs, and the complete and general satisfaction with his entire administration, made

President McKinley the logical and unanimous choice of the party for the nomination in 1900, and the only question in the convention would be as to who would have the honor of the second place on the ticket. All of the minor parties held their conventions in 1900 before the conventions of the old parties. The Social Democrats were first, with their convention at Indianapolis, March 6, 1900, at which Eugene V. Debs was nominated for President. The People's Party met at Sioux Falls, South Dakota, May 9-10, 1900, and nominated William J. Bryan for President and Charles A. Towne for Vice-President. Their platform denounced the gold standard Act of March 14, 1900, advocated free silver, an income tax, and condemned the war policy of the Republican Party. A faction of the People's Party opposed to fusion with the Democrats had seceded in 1896, and became known as the Middle-of-the-Road People's Party; they met in convention at Cincinnati May 9-10, 1900, and nominated Wharton Barker, of Pennsylvania, and Ignatius Donnelly, of Minnesota. The Socialist-Labor Party met at New York June 2-8, 1900, and nominated Joseph F. Malloney, of Massachusetts, and Valentine Remmel, of Pennsylvania. The Prohibition Convention was held in Chicago, Illinois, June 27-28, and nominated John G. Woolley, of Illinois, and Henry B. Metcalf, of Rhode Island.

The Twelfth Republican National Convention began its session Tuesday, June 19, 1900, at Philadelphia, in the National Export Exposition Building. About 12:35 p. m. on that day, Senator Marcus A. Hanna, Chairman of the

National Committee, faced the vast assemblage of delegates and spectators and called the Convention to order.
After the opening prayer by Rev. J. Gray Bolton, Chairman Hanna, in a short speech, which was received with
great applause, introduced Senator Wolcott, of Colorado,
as Temporary Chairman. Senator Wolcott accepted the
honor in a strong speech, and after the roll-call of States
for the naming of the various committees, a motion to adjourn was made, and then Rev. Edgar M. Levy, who had
uttered the invocation at the first Republican National
Convention, forty-four years since, delivered a benedic-
tion, and about 3 p. m. the session was over for the day.
At the opening of the second day, Chairman Wolcott
stated that fifteen survivors of the preliminary Republican
Convention at Pittsburg in 1856 were present with the
same old flag used in that convention, and as these men
came forward, with their tattered flag, they received a remarkable and stirring ovation. Sereno E. Payne, of New
York, reported for the Committee on Credentials, and the
report was adopted without debate. Gen. Charles E. Gros-
venor, of Ohio, Chairman of the Committee on Permanent
Organization, now reported the name of Senator Henry
Cabot Lodge, of Massachusetts, as Permanent President of
the Convention, and that the rest of the temporary officers
be made permanent; the report was adopted, and Senator
Lodge delivered a scholarly and eloquent speech, reviewing
the history of the country for the past forty-four years.
Senator Chas. W. Fairbanks, of Indiana, Chairman of the
Committee on Resolutions, then read the platform, which
was adopted with displays of the utmost enthusiasm.

REPUBLICAN PLATFORM, 1900.

The Republicans of the United States, through their chosen representatives, met in national convention, looking back upon an unsurpassed record of achievement and looking forward into a great field of duty and opportunity, and appealing to the judgment of their countrymen, make these declarations:

EXPECTATIONS FULFILLED.

The expectation in which the American people, turning from the Democratic Party, intrusted power four years ago to a Republican Chief Magistrate and Republican Congress, has been met and satisfied. When the people then assembled at the polls, after a term of Democratic legislation and administration, business was dead, industry paralyzed, and the national credit disastrously impaired. The country's capital was hidden away and its labor distressed and unemployed. The Democrats had no other plan with which to improve the ruinous condition which they had themselves produced than to coin silver at the ratio of 16 to 1.

PROMISE OF PROSPERITY REDEEMED.

The Republican Party, denouncing this plan as sure to produce conditions even worse than those from which relief was sought, promised to restore prosperity by means of two legislative measures: a protective tariff and a law making gold the standard of value. The people by great majorities issued to the Republican Party a commission to enact these laws. The commission has been executed, and the Republican promise is redeemed.

Prosperity more general and more abundant than we have ever known has followed these enactments. There is no longer controversy as to the value of any government obligations. Every American dollar is a gold dollar or its assured equivalent, and American credit stands higher than that of any nation. Capital is fully employed, and labor everywhere is profitably occupied.

GROWTH OF EXPORT TRADE.

No single fact can more strikingly tell the story of what Republican government means to the country than this, that while during the whole period of one hundred and seven years, from 1790 to 1897, there was an excess of exports over imports of only $383,028,-497, there has been in the short three years of the present Republican administration an excess of exports over imports in the enormous sum of $1,483,537,094.

THE WAR WITH SPAIN.

And while the American people, sustained by this Republican legislation, have been achieving these splendid triumphs in their business and commerce, they have conducted and in victory concluded a war for liberty and human rights. No thought of national aggrandizement tarnished the high purpose with which American standards were unfurled. It was a war unsought and patiently resisted, but when it came, the American government was ready. Its fleets were cleared for action; its armies were in the field, and the quick and signal triumph of its forces on land and sea bore equal tribute to the courage of American soldiers and sailors, and to the skill and foresight of Republican statesmanship. To ten millions of the human race there was given "a new birth of freedom," and to the American people a new and noble responsibility.

McKINLEY'S ADMINISTRATION INDORSED.

We indorse the administration of William McKinley. Its acts have been established in wisdom and in patriotism, and at home and abroad it has distinctly elevated and extended the influence of the American nation. Walking untried paths and facing unforeseen responsibilities, President McKinley has been in every situation the true American, patriot and the upright statesman, clear in vision, strong in judgment, firm in action, always inspiring and deserving the confidence of his countrymen.

DEMOCRATIC INCAPACITY A MENACE TO PROSPERITY.

In asking the American people to indorse this Republican record. and to renew their commission to the Republican Party, we remind them of the fact that the menace to their prosperity has always resided in Democratic principles, and no less in the general incapacity of the Democratic Party to conduct public affairs. The prime essential of business prosperity is public confidence in the good sense of the government and in its ability to deal intelligently with each new problem of administration and legislation. That confidence the Democratic Party has never earned. It is hopelessly inadequate, and the country's prosperity, when Democratic success at the polls is announced, halts and ceases in mere anticipation of Democratic blunders and failures.

MONETARY LEGISLATION.

We renew our allegiance to the principle of the gold standard and declare our confidence in the wisdom of the legislation of the Fifty-Sixth Congress, by which the parity of all our money and the stability of our currency upon a gold basis has been secured. We recognize that interest rates are a potent factor in production and business activity, and for the purpose of further equalizing and of further lowering the rates of interest, we favor such monetary legislation as will enable the varying needs of the season and of all sections to be promptly met, in order that trade may be evenly sustained, labor steadily employed, and commerce enlarged. The volume of money in circulation was never so great per capita as it is today.

FREE COINAGE OF SILVER OPPOSED.

We declare our steadfast opposition to the free and unlimited coinage of silver. No measure to that end could be considered which was without the support of the leading commercial countries of the world. However firmly Republican legislation may seem to have secured the country against the peril of base and discredited currency, the election of a Democratic President could not fail to impair the country's credit and to bring once more into question the intention of the American people to maintain upon the gold standard the parity of their money circulation. The Democratic Party must be convinced that the American people will never tolerate the Chicago platform.

TRUSTS.

We recognize the necessity and propriety of the honest co-operation of capital to meet new business conditions, and especially to extend our rapidly increasing foreign trade; but we condemn all conspiracies and combinations intended to restrict business, to create monopolies, to limit production, or to control prices, and favor such legislation as will effectively restrain and prevent all such abuses, protect and promote competition, and secure the rights of producers, laborers, and all who are engaged in industry and commerce.

PROTECTION POLICY REAFFIRMED.

We renew our faith in the policy of protection to American labor. In that policy our industries have been established, diversified, and maintained. By protecting the home market, competition has been stimulated and production cheapened. Opportunity to the inventive genius of our people has been secured and wages in every department of labor maintained at high rates—higher now than ever before, and always distinguishing our working people in their better conditions of life from those of any competing country. Enjoying the blessings of the American common school, secure in the right of self-government, and protected in the occupancy of their own markets, their constantly increasing knowledge and skill have enabled them to finally enter the markets of the world.

RECIPROCITY FAVORED.

We favor the associated policy of reciprocity, so directed as to open our markets on favorable terms for what we do not ourselves produce, in return for free foreign markets.

RESTRICTION OF IMMIGRATION, AND OTHER LABOR LEGISLATION.

In the further interest of American workmen we favor a more effective restriction of the immigration of cheap labor from foreign lands, the extension of opportunities of education for working-children, the raising of the age limit for child-labor, the protection of free labor as against contract convict labor, and an effective system of labor insurance.

SHIPPING.

Our present dependence upon foreign shipping for nine-tenths of our foreign-carrying trade is a great loss to the industry of this country. It is also a serious danger to our trade, for its sudden withdrawal in the event of European war would seriously cripple our expanding foreign commerce. The national defense and naval efficiency of this country, moreover, supply a compelling reason for legislation which will enable us to recover our former place among the trade carrying fleets of the world.

DEBT TO SOLDIERS AND SAILORS.

The nation owes a debt of profound gratitude to the soldiers and sailors who have fought its battles, and it is the government's duty to provide for the survivors and for the widows and orphans of those who have fallen in the country's wars. The pension laws, founded on this just sentiment, should be liberally administered, and preference should be given, wherever practicable, with respect to employment in the public service, to soldiers and sailors and to their widows and orphans.

THE CIVIL SERVICE.

We commend the policy of the Republican Party in maintaining the efficiency of the civil service. The administration has acted wisely in its effort to secure for public service in Cuba, Porto Rico, Hawaii, and the Philippine Islands, only those whose fitness has been determined by training and experience. We believe that employment in the public service in these territories should be confined, as far as practicable, to their inhabitants.

THE RACE QUESTION.

It was the plain purpose of the Fifteenth Amendment to the Constitution to prevent discrimination on account of race or color in regulating the elective franchise. Devices of state governments, whether by statutory or constitutional enactment, to avoid the purpose of this amendment are revolutionary and should be condemned.

PUBLIC ROADS.

Public movements looking to a permanent improvement of the roads and highways of the country meet with our cordial approval, and we recommend this subject to the earnest consideration of the people and of the legislatures of the several states.

RURAL FREE DELIVERY.

We favor the extension of the rural free delivery service wherever its extension may be justified.

LAND LEGISLATION.

In further pursuance of the constant policy of the Republican Party to provide free homes on the public domain we recommend adequate national legislation to reclaim the arid lands of the United States, reserving control of the distribution of water for irrigation to the respective states and territories.

NEW STATES PROPOSED.

We favor home-rule for, and the early admission to statehood of, the territories of New Mexico, Arizona and Oklahoma.

REDUCTION OF WAR TAXES.

The Dingley Act, amended to provide sufficient revenue for the conduct of the war, has so well performed its work that it has been possible to reduce the war debt in the sum of $40,000,000. So ample are the government's revenues and so great is the public confidence in the integrity of its obligations, that its newly funded 2 per cent. bonds sell at a premium. The country is now justified in expecting, and it will be the policy of the Republican Party to bring about, a reduction of the war taxes.

ISTHMIAN CANAL AND NEW MARKETS.

We favor the construction, ownership, control, and protection of an isthmian canal by the government of the United States. New markets are necessary for the increasing surplus of our farm products. Every effort should be made to open and obtain new markets, especially in the Orient, and the administration is to be warmly commended for its successful efforts to commit all trading and colonizing nations to the policy of the open door in China.

DEPARTMENT OF COMMERCE.

In the interest of our expanding commerce we recommend that Congress create a Department of Commerce and Industries, in the charge of a secretary with a seat in the cabinet. The United States consular system should be reorganized under the supervision of this new department, upon such a basis of appointment and tenure as will render it still more servicable to the nation's increasing trade.

PROTECTION OF CITIZENS.

The American government must protect the person and property of every citizen wherever they are wrongfully violated or placed in peril.

SERVICES OF WOMEN.

We congratulate the women of America upon their splendid record of public service in the Volunteer Aid Association and as nurses in camp and hospital during the recent campaigns of our armies in the East and West Indies, and we appreciate their faithful co-operation in all works of education and industry.

FOREIGN AFFAIRS, SAMOAN AND HAWAIIAN ISLANDS.

President McKinley has conducted the foreign affairs of the United States with distinguished credit to the American people. In releasing us from vexatious conditions of a European alliance for the government of Samoa, his course is especially to be commended. By securing to our undivided control the most important island of the Samoan group and the best harbor in the Southern Pacific, every American interest has been safeguarded.

We approve the annexation of the Hawaiian islands to the United States.

THE HAGUE CONFERENCE, THE MONROE DOCTRINE, THE SOUTH AFRICAN WAR.

We commend the part taken by our government in the Peace Conference at The Hague. We assert our steadfast adherence to the policy announced in the Monroe doctrine. The provisions of The Hague convention was wisely regarded when President McKinley tendered his friendly offices in the interest of peace between Great Britain and the South African Republic. While the American Government must continue the policy prescribed by Washington, affirmed by every succeeding president, and imposed upon us by The Hague Treaty, of non-intervention in European controversies, the American people earnestly hope that a way may soon be found, honorable alike to both contending parties, to terminate the strife between them.

SOVEREIGNTY IN NEW POSSESSIONS.

In accepting, by the Treaty of Paris, the just responsibility of our victories in the Spanish War, the President and the Senate won the undoubted approval of the American people. No other course was possible than to destroy Spain's sovereignty throughout the West Indies and in the Philippine Islands. That course created our responsibility before the world and with the unorganized population whom our intervention had freed from Spain, to provide for the maintenance of law and order, and for the establishment of good government, and for the performance of international obligations.

Our authority could not be less than our responsibility, and wherever sovereign rights were extended it became the high duty of the government to maintain its authority, to put down armed insurrection, and to confer the blessings of liberty and civilization upon all the rescued people.

The largest measure of self-government consistent with their welfare and our duties shall be secured to them by law.

INDEPENDENCE OF CUBA.

To Cuba, independence and self-government were assured in the same voice by which war was declared, and to the letter this pledge shall be performed.

INVOKES THE JUDGMENT OF THE PEOPLE.

The Republican Party, upon its history and upon this declaration of its principles and policies, confidently invokes the considerate and approving judgment of the American people.

On the third day of the Convention, Thursday, June 21 1900, Mr. Quay, of Pennsylvania, withdrew a plan of representation which he had presented the previous day, and the Convention proceeded to the nominations for President and Vice-President. Alabama yielded to Ohio, and Senator Joseph B. Foraker, of Ohio, who had the same great honor four years previous, went to the platform and in a speech of great vigor and eloquence nominated William McKinley, of Ohio, for President. The nomination was seconded by Theodore Roosevelt, of New York, Senator John M. Thurston, John W. Yerkes, of Kentucky, George Knight, of California, and Governor James A. Mount, of Indiana. There were no further nominations. The ballot showed that 930 votes had been cast, and that William McKinley had received 930, and pandemonium broke loose. After it had subsided, Col. Lafe Young, in a remarkable speech, withdrew the name of Jonathan P. Dolliver for Vice-President and nominated Theodore Roosevelt of New York. Butler Murray, of Massachusetts, and James A. Ashton, of Washington, seconded the nomination, and in response to demands for "Depew! Depew!" that gentleman came forward and with his customary eloquence and wit also seconded the nomination. The balloting then proceeded and Theodore Roosevelt received 929 votes, he having refrained from voting for himself. Thus, in this Convention, for the first time in the history of the party, the candidates for President and Vice-President were practically nominated by acclamation.

The Democratic National Convention met at Kansas City, Mo., July 4-6, 1900. There was a long wrangle in the Committee on Resolutions over the silver plank in the platform, but it was finally adopted by a vote of 26 to 24, and the Convention adopted the platform by acclamation. The platform declared that while not taking a backward step from any position of the party, Imperialism growing out of the Spanish war was the paramount issue. The Kansas City platform is here given in full as of great interest in the pending campaign.

Democratic Platform 1900.

We, the representatives of the Democratic Party of the United States, assembled in national convention, on the anniversary of the adoption of the declaration of independence, do reaffirm our faith in that immortal proclamation of the inalienable rights of man, and our allegiance to the constitution framed in harmony therewith by the fathers of the republic. We hold with the United States Supreme Court that the declaration of independence is the spirit of our government, of which the constitution is the form and letter.

We declare again that all governments instituted among men derive their just powers from the consent of the governed; that any government not based upon the consent of the governed is a tyranny, and that to impose upon any people a government of force is to substitute the methods of imperialism for those of a republic. We hold that the constitution follows the flag, and denounce the doctrine that an executive or Congress, deriving their existence and their powers from the constitution, can exercise lawful authority beyond it, or in violation of it.

We assert that no nation can long endure half republic and half empire, and we warn the American people that imperialism abroad will lead quickly and inevitably to despotism at home.

PORTO RICO LAW DENOUNCED.

Believing in these fundamental principles, we denounce the Porto Rico law, enacted by a Republican Congress against the protest and opposition of the Democratic minority, as a bold and open violation of the nation's organic law, and a flagrant breach of the national good faith.

It imposes upon the people of Porto Rico a government without their consent, and taxation without representation. It dishonors the American people by repudiating a solemn pledge made in their behalf by the commanding General of our army, which the Porto Ricans welcomed to a peaceful and unresisted occupation of their land. It doomed to poverty and distress a people whose helplessness appeals with peculiar force to our justice and magnanimity.

In this, the first act of its imperialistic programme, the Republican party seeks to commit the United States to a colonial policy, inconsistent with Republican institutions, and condemned by the Supreme Court in numerous decisions.

PLEDGES TO THE CUBANS.

We demand the prompt and honest fulfillment of our pledge to the Cuban people and the world that the United States has no disposition or intention to exercise sovereignty, jurisdiction, or control over the Island of Cuba, except for its pacification. The war ended nearly two years ago, profound peace reigns over all the island, and still the administration keeps the government of the island from its people, while Republican carpet-bag officials plunder its revenues and exploit the colonial theory, to the disgrace of the American people.

THE PHILIPPINE QUESTION.

We condemn and denounce the Philippine policy of the present administration. It has involved the republic in unnecessary war, sacrificed the lives of many of our noblest sons, and placed the United States, previously known and applauded throughout the world as the champion of freedom, in the false and un-American position of crushing with military force the efforts of our former allies to achieve liberty and self-government. The Filipinos cannot become citizens without endangering our civilization; they cannot become subjects without imperiling our form of government, and we are not willing to surrender our civilization or to convert the republic into an empire; we favor an immediate declaration of the nation's purpose to give to the Filipinos first, a stable form of government; second, independence; and, third, protection from outside interference such as has been given for nearly a century to the republics of Central and South America.

The greedy commercialism which dictated the Philippine policy of the Republican administration attempts to justify it with the plea that it will pay, but even this sordid and unworthy plea fails when brought to the test of facts. The war of criminal aggression against the Filipinos, entailing an annual expense of many millions, has already cost more than any possible profit that could accrue from the entire Philippine trade for years to come. Furthermore, when trade is extended at the expense of liberty the price is always too high.

We are not opposed to territorial expansion when it takes in desirable territory which can be erected into states in the Union and whose people are willing and fit to become American citizens.

We favor trade expansion by every peaceful and legitimate means. But we are unalterably opposed to the seizing or purchasing of distant islands to be governed outside the constitution and whose people can never become citizens.

We are in favor of extending the republic's influence among the nations, but believe that influence should be extended, not by force and violence, but through the persuasive power of a high and honorable example.

The importance of other questions now pending before the American people is in no wise diminished, and the Democratic party takes no backward step from its position on them, but the burning issue of imperialism growing out of the Spanish war in-

MARCUS A. HANNA.

volves the very existence of the republic and the destruction of our free institutions. We regard it as the paramount issue of the campaign.

THE MONROE DOCTRINE.

The declaration in the Republican platform adopted at the Philadelphia convention, held in June, 1900, that the Republican party "steadfastly adheres to the policy announced in the Monroe doctrine" is manifestly insincere and deceptive. This profession is contradicted by the avowed policy of that party in opposition to the spirit of the Monroe doctrine to acquire and hold sovereignity over large areas of territory and large numbers of people in the Eastern hemisphere. We insist on the strict maintenance of the Monroe doctrine and in all its integrity, both in letter and in spirit, as necessary to prevent the extension of European authority on this continent and as essential to our supremacy in American affairs. At the same time we declare that no American people shall ever be held by force in unwilling subjection to European authority.

OPPOSITION TO MILITARISM.

We oppose militarism. It means conquest abroad and intimidation and oppression at home. It means the strong arm which has ever been fatal to free institutions. It is what millions of our citizens have fled from in Europe. It will impose upon our peace-loving people a large standing army and unnecessary burden of taxation and a constant menace to their liberties.

A small standing army with a well-disciplined state militia are amply sufficient in time of peace. This republic has no place for a vast military service and conscription.

When the nation is in danger the volunteer soldier is his country's best defender. The national guard of the United States should ever be cherished in the patriotic hearts of a free people. Such organizations are ever an element of strength and safety.

For the first time in our history and co-evil with the Philippine conquest has there been a wholesale departure from our time-honored and approved system of volunteer organization. We denounce it as un-American, un-Democratic, and un-Republican, and as a subversion of the ancient and fixed principles of a free people.

TRUSTS DENOUNCED.

Private monopolies are indefensible and intolerable. They destroy competition, control the price of all material, and of the finished product, thus robbing both producer and consumer. They lessen the employment of labor and arbitrarily fix the terms and conditions thereof, and deprive individual energy and small capital of their opportunity for betterment. They are the most efficient means yet devised for appropriating the fruits of industry to the benefit of the few at the expense of the many, and unless their insatiate greed is checked all wealth will be aggregated in a few hands and the republic destroyed.

The dishonest paltering with the trust evil by the Republican party in state and national platforms is conclusive proof of the truth of the charge that trusts are the legitimate product of Republican policies; that they are fostered by Republican laws, and that they are protected by the Republican administration in return for campaign subscriptions and political support.

We pledge the Democratic party to an increasing warfare in nation, state, and city against private monopoly in every form. Existing laws against trusts must be enforced and more stringent ones must be enacted providing for publicity as to the affairs of corporations engaged in interstate commerce and requiring all corporations to show, before doing business outside the state of their origin, that they have no water in their stock and that they have not attempted and are not attempting, to monopolize any branch of business or the production of any articles of merchandise, and the whole constitutional power of Congress over interstate commerce, the mails, and all modes of interstate communication shall be exercised by the enactment of comprehensive laws upon the subject of trusts.

Tariff laws should be amended by putting the products of trusts upon the free list to prevent monopoly under the plea of protection.

The failure of the present Republican administration, with an absolute control over all the branches of the national government, to enact any legislation designed to prevent or even curtail the absorbing power of trusts and illegal combinations, or to enforce the anti-trust laws already on the statute books, proves the insincerity of the high-sounding phrases of the Republican platform.

Corporations should be protected in all their rights and their legitimate interests should be respected, but any attempt by corporations to interfere with the public affairs of the people or to control the sovereignity which creates them should be forbidden under such penalties as will make such attempts impossible.

We condemn the Dingley tariff law as a trust-breeding measure, skillfully devised to give the few favors which they do not deserve and to place upon the many burdens which they should not bear.

INTERSTATE COMMERCE LAW.

We favor such an enlargement of the scope of the interstate commerce law as will enable the commission to protect individuals and communities from discriminations and the public from unjust and unfair transportation rates.

DECLARATION FOR 16 TO 1.

We reaffirm and indorse the principles of the national Democratic platform adopted at Chicago in 1896, and we reiterate the demand of that platform for an American financial system, made by the American people for themselves, which shall restore and maintain a bimetalic level, and as part of such system the immediate restoration of the free and unlimited coinage of silver and gold at the present legal ratio of 16 to 1, without waiting for the aid or consent of any other nation.

CURRENCY LAW DENOUNCED.

We denounce the currency bill enacted at the last session of Congress as a step forward in the Republican policy which aims to discredit the sovereign right of the national government to issue all money, whether coin or paper, and to bestow upon national banks the power to issue and control the volume of paper money for their own benefit.

A permanent national bank currency, secured by government bonds, must have a permanent debt to rest upon, and if the bank currency is to increase with population and business the debt must also increase. The Republican currency scheme is therefore a scheme for fastening upon taxpayers a perpetual and growing debt for the benefit of the banks.

We are opposed to this private corporation paper circulated as

money, but without legal-tender qualities, and demand the retire-
ment of the national bank notes as fast as government paper or
silver certificates can be substituted for them.

SENATORS ELECTED BY THE PEOPLE.

We favor an amendment to the Federal constitution providing
for the election of United States Senators by direct vote of the
people, and we favor direct legislation wherever practicable.

GOVERNMENT BY INJUNCTION.

We are opposed to government by injunction; we denounce the
blacklist, and favor arbitration as a means of settling disputes between corporations and their employes.

DEPARTMENT OF LABOR.

In the interest of American labor and the uplifting of the
workingmen, as the cornerstone of the prosperity of our country,
we recommend that Congress create a department of labor, in
charge of a secretary, with a seat in the Cabinet, believing that the
elevation of the American labor will bring with it increased production and increased prosperity to our country at home and
to our commerce abroad.

PENSIONS.

We are proud of the courage and fidelity of the American
soldier and sailors in all our wars; we favor liberal pensions to
them and their dependents, and we reiterate the position taken
in the Chicago platform in 1896, that the fact of enlistment and
service shall be deemed conclusive evidence against disease and
disability before enlistment.

NICARAGUA CANAL.

We favor the immediate construction, ownership, and control
of the Nicaraguan canal by the United States and we denounce the
insincerity of the plank in the national Republican platform for an
Isthmian canal in face of the failure of the Republican majority
to pass the bill pending in Congress.

We condemn the Hay-Pauncefote treaty as a surrender of American rights and interests, not to be tolerated by the American people.

STATEHOOD FOR THE TERRITORIES.

We denounce the failure of the Republican party to carry out its pledges, to grant statehood to the territories of Arizona, New Mexico, and Oklahoma, and we promise the people of those territories immediate statehood and home rule during their condition as territories, and we favor home rule and a territorial form of government for Alaska and Porto Rico.

ARID LANDS.

We favor an intelligent system of improving the arid lands of the West, storing the waters for purposes of irrigation, and the holding of such lands for actual settlers.

CHINESE EXCLUSION LAW.

We favor the continuance and strict enforcement of the Chinese exclusion law and its application to the same classes of all Asiatic races.

ALLIANCE WITH ENGLAND.

Jefferson said: "Peace, commerce, and honest friendship with all nations; entangling alliances with none."

We approve this wholesome doctrine and earnestly protest against the Republican departure which has involved us in so-called politics, including the diplomacy of Europe and the intrigue and land-grabbing of Asia, and we especially condemn the ill-concealed Republican alliance with England, which must mean discrimination against other friendly nations, and which has already stifled the nation's voice while liberty is being strangled in Africa.

SYMPATHY FOR THE BOERS.

Believing in the principles of self-government, and rejecting, as did our forefathers, the claim of monarchy, we view with indignation the purpose of England to overwhelm with force the South African republics. Speaking, as we do, for the entire Ameri-

can nation except its Republican officeholders, and for all free men
everywhere, we extend our sympathy to the heroic burghers in
their unequal struggle to maintain their liberty and independence.

REPUBLICAN APPROPRIATIONS.

We denounce the lavish appropriations of recent Republican
Congresses, which have kept taxes high, and which threaten the
perpetuation of the oppressive war levies.

SHIP SUBSIDY BILL.

We oppose the accumulation of a surplus to be squandered in
such bare-faced frauds upon the taxpayers as the shipping sub-
sidy bill, which under the false pretense of prospering American
ship-building, would put unearned millions into the pockets of
favorite contributors to the Republican campaign fund.

REPEAL OF THE WAR TAXES.

We favor the reduction and speedy repeal of the war taxes,
and a return to the time-honored Democratic policy of strict
economy in governmental expenditures.

CONCLUDING PLEA TO THE PEOPLE.

Believing that our most cherished institutions are in great peril,
that the very existence of our constitutional republic is at stake,
and that the decision now to be rendered will determine whether
or not our children are to enjoy those blessed privileges of free
government which have made the United States great, prosperous,
and honored, we earnestly ask for the foregoing declaration of
principles the hearty support of the liberty-loving American people, regardless of previous party affiliations.

William J. Bryan, of Nebraska, was again nominated
for President, and Adlai E. Stevenson, of Illinois, for
Vice-President, both on the first ballots. While the Democratic Convention was in session, the Silver Republicans

met in Convention in the same city. The Chairman *pro tem.* was Henry M. Teller, who had withdrawn from the Republican Convention in 1896. This Convention nominated William J. Bryan for President, and the National Committee was authorized to name the Vice-President, which they did on July 7th, by endorsing Adlai E. Stevenson.

The campaign of 1900 was as animated throughout as was that of 1896. Imperialism was the issue raised by the Democrats, and the result in November was an overwhelming victory for the Republican candidates, McKinley and Roosevelt, who carried enough States to assure them of 292 electoral votes to 155 for Bryan and Stevenson. The popular vote for the leading candidates was as follows: McKinley (Rep.), 7,207,923; Bryan (Dem.), 6,358,133; Woolley (Prohib.), 208,914; Debs (Soc. Dem.), 87,814; Barker (M. R. Peop.), 50,373; Malloney (Soc. L.), 39,739.

William McKinley was inaugurated for his second term on March 4, 1901. On September 6, 1901, the almost unbelievable news was telegraphed over the country that President McKinley, while in the Temple of Music at the Pan-American Exposition at Buffalo, had been shot twice by an assassin, an anarchist named Leon Czolgosz. But it proved only too true, and for a week the people of the country watched the bulletins and prayed for the President, who fought bravely against death. The wound in the stomach was fatal, and William McKinley, the third martyred President of the Republican Party, passed away on

September 14, 1901, at the home of John G. Milburn in Buffalo. The great purity and simplicity of his life, his devotion to his wife, his courageous struggle for the great economical principles which had brought the country to the highest degree of prosperity ever known, and the splendid record of his administration made his loss deeply felt by the nation, and he was enshrined beside Lincoln in American history. The last words of William McKinley exhibited the Christian character of a great life: "It is God's way; His will be done."

By special permission of C. M. Bell Photo Co., Washington, D. C.

THEODORE ROOSEVELT.

CHAPTER XX.

"I feel that we have a right to appeal not merely to Republicans, but to all good citizens, no matter what may have been their party affiliations in the past, and to ask them, on the strength of the record . to stand shoulder to shoulder with us, perpetuating the conditions under which we have reached a degree of prosperity never before attained in the Nation's history and under which, abroad, we have put the American Flag on a level which it never before in the history of the country has been placed."

Theodore Roosevelt, to the Notification Committee, Sagamore Hill, L. I., July, 1900.

Theodore Roosevelt took the oath of office as President at Buffalo, New York, on September 14, 1901, and became the twenty-sixth President of the United States, and the third to succeed a martyred Republican President. He was born in New York City, October 27, 1858. He graduated from Harvard and spent some years in traveling; served in the New York Legislature in 1882, 1883 and 1884, and was prominent as a champion of Civil Service Reform. Was Chairman of the New York delegation to the Convention in 1884, and ran for Mayor of New York in 1886, as the Independent candidate, endorsed by the Republicans, but was defeated; was appointed Civil Service Commissioner in May, 1889, by President Harrison, and served till 1895, exhibiting great energy and establishing

(285)

Civil Service principles in all Executive Departments, acquiring a splendid reputation throughout the country for fearlessness and honesty. He resigned from the Civil Service Commission to accept the appointment of Police Commissioner of New York City in May, 1895, and displayed his usual energy in the suppression of corruption and in the establishment of law and order in New York City. He was appointed Assistant Secretary of the Navy by President McKinley, and worked with great vigor to place the Navy on a proper footing, and the success of the Navy in the Spanish-American war was due in no small degree to his preliminary work. When the war broke out in April, 1898, he resigned his position in the Navy Department and organized a volunteer cavalry regiment, recruited mainly from the Western plains, the members of which were called the "Rough Riders." They were commanded at first by Col. Leonard Wood, and Mr. Roosevelt was made Lieutenant-Colonel. His previous military experience had been several years' service in the New York National Guard. For his gallant conduct at San Juan Hill and in the Cuban campaign he was commissioned Colonel July 11, 1898, though many of the officers at Washington were opposed to him. He was elected Governor of New York in the Fall of 1898. In all of these positions he devoted himself to his work with energy and enthusiasm amazing to all. His published works on American History rank him as one of the great historians of the country, and his interests in out-door sports and his delightful home life have endeared him to the people as a typical American. The nomination for Vice-President came to him unsought and undesired, but in response to the demands of the people he fell in line promptly. Coming to the Presidential Chair under trying circumstances he immediately displayed the highest ability and tact in taking charge of the administration of the national affairs. The policies of President McKinley were pursued without deviation, and President Roosevelt conducted the domestic and foreign affairs in a way that has marked him as a great statesman, and the country and its new possessions are eminently in a condition of prosperity and satisfaction.

On May 20, 1902, the United States partially redeemed its pledge in regard to Cuba by hauling down its flag at the Government Palace, Havana, after which the flag of the new Republic of Cuba was raised. This pledge fulfilled, the Republican Party rounded it out with the approval of the Cuban Reciprocity Treaty, ratified in the Senate March 19, 1903.

The long continued agitation for the construction of a canal, by the United States, connecting the waters of the Atlantic and Pacific oceans, resulted in the Isthmian Canal Act, approved June 28, 1902, in which the President was authorized to acquire the rights of the new Panama Canal Company of France, and if the title proved satisfactory, and a treaty could be obtained from the Republic of Colombia for the necessary territory, the President was authorized to pay the Canal Company $40,000,000 for this property, but if this could not be done within a reasonable time then the Nicaraguan route was to be considered. An

Isthmian Canal Commission was created. Attorney General P. C. Knox reported to the President (October 26, 1902) that the title to the canal was valid, and on January 22, 1903, a treaty between the United States and Colombia for the construction of the canal was signed at Washington and was ratified by the United States Senate March 17, 1903, but was rejected by the Colombian Senate September 14, 1903, who suggested the negotiation of a new treaty. But early in November, 1903, Panama declared its independence, and was recognized as a Republic by the United States on November 6th. A new Canal Treaty was signed at Washington by Secretary of State John Hay, representing the United States, and Philippe Bunau-Varilla representing Panama, and the treaty was ratified by the Government of Panama on December 2, 1903, and is now under consideration in the United States Senate. These various events, all justified by the laws of nations, brought Colombia to terms, and late in November, 1903, she offered the United States a free canal concession if the latter would permit the subjugation of Panama, but the matter had gone too far, and it is now probable that the Panama Canal will be built by this Government, acting with the new Republic of Panama.

The legislation and the course of events in the Philippines has been equally satisfactory. On July 1, 1902, Congress provided for the termination of military rule in these islands and the establishment of civil government. William H. Taft, of Ohio, who had been President of the Commission, was appointed Governor, and in that capacity continued the splendid work which had been begun by the Commission. In December, 1903, Governor Taft was appointed Secretary of War by President Roosevelt, taking the place of Elihu Root, resigned, and his successor in the Philippines is Luke E. Wright, of Tennessee. On July 4, 1902, the insurrection in the Philippines against the authority of the United States having ended in 'all parts of the Islands except in the part inhabited by the Moro Tribes, President Roosevelt issued a Proclamation of pardon and amnesty to all political offenders on their taking the oath of allegiance to the United States.

The great combinations of capital called Trusts, in so far as they concentrate the industries of the country in the hands of a few, stifling competiton and dictating wages and prices, have received the emphatic condemnation of the Republican Party, and President Roosevelt and Attorney General Knox have done their utmost, under the existing laws, to suppress these combinations when unlawful. The Republican Party has done more than any other party to curb the evils of the Trusts, and it is probable that the question can only be adequately handled by an amendment to the United States Constitution giving Congress direct supervision over their organization. The settlement of the coal strike in the United States by President Roosevelt is remembered gratefully, and was to the satisfaction of both sides, and was in keeping with his record of direct and fearless action in emergencies. His administration saw the dedication of the Louisiana Purchase Exposition buildings at St. Louis on April 30, 1903, and on

July 4, 1903, the completion of the Pacific Cable, the first message having been sent by the President to Governor Taft. The report of the Alaskan Boundary Commission on October 7, 1903, gave to the United States all points, except one, in dispute. This called attention to the work of the Department of State, but we are too close to the splendid diplomacy of John Hay to fully appreciate its far-reaching effect for the advancement of the interests of this country.

Such is a brief record of recent events that will close this history of the splendid achievements of the Republican Party. The history of the administrations of the eight Republican Presidents, Lincoln, Grant, Hayes, Garfield, Arthur, Harrison, McKinley and Roosevelt, may be read at least with interest by every citizen of the United States, regardless of his party affiliations, and assuredly with pride and satisfaction by those who count themselves as members of the Grand Old Party.

APPENDIX

THE REPUBLICAN NATIONAL COMMITTEE.

The Republican National Committee is composed of one member from each State and Territory. The Committee is chosen by the several State delegations at the National Conventions of the party.

The Committee is the national executive head of the Republican Party. It decides the time and place, and issues the calls for the National Conventions. The call states the number of delegates to be chosen for each district, and sometimes prescribes the manner of their selection. The National Committee also selects the temporary officers of the convention, subject to its ratification, and after the nominations have been made takes general charge of the campaign. The Chairmen of the Republican National Committee have been as follows:

1856. Edwin D. Morgan, New York.
1860. Edwin D. Morgan, New York.
1864. Marcus L. Ward, New Jersey.
1868. William Claflin, Massachusetts.
1872. Edwin D. Morgan, New York.
1876. { Zachariah Chandler, Michigan.
{ J. Donald Cameron, Pennsylvania.
1880. { M. Jewell, Connecticut.
{ Dwight M. Sabin, Minnesota.
1884. B. F. Jones, Pennsylvania.
1888. M. S. Quay, Pennsylvania.
1892. Thomas H. Carter, Montana.
1896. Marcus A. Hanna, Ohio.
1900. Marcus A. Hanna, Ohio.

THE NATIONAL REPUBLICAN LEAGUE.

The National Republican League, an organization of the greatest help to the party in National and State Campaigns, was organized in Chickering Hall, New York City, December 15-17, 1887. It is made up of the active Republican Clubs of the country, which are first organized into a State League, and then joined in the National League. It now has a membership of fully 500,000. The first President of the League was Jas. P. Foster, of New York, who was most active in the founding of the organization. National Conventions of the League have been held as follows: Baltimore, 1889; Nashville, 1890; Cincinnati, 1891; Buffalo, 1892; Louisville, 1893; Denver, 1894; Cleveland, 1895; Milwaukee, 1896; Detroit, 1897; Omaha, 1898; St. Paul, 1900; Chicago, 1902. The Conventions have been held biennially since 1898. The 1904 Convention will be held at Indianapolis. The following have served as Presidents of the National Republican League:

1889–1890. Jas. P. Foster, New York.
1890–1892. John M. Thurston, Nebraska.
1892–1893. John S. Clarkson, Iowa.
1893–1895. W. W. Tracy, Illinois.
1895–1896. E. A. McAlpin, New York.
1896–1897. D. D. Woodmansee, Ohio.
1897–1898. L. J. Crawford, Kentucky.
1898–1900. Wm. Stone, California.
1900–1902. I. N. Hamilton, Illinois.
1902. J. Hampton Moore, Pennsylvania.

REPUBLICAN NATIONAL CONVENTIONS.

TIME.	PLACE.	NOMINEES.
June 17-18, 1856.	Philadelphia, Pa.	John C. Fremont, Cal. / Wm. L. Dayton, N. J.
May 16-18, 1860.	Chicago, Ill.	Abraham Lincoln, Ill. / Hannibal Hamlin, Me.
June 7-8, 1864.	Baltimore, Md.	Abraham Lincoln, Ill. / Andrew Johnson, Tenn.
May 20-22, 1868.	Chicago, Ill.	Ulysses S. Grant, Ill. / Schuyler Colfax, Ind.
June 5-6, 1872.	Philadelphia, Pa.	Ulysses S. Grant, Ill. / Henry Wilson, Mass.
June 14-16, 1876.	Cincinnati, O.	Rutherford B. Hayes, Ohio. / Wm. A. Wheeler, N. Y.
June 2-8, 1880.	Chicago, Ill.	Jas. A. Garfield, Ohio. / Chester A. Arthur, N. Y.
June 3-6, 1884.	Chicago, Ill.	James G. Blaine, Me. / John A. Logan, Ill.
June 19-25, 1888.	Chicago, Ill.	Benj. Harrison, Ind. / Levi P. Morton, N. Y.
June 7-11, 1892.	Minneapolis, Minn.	Benj. Harrison, Ind. / Whitelaw Reid, N. Y.
June 16-18, 1896.	St. Louis, Mo.	Wm. McKinley, Ohio. / Garret A. Hobart, N. J.
June 19-21, 1900.	Philadelphia, Pa.	Wm. McKinley, Ohio. / Theodore Roosevelt, N. Y.
June 21, 1904.	Chicago, Ill.	

PRESIDENTIAL ELECTIONS.

The Constitution requires each State to appoint, in such manner as the Legislature thereof may direct, a number of electors, equal to the whole number of Senators and Representatives to which the State may be entitled in Congress; but no Senator or Representative, or person holding an office of trust or profit under the United States, shall be appointed an elector.

The original clause in the Constitution provided that after the electors had been chosen they should elect the President as follows: The electors shall meet in their respective States and vote by ballot for two persons, of whom one at least shall not be an inhabitant of the same State with themselves. A list of the votes shall then be sent to the President of the Senate; the person having the greatest number of votes shall be President, if such number be a majority of the whole number of electors appointed; but in the event of no person having a majority, or in case of a tie vote, the House of Representatives shall immediately choose the President. In every case, after the choice of President, the person having the greatest number of votes shall be Vice-President. But, if there should remain two or more having equal votes, then the Senate shall choose from them by ballot the Vice-President.

Under this clause in the original Constitution there were four elections: Washington (two terms), John Adams and Jefferson. The last election (Jefferson) brought on a contest that resulted in the Twelfth Amendment of the Constitution. It will be noticed that the original clause did not require the electors to name the person they voted for as President and the person voted for as Vice-President; they were simply to vote for two persons. On counting the electoral votes as a result of the election of 1800, it was found that Thomas Jefferson, of Virginia, and Aaron Burr, of New York, had an equal electoral vote—73. This threw the election into the House, and a bitter contest followed, which resulted in the victory of Jefferson, making Burr Vice-President; and the curious situation was present of an aspirant to the presidency occupying the subordinate position of Vice-President.

To correct this evil, the Twelfth Amendment was proposed, ratified by a sufficient number of States, and went into effect in 1804, and has governed the presidential elections to this day. This amendment provides that the electors, instead of voting for two candidates for President, shall distinctly name in their ballots the person voted for as President and the person voted for as Vice-President. The certificates of the ballots are opened by the President of the Senate in the presence of the Senate and the House. If no person have a majority, then the House chooses the President, each State having one vote. The person having the greatest number of votes as Vice-President shall be Vice-President. But if no person has a majority, then the Senate chooses the Vice-President. But no person constitutionally ineligible to the office of President is eligible to the vice-presidency.

Since the Jefferson-Burr contest there has been but one election by the House of Representatives, that of 1824, when none of the candidates having received a majority of the electoral vote, the House, between Andrew Jackson, John Q. Adams and William H. Crawford, selected John Q. Adams as President. John Q. Adams was a son of John Adams, the second President, and this has been the only time in the history of the nation that father and son have occupied the Presidential chair. There has been but one instance of an election of a Vice-President by the Senate, that of R. M. Johnston, in 1837.

Two methods of choosing the presidential electors preceded the present system. It will be remembered that the Constitution gives the various Legislatures the power of naming the manner in which the electors shall be chosen. Originally, the Legislatures exercised this power themselves; then the district system was tried; that is, each voter cast a ballot for three electors, two for the State at large (representing the Senators) and one for the Congressional district in which he lived. The system now in vogue is an election by a "general ticket;" that is to say, each voter uses a ballot on which are printed the names of all the electors to which his State is entitled.

The tendency of the district system was to divide the electoral vote, while the "general ticket" tends to a solid vote from each State. In the "Mugwump" campaign of 1884—Cleveland-Blaine—no State divided its electoral votes. No State divided its vote in the Harrison-Cleveland election of 1888. In 1892, owing to the People's Party candidate breaking the vote, and owing to other circumstances, five States divided their votes. In the McKinley-Bryan contest of 1896 the votes were only divided in two States—California and Kentucky—where the popular voting was so close that each State named one Bryan elector.

The present system of naming electors increases the chances of electing Presidents who have received less than a majority of the popular vote, and it is even possible to elect a President who has received less than a plurality of votes, which has happened in two instances—the election of Hayes and Benjamin Harrison. It can be seen in the following instances how both of the cases may happen: A candidate may carry Kansas by a majority of 43,000, as Blaine did in 1884, and gain nine electoral votes, and lose New York, with its thirty-six electoral votes by 1,149 popular votes, as happened in the same election; or in 1896, when Bryan carried Colorado by 133,000 majority and gained four electoral votes, and perhaps lost twelve electoral votes in Kentucky by the narrow margin of 281 popular votes.

The following Presidents have failed to receive a majority of the total popular vote: Adams in 1824 (elected by the House), Polk in 1844, Taylor in 1848, Buchanan in 1856, Lincoln in 1860, Hayes in 1876, Garfield in 1880, Cleveland in 1884, Harrison in 1888, and Cleveland in 1892. McKinley, in 1896, was the first President since 1872 to receive a clear majority of the popular votes.

Only States vote at the presidential elections, each State being entitled to a number of electors equal to the whole number of Senators and Representatives to which the State may be entitled in Congress. New York, Pennsylvania, Illinois and Ohio rank in the order named as to largest number of electors. Since the first election of Jackson, in 1828, no President has been chosen in direct opposition to the combined votes of New York and Pennsylvania.

The theory of the electoral college, as conceived by the Federal Convention, was never realized. The aim was to constitute this peculiar body as a check on the popular excitement attendant on these elections. It was meant that the electors should meet some time after the election day and calmly discuss the merits of the best men Under the present system, the National Conventions of the various parties present their candidates; on the Tuesday next after the first Monday in November of every fourth year the people vote for the electors, and the result is known the next day, although the electors do not meet until the second Monday in January next after the election. There is nothing in the Constitution to compel an elector to vote for any particular candidate, yet custom is often stronger than law, and the elector who would frustrate the wishes of the people who elected him would be guilty of the basest of political treachery, although no law could punish him.

In the early history of the country, presidential candidates were first presented by the party leaders, then by Congressional caucuses, by State Legislatures, local conventions, and since 1832 the method of nominating has been by National Conventions of the various parties. Each State is generally allowed twice as many delegates as it has electors. In the Democratic Conventions a two-thirds vote of the delegates is necessary for choice, while the Republican Conventions only require a majority vote of the delegates for choice.

The Constitution requires, among other things, that the President shall be thirty-five years of age. Mr. Roosevelt is the youngest President we have had, being three years younger than Ulysses S. Grant, who was forty-seven years old when inaugurated. The eldest was William H. Harrison, who was sixty-eight years of age when inaugurated.

The manner of counting the electoral vote is prescribed in the Twelfth Amendment to the Constitution as follows:

"The President of the Senate shall, in the presence of the Senate and House of Representatives, open all the certificates, and the votes shall then be counted; the person having the greatest number of votes for President shall be President, if such number be a majority of the whole number of electors appointed; and if no person have such majority, then from the persons having the highest numbers, not exceeding three, on the list of those voted for as President, the House of Representatives shall choose immediately, by ballot, the President. But in choosing the President the votes shall be taken by States, the representation from each State having one vote; a quorum for this purpose shall consist of a member or members from two-thirds of the States, and a majority of all the States shall be necessary to a choice. And if the House of Representatives shall not choose a President, whenever the right of choice shall devolve upon them, before the fourth day of March next following, then the Vice-President shall act as President, as in the case of the death or other constitutional disability of the President. The person having the greatest number of votes as Vice-President shall be the Vice-President, if such number be a majority of the whole number of electors appointed; and if no person have a majority, then from the two highest numbers on the list the Senate shall choose the Vice-President; a quorum for the purpose shall consist of two-thirds of the whole number of Senators, and a majority of the whole number shall be necessary to a choice."

The procedure of the two houses, in case the returns of the election of electors from any State are disputed, is provided in the "Electoral Count" Act, passed in 1886. The "Electoral Count" Act remedied the strained situation brought about by the Hayes-Tilden controversy in 1876. Congress counts the ballots on the second Wednesday in February succeeding the meeting of the electors.

THE ELECTORAL VOTE IN 1904.

STATES.	ELECTORAL VOTES.	STATES.	ELECTORAL VOTES.
Alabama	11	Nevada	3
Arkansas	9	New Hampshire	4
California	10	New Jersey	12
Colorado	5	New York	39
Connecticut	7	North Carolina	12
Delaware	3	North Dakota	4
Florida	5	Ohio	23
Georgia	13	Oregon	4
Idaho	3	Pennsylvania	34
Illinois	27	Rhode Island	4
Indiana	15	South Carolina	9
Iowa	13	South Dakota	4
Kansas	10	Tennessee	12
Kentucky	13	Texas	18
Louisiana	9	Utah	3
Maine	6	Vermont	4
Maryland	8	Virginia	12
Massachusetts	16	Washington	5
Michigan	14	West Virginia	7
Minnesota	11	Wisconsin	13
Mississippi	10	Wyoming	2
Missouri	18		
Montana	3	Total	476
Nebraska	8	Necessary to a choice.	239

PRESIDENTS AND THEIR CABINETS SINCE THE ORGANIZA-
TION OF THE REPUBLICAN PARTY.

1856.

JAMES BUCHANAN, Pa., *Dem.*
Lewis Cass ....Sec. State.
Jeremiah S. Black.... "
Howell Cobb ....Sec. Treas.
Jacob Thomas .... "
John A. Dix......... "
John B. Floyd ......Sec. War.
Joseph Holt .... "
Isaac Toucey.......Sec. Navy.

J. C. BRECKINRIDGE, Ky., *Dem.*
Jacob Thompson ....Sec. Int'r.
Moses Kelly .... "
Jeremiah S. Black...Att. Gen'l.
Edwin M. Stanton... "
Aaron V. Brown....Post. Gen'l.
J. Holt .... "
H. King .... "

1860.

ABRAHAM LINCOLN, Ill., *Rep.*
Wm. H. Seward ....Sec. State.
Simon Cameron .....Sec. War.
Edwin M. Stanton... "
Caleb B. Smith.......Sec. Int'r.
John P. Usher....... "
Gideon Welles ......Sec. Navy.

HANNIBAL HAMLIN, Me., *Rep.*
Salmon P. Chase....Sec. Treas.
Wm. P. Fessenden... "
Edward Bates ......Att. Gen'l.
James Speed
Montgomery Blair ..Post. Gen'l.
William Denison .... "

1864.

ABRAHAM LINCOLN, Ill., *Rep.*
William H. Seward..Sec. State.
Edwin M. Stanton....Sec. War.
John P. Usher.......Sec. Int'r.
Henry Harlan

ANDREW JOHNSON, Tenn., *Rep.*
Hugh McCulloch ....Sec. Treas.
Gideon Welles ......Sec. Navy.
James Speed ....Att. Gen'l.
Wm. Denison ......Post. Gen'l.

1865.

ANDREW JOHNSON, Tenn., *Rep.*

Wm. H. Seward.....Sec. State.
Edwin M. Stanton....Sec. War.
Lorenzo Thomas .... "
John Schofield ...... "
Hugh McCulloch ....Sec. Treas.
Henry Harlan ....Sec. Int'r.
Orville H. Browning.. "

Gideon Welles ......Sec. Navy.
James Speed ....Att. Gen'l.
Henry Stanbery ..... "
Wm. M. Evarts...... "
Wm. Denison ......Post. Gen'l.
Alex. W. Randall.... "

1868.

ULYSSES S. GRANT, Ill., *Rep.*
E. B. Washburne....Sec. State.
Hamilton Fish ...... "
G. S. Boutwell.....Sec. Treas.
J. A. Rawlins........Sec. War.
Wm. W. Belknap.... "

SCHUYLER COLFAX, Ind., *Rep.*
J. D. Cox..........Sec. Int'r.
Columbus Delano .... "
George M. Robeson...Sec. Navy.
George A. Williams..Att. Gen'l.
John A. J. Creswell.Post. Gen'l.

1872.

ULYSSES S. GRANT, Ill.. *Rep.*
Hamilton Fish ......Sec. State.
Wm. M. Belknap.....Sec. War.
Alphonso Taft "
J. D. Cameron. "
John A. J. Creswell..Post. Gen'l.
Marshall Jewell ..... "
James N. Tyner...... "
George M. Robeson....Sec. Navy.

HENRY WILSON, Mass., *Rep.*
Columbus Delano ....Sec. Int'r.
Zachariah Chandler . "
Wm. M. Richardson..Sec. Treas.
Benj. H. Bristow. "
Lot M. Morrill .. "
George A. Williams..Att. Gen'l.
Edwards Pierrepont . "
Alphonso Taft ...... "

1876.

RUTH'FORD B. HAYES, O., *Rep.*
Wm. M. Evarts .....Sec. State.
R. W. Thompson.....Sec. Navy.
Nathan Goff, Jr..... "
D. M. Key.........Post. Gen'l.
Horace Maynard .... "

WM. A. WHEELER, N. Y., *Rep.*
John Sherman ......Sec. Treas.
G. W. McCrary.......Sec. War.
Alex. Ramsay .... "
Carl Schurz ....Sec. Int'r.
Charles Devens .....Att. Gen'l.

1880.

JAMES A GARFIELD, Ohio, *Rep.*
J. G. Blaine........Sec. State.
R. T. Lincoln ....Sec. War.
W. H. Hunt........Sec. Navy.
Wayne McVeagh ....Att. Gen'l.

CHESTER A. ARTHUR, N. Y., *Rep.*
Wm. Windom ......Sec. Treas.
S. J. Kirkwood .....Sec. Int'r.
T. L. James Post. Gen'l.

1881.

CHESTER A. ARTHUR, N. Y.. *Rep.*

J. G. Blaine........Sec. State.
F. T. Frelinghuysen.. "
R. T. Lincoln ....Sec. War.
W. H. Hunt........Sec. Navy.
W. E. Chandler...... "
Wayne McVeagh ....Att. Gen'l.
B. H. Brewster...... "

Wm. Windom ......Sec. Treas.
C. J. Folger .... "
S. J. Kirkwood .....Sec. Int'r.
H. M. Teller .... "
T. L. James ....Post. Gen'l.
T. O. Howe .... "

1884

G. CLEVELAND, N. Y., *Dem.*
Thos. F. Bayard ....Sec. State.
Wm. C. Endicott .....Sec. War.
Wm. C. Whitney ....Sec. Navy.
Wm. F. Vilas ......Post. Gen'l.
Don M. Dickinson.... "

Thos. A. Hendricks, Ind., *Dem.*
Daniel Manning   Sec. Treas.
Chas. Fairchild   "
Augustus Garland ..Att. Gen'l.
Lucius Q. C. Lamar..Sec. Int'r.
William F. Vilas   "
Norman J. Coleman..Sec. Agric.

1888.

BENJ. HARRISON, Ind., *Rep.*
James G. Blaine.....Sec. State.
Redfield Proctor .....Sec. War.
Benj. F. Tracy ......Sec. Navy.
John Wanamaker ..Post. Gen'l.

Levi P. Morton, N. Y., *Rep.*
William Windom ...Sec. Treas.
Wm. H. H. Miller....Att. Gen'l.
John W. Noble   .Sec. Int'r.
Jeremiah M. Rusk...Sec. Agric.

1892.

G. CLEVELAND, N. Y., *Dem.*
Richard Olney ......Sec. State.
Daniel S. Lamont....Sec. War.
Hilary A. Herbert...Sec. Navy.
Wm. L. Wilson.....Post. Gen'l.

Adlai E. Stevenson, Ill., *Dem.*
John G. Carlisle....Sec. Treas.
Judson Harmon ....Att. Gen'l.
David R. Francis....Sec. Int'r.
J. Sterling Morton..Sec. Agric.

1896.

WM. McKINLEY, Ohio, *Rep.*
John Sherman ......Sec. State.
William R. Day......   "
John Hay   "
Russell A. Alger.....Sec. War.
Elihu Root   "
John D. Long.......Sec. Navy.
James A. Gary   Post. Gen'l.
Chas. Emory Smith..   "

Garret A. Hobart, N. J., *Rep.*
Lyman J. Gage......Sec. Treas.
Jos. McKenna ......Att. Gen'l.
John W. Griggs .....   "
Cornelius N. Bliss....Sec. Int'r.
Ethan A. Hitchcock..   "
James Wilson   Sec. Agric.

1900.

WM. McKINLEY, Ohio, *Rep.*
John Hay ....Sec. State.
Lyman J. Gage.....Sec. Treas.
Elihu Root ....Sec. War.
Ethan A. Hitchcock..Sec. Int'r.

Theo. Roosevelt, N. Y., *Rep.*
John D. Long.......Sec. Navy.
Chas. Emory Smith.Post. Gen'l.
Philander C. Knox...Att. Gen'l.
Jas. Wilson ....Sec. Agric.

1901.

THEO. ROOSEVELT, N. Y., *Rep.*

John Hay ....Sec. State.
Lyman J. Gage .....Sec. Treas.
Leslie M. Shaw...... "
Elihu Root ....Sec. War.
Wm. H. Taft .... "
Chas. Emory Smith.Post. Gen'l.
Henry C. Payne..... "

John D. Long ......Sec. Navy.
Wm. H. Moody...... "
Philander C. Knox...Att. Gen'l.
Ethan A. Hitchcock..Sec. Int'r.
Jas. Wilson . . .Sec. Agric.
G. B. Cortelyou.Sec. Com. & Lab.

PRESIDENTS PRO TEM. OF THE UNITED STATES SENATE SINCE THE ORGANIZATION OF THE REPUBLICAN PARTY.

CONGRESS.	YEAR.	NAME.
32–33	1852–54	D. R. Atchison, Missouri.
33–34	1854–57	Jesse D. Bright, Indiana.
34	1857	James M. Mason, Virginia.
35–36	1857–61	Benj. Fitzpatrick. Alabama.
36–38	1861–64	Solomon Foot, Vermont.
38	1864–65	Daniel Clark, New Hampshire.
39	1865–67	Lafayette S. Foster, Connecticut.
40	1867–69	Benj. F. Wade, Ohio.
41–42	1869–73	Henry B. Anthony, Rhode Island.
43	1873–75	M. H. Carpenter, Wisconsin.
44–45	1875–79	Thos. W. Ferry, Michigan.
46	1879–81	A. G. Thurman, Ohio.
47	1881	Thos. F. Bayard, Delaware.
47	1881–83	David Davis, Illinois.
48	1883–85	Geo. F. Edmunds, Vermont.
49	1885–87	John Sherman, Ohio.
49–51	1887–91	Jno. J. Ingalls, Kansas.
52	1891–93	C. F. Manderson, Nebraska.
53	1893–95	Isham G. Harris, Tennessee.
54–58	1895	Wm. P. Frye, Maine.

SPEAKERS OF THE U. S. HOUSE OF REPRESENTATIVES
SINCE THE ORGANIZATION OF THE REPUBLICAN PARTY.

CONGRESS.	YEAR.	NAME.
32–33	1851–55	Linn Boyd, Kentucky.
34	1855–57	Nathaniel P. Banks, Massachusetts.
35	1857–59	Jas. L. Orr, South Carolina.
36	1859–61	Wm. Pennington, New Jersey.
37	1861–63	Galusha A. Grow, Pennsylvania.
38–40	1863–69	Schuyler Colfax, Indiana.
41–43	1869–75	Jas. G. Blaine, Maine.
44	1875–76	Michael C. Kerr, Indiana.
44–46	1876–81	Samuel J. Randall, Pennsylvania.
47	1881–83	J. Warren Keifer, Ohio.
48–50	1883–89	John G. Carlisle, Kentucky.
51	1889–91	Thos. B. Reed, Maine.
52–53	1891–95	Chas. F. Crisp, Georgia.
54–55	1895–99	Thos. B. Reed, Maine.
56–57	1899–1903	David B. Henderson, Iowa.
58	1903	Jos. G. Cannon, Illinois.

THE PRESIDENTIAL SUCCESSION.

By Act approved January 18, 1886, the presidential succession
is fixed as follows: In case of the removal, death, resignation, or inability of both the President and Vice-President of the United States,
the Secretary of State, or if there be none, or in case of his removal,
death, etc., then the Secretary of the Treasury, the Secretary of War,
the Attorney-General, the Postmaster-General, Secretary of the Navy,
and Secretary of the Interior, shall act until the disability is removed, or a President elected; if Congress is not in session when the
presidential powers devolve on any of these persons, or does not meet
twenty days thereafter, then the said person must call an extraordinary session. This law applies only to such persons who are appointed by the advice and with the consent of the Senate, and who
are eligible under the Constitution for the office of President.

POPULAR AND ELECTORAL VOTE, 1856.

STATES	Popular Vote			Electoral Vote		
	Buchanan and Breckinridge Dem.	Fremont and Dayton Rep.	Fillmore and Donelson American and Whigs	Buchanan and B	Fremont and D	Fillmore and D
Alabama	46,739	.....	28,552	9	...	...
Arkansas	21,910		10,787	4		
California	53,365	20,691	36,165	4		
Connecticut	34,995	42,715	2,615		6	
Delaware	8,004	308	6,175	3		
Florida	6,358		4,833	3		
Georgia	56,578		42,228	10		
Illinois	105,348	96,189	37,444	11		
Indiana	118,670	94,375	22,386	13		
Iowa	36,170	43,954	9,180			
Kentucky	74,642	314	67,416	12		
Louisiana	22,164		20,709	6		
Maine	39,080	67,379	3,325		8	
Maryland	39,115	281	47,460			
Massachusetts	39,240	108,190	19,626		13	
Michigan	52,136	71,762	1,660		6	
Mississippi	35,446		24,195	7		
Missouri	58,164		48,524	9		
New Hampshire	32,789	38,345	422		5	
New Jersey	46,943	28,338	24,115	7		
New York	195,878	276,007	124,604		35	
North Carolina	48,246		36,886	10		
Ohio	170,874	187,497	28,126		23	
Pennsylvania	230,710	147,510	82,175	27		
Rhode Island	6,680	11,467	1,675			
*South Carolina	.....	.....	.....	8		
Tennessee	73,638		66,178	12		
Texas	31,169		15,639	4		
Vermont	10,569	39,561	545			
Virginia	89,706	291	60,310	15		
Wisconsin	52,843	66,090	579	...		

POPULAR AND ELECTORAL VOTE, 1860.

STATES	Lincoln and Hamlin Rep.	Douglas and Johnson Dem.	Breckinridge and Lane Ind. Dem.	Bell and Everet Constitutional Union	Lincoln and H	Douglas and J	Breckinridge and L	Bell and E
	Popular Vote				Electoral Vote			
Alabama		13,651	48,831	27,825	. .	. .	9	. .
Arkansas		5,227	28,732	20,094	. .	. .	4	. .
California	39,173	38,516	34,334	6,817	4	. .		
Connecticut	43,692	15,522	14,641	3,291	6	. .		
Delaware	3,815	1,023	7,347	3,864	. .	. .	3	. .
Florida	. . . . . .	367	8,543	5,437	. .	. .	3	. .
Georgia	. . . . . .	11,590	51,889	42,886	. . .		10	
Illinois	172,161	160,215	2,404	3,913	11			
Indiana	139,033	115,509	12,295	5,306	13			
Iowa .	70,409	55,111	1,048	1,763	4			. .
Kentucky	1,364	25,651	53,143	66,058	. . .	. .		12
Louisiana	. . . . . .	7,625	22,681	20,204	. . .	. .	6	. .
Maine	62,811	26,693	6,368	2,046	8	. .		
Maryland	2,294	5,966	42,482	41,760	. . .	. .	8	. .
Massachusetts . . .	106,533	34,372	5,939	22,331	13	. .	. . . .	
Michigan	88,480	65,057	805	405	6	. .		
Minnesota	22,069	11,920	748	62	4			
Mississippi	. . . . . .	3,283	40,797	25,040	. . .	. .	7	. .
Missouri .	17,028	58,801	31,317	58,372	. . .	9	. .	. .
New Hampshire . .	37,519	25,881	2,112	441	5	. .		
New Jersey	58,324	62,801	. . . . . .	. . . . . .	4	3	. .	. .
New York .	362,646	312,510	. . . . . .	. . . . . .	35	. .	. .	. .
North Carolina . .	. . . . . .	2,701	48,339	44,990	. . .		10	
Ohio	231,610	187,232	11,405	12,194	23			
Oregon	5,270	3,951	3,006	183	3	.		
Pennsylvania	268,030	16,765	178,871	12,776	27	. .		
Rhode Island	12,244	7,707	. . . . . .	. . . . . .	4	. .	. .	. .
*South Carolina .	. . . . . .	. . . . . .	. . . . . .	. . . . . .	. . .	. .	8	. .
Tennessee		11,350	64,709	69,274	. . .	. .		12
Texas	. . . . . .	. . . . . .	47,548	15,438	. . .	. .	4	. .
Vermont	33,808	6,849	1,969	218	5	. .		. .
Virginia	1,929	16,290	74,323	74,681	. . .	. .	. .	15
Wisconsin	86,110	65,021	888	161	5	. .	. .	. .
Total	1,866,352	1,375,157	847,514	587,830	180	12	72	39

*Electors chosen by Legislature.

POPULAR, ARMY AND ELECTORAL VOTES, 1864.

STATES	Popular Vote		Army Vote		Electoral Vote	
	Lincoln and Johnson Rep.	McClellan and Pendleton Dem.	Lincoln and Johnson	McClellan and Pendleton	Lincoln and J	McClell and P
California	62,134	43,841	2,600	237	5	
Connecticut	44,693	42,288	.....	.....	6	
Delaware	8,155	8,767	.....	.....	...	
Illinois	189,487	158,349	.....	.....	16	
Indiana	150,422	130,233	.....	.....	13	
Iowa	87,331	49,260	15,178	1,364	8	
Kansas	14,228	3,871	.....	.....	3	
Kentucky	27,786	64,301	1,194	2,823		11
Maine	72,278	47,736	4,174	741	7	
Maryland	40,153	32,739	2,800	321	7	
Massachusetts	126,742	48,745	.....	.....	12	..
Michigan	85,352	67,370	9,402	2,959	8	
Minnesota	25,060	17,375	v	.....	4	
Missouri	72,991	31,026	.....	.....	11	
*Nevada	9,826	6,594	.....	.....	6	
New Hampshire	36,595	33,034	2,066	690	5	
New Jersey	60,723	68,014	.....	.....	...	
New York	368,726	361,986	.....	.....	33	
Ohio	265,154	205,568	41,146	9,757	21	
Oregon	9,888	8,457	.....	.....	3	
Pennsylvania	296,389	276,308	26,712	12,349	26	
Rhode Island	14,343	8,718	.....	.....		
Vermont	42,422	13,325	243	49		
West Virginia	23,223	10,457	.....	.....	4	
Wisconsin	79,564	63,875	11,372	2,458	8	
Total	2,213,665	1,802,237	116,887	33,748	212	21

*Nevada chose three electors, one of whom died before the election.

The Army votes of Kansas and Minnesota arrived too late to be counted.

POPULAR AND ELECTORAL VOTE, 1868.

STATES	Popular Vote		Electoral Vote	
	Grant and Colfax Rep.	Seymour and Blair Dem.	Grant and C	Seymour and B
Alabama	76,366	72,080	8	
Arkansas	22,152	19,078	5	
California	54,592	54,078	5	
Connecticut	50,641	47,600	6	
Delaware	7,623	10,980		3
Florida	. . . . . .	. . . . . .	3	
Georgia	57,134	102,822		9
Illinois	250,293	199,143	16	
Indiana	176,552	166,980	13	
Iowa	120,399	74,040	8	
Kansas	31,049	14,019	3	
Kentucky	39,566	115,889		11
Louisiana	33,263	80,225		7
Maine	70,426	42,396	7	
Maryland	30,438	62,357		
Massachusetts	136,477	59,408	12	
Michigan	128,550	97,069	8	
Minnesota	43,542	28,072	4	
Missouri	85,671	59,788	11	
Nebraska	9,729	5,439	3	
Nevada	6,480	5,218	3	
New Hampshire	38,191	31,224	5	
New Jersey	80,121	83,001		
New York	419,883	429,883		3⅞
North Carolina	96,226	84,090	9	
Ohio	280,128	238,700	21	
Oregon	10,961	11,125	. . .	3
Pennsylvania	342,280	313,382	26	
Rhode Island	12,993	6,548	4	
South Carolina	62,301	45,237		
Tennessee	56,757	26,311	1	
Vermont	44,167	12,045		
West Virginia	29,025	20,306		. . .
Wisconsin	108,857	84,710	8	. . .
Totals	3,012,833	2,703,249	214	80

Florida electors chosen by Legislature.

POPULAR AND ELECTORAL VOTE, 1872.

STATES	Popular Vote			Electoral Vote
	Grant and Wilson Rep.	Greeley and Brown Liberal Rep. and Dem.	O'Conor and Adams Straightout Dem	Grant and Wilson
Alabama	90,272	79,444	....	10
Arkansas	41,373	37,927	....	
California	54,020	40,718	1,068	6
Connecticut	50,638	45,880	204	6
Delaware	11,115	10,206	487	3
Florida	17,763	15,427		4
Georgia	62,550	76,356	4,000	.
Illinois	241,944	184,938	3,058	21
Indiana	186,147	163,632	1,417	15
Iowa	131,566	71,196	2,221	11
Kansas	67,048	32,970	596	5
Kentucky	88,766	99,995	2,374	
Louisiana	71,663	57,029	.,...	...
Maine	61,422	29,087		.
Maryland	66,760	67,687	19	
Massachusetts	133,472	59,260	....	13
Michigan	138,455	78,355	2,861	11
Minnesota	55,117	34,423		5
Mississippi	82,175	47,288	....	8
Missouri	119,196	151,434	2,429	
Nebraska	18,329	7,812		3
Nevada	8,413	6,236		3
New Hampshire	37,168	31,424	100	5
New Jersey	91,656	76,456	630	9
New York	440,736	387,281	1,454	35
North Carolina	94,769	70,094		10
Ohio	281,852	244,321	1,163	♭2
Oregon	11,819	7,730	572	3
Pennsylvania	349,589	212,041		29
Rhode Island	13,665	5,329		4
South Carolina	72,290	22,703	187	7
Tennessee	85,655	94,391	....	
Texas	47,406	66,500	2,499	
Vermont	41,481	10,927	593	5
Virginia	93,468	91,654	42	11
West Virginia	32,315	29,451	600	5
Wisconsin	104,997	86,477	834	10
Total	3,597,070	2,834,079	29,408	286

The Prohibition candidate (Jas. Black) received 5,608 votes.
The total electoral vote was 366; Mr. Greeley's death, on November 29, 1873, made it necessary for the Democratic and Liberal Republican electors to vote for other persons; Thos. A. Hendricks received 42. B. Gratz Brown 18. Chas. J. Jenkins 2. David Davis 1. On objection, Congress excluded the vote of Arkansas, Louisiana and Georgia, a total of 17. The foregoing refers to the electoral vote for President; the vote for Vice-President was divided among eight persons.

POPULAR AND ELECTORAL VOTE, 1876.

STATES	Popular Vote. Tilden and Hendricks Dem.	Hayes and Wheeler Rep.	Cooper and Cary Greenback	Electoral Vote. Hayes and Wheeler	Tilden and Hendricks
Alabama	102,002	68,230	......	...	10
Arkansas	58,071	38,669	289	...	6
California	76,465	79,269	47	6	
Colorado	......	......	......		
Connecticut	61,934	59,034	774		
Delaware	13,381	10,752	......	...	6
Florida	22,923	23,849		4	
Georgia	130,088	50,446		...	11
Illinois	258,601	278,232	17,233	21	
Indiana	213,526	208,011	9,533	...	15
Iowa	112,099	171,327	9,001	11	
Kansas	37,902	78,322	7,776	5	
Kentucky	159,690	97,156	1,944		12
Louisiana	70,508	75,135			
Maine	49,823	66,300	663	8	
Maryland	91,780	71,981	33	...	8
Massachusetts	108,777	150,063	779	13	
Michigan	141,095	166,534	9,060	11	
Minnesota	48,799	72,962	2,311	5	
Mississippi	112,173	52,605	......	...	8
Missouri	203,077	145,029	3,498	...	15
Nebraska	17,554	31,916	2,320	3	
Nevada	9,308	10,383	......		
New Hampshire	38,509	41,539	76	[illegible]	...
New Jersey	115,962	103,517	712	.	9
New York	521,949	489,207	1,987	.	35
North Carolina	125,427	108,417	......	...	10
Ohio	323,182	330,698	3,057	2	
Oregon	14,149	15,206	510	3	
Pennsylvania	366,158	384,122	7,187	29	
Rhode Island	10,712	15,787	68	4	
South Carolina	90,906	91,870			
Tennessee	133,166	89,566	......	...	12
Texas	104,755	44,800	......	...	8
Vermont	20,254	44,092			
Virginia	139,670	95,558	......	...	11
West Virginia	56,455	42,698	1,373	...	5
Wisconsin	123,927	130,668	1,509	10	...
Total	4,284,757	4,033,950	81,740	185	184

Green C. Smith, Prohibitionist, received a total of 9,522 votes. There were 2,636 scattering votes for the Anti-Masonic and American Alliance tickets.

The Colorado electors were chosen by the Legislature.

The Returning Boards' counts are given for the popular votes in Florida and Louisiana, where there was a dispute as to Tilden's majority.

STATES	Popular Vote			Electoral Vote	
	Garfield and Arthur Rep.	Hancock and English Dem.	Weaver and Chambers Greenback	Garfield and Arthur	Hancock and English
Alabama	56,221	91,185	4,642	...	10
Arkansas	42,436	60,775	4,079		6
California	80,348	80,426	3,392		5
Colorado	27,450	24,647	1,435	3	
Connecticut	67,071	64,415	868	6	
Delaware	14,133	15,275	120		3
Florida	23,654	27,964	......	...	4
Georgia	54,086	102,470	969	...	11
Illinois	318,037	277,321	26,358	21	
Indiana	232,164	225,522	12,986	15	
Iowa	183,927	105,845	32,701	11	...
Kansas	121,549	59,801	19,851	5	...
Kentucky	106,306	149,068	11,499	...	12
Louisiana	38,637	65,067	439	...	8
Maine	74,039	65,171	4,408	7	
Maryland	78,515	93,706	818	...	8
Massachusetts	165,205	111,960	4,548	13	
Michigan	185,431	131,597	34,895	11	
Minnesota	93,903	53,315	3,267	5	...
Mississippi	34,854	75,750	5,797	...	
Missouri	153,567	208,609	35,135	...	15
Nebraska	54,979	28,523	3,950	3	...
Nevada	8,732	9,613	......	...	
New Hampshire	44,852	40,794	528	5	
New Jersey	120,555	122,565	2,617	...	9
New York	555,544	534,511	12,373	35	
North Carolina	115,874	124,208	1,126	...	10
Ohio	375,048	340,821	6,456	22	
Oregon	20,619	19,948	249	3	
Pennsylvania	444,704	407,428	20,668	29	
Rhode Island	18,195	10,779	236	4	
South Carolina	58,071	112,312	566		7
Tennessee	107,677	128,191	5,917	...	12
Texas	57,893	156,428	27,405	...	8
Vermont	45,567	18,316	1,215	5	
Virginia	84,020	128,586	......		11
West Virginia	46,243	57,391	9,079	..	5
Wisconsin	144,400	114,649	7,986	10	...
Total	4,454,416	4,444,952	308,578	214	155

Neal Dow. Prohibition candidate, received a total vote of 10,305.
Two Republican tickets were voted for in Louisiana. The Democratic
vote for Maine is given for the fusion vote for the electoral ticket, made
up of three Democrats and four Greenbackers A straight Greenback
ticket was also voted for in Maine
 Two Democratic tickets were voted in Virginia. The Regular received 96,912; the "Readjusters" 31,674.

POPULAR AND ELECTORAL VOTE, 1884.

STATES	Blaine Rep.	Cleveland Dem.	Butler Greenback	St. John Pro.	Cleveland and H	Blaine and L
	Popular Vote				Electoral Vote	
Alabama	59,591	93,951	873	612	10	...
Arkansas	50,895	72,927	1,847		7	
California	102,416	89,288	2,017	2,920	...	8
Colorado	36,290	27,723	1,958	761	...	3
Connecticut	65,923	67,199	1,688	2,305	6	
Delaware	12,951	16,964	6	55	3	
Florida	28,031	31,766		72	4	
Georgia	48,603	94,667	145	195	12	
Illinois	337,474	312,355	10,910	12,074	...	22
Indiana	238,463	244,990	8,293	3,028	15	
Iowa	197,089	177,316		1,472	...	13
Kansas	154,406	90,132	16,341	4,495	...	9
Kentucky	118,122	152,961	1,691	3,139	13	
Louisiana	46,347	62,540			8	
Maine	72,209	52,140	3,953	2,160	...	6
Maryland	85,699	96,932	531	2,794	8	
Massachusetts	146,724	122,481	24,433	10,026	...	14
Michigan	192,669	149,835	42,243	18,403	...	13
Minnesota	111,923	70,144	3,583	4,684		7
Mississippi	43,509	76,510			9	
Missouri	202,929	235,988		2,153	16	
Nebraska	76,912	54,391		2,899		5
Nevada	7,193	5,578	26		...	3
New Hampshire	43,249	39,183	552	1,571	...	4
New Jersey	123,440	127,798	3,496	6,159	9	
New York	562,005	563,154	16,994	25,016	36	
North Carolina	125,068	142,952		454	11	
Ohio	400,082	368,280	5,179	11,069		23
Oregon	26,860	24,604	726	492		3
Pennsylvania	473,804	392,785	16,992	15,283		30
Rhode Island	19,030	12,391	422	928		4
South Carolina	21,733	69,890			9	
Tennessee	124,078	133,258	957	1,131	12	
Texas	93,141	225,309	3,321	3,534	13	
Vermont	39,514	17,331	785	1,752	...	4
Virginia	139,356	145,497		138	12	
West Virginia	63,096	67,317	810	939	6	
Wisconsin	161,157	146,459	4,598	7,656	...	11
Total	4,851,981	4,874,986	175,370	150,369	219	182

POPULAR AND ELECTORAL VOTE, 1888.

STATES	Cleve and Dem.	Harrison Rep.	Fisk Pro.	Streeter U. Labor	Harrison and M	Cleve and and T
Alabama	117,320	56,197	583	. . . . . .	. . .	10
Arkansas	85,962	58,752	641	10,613		7
California	117,729	124,816	5,761		8	
Colorado	37,567	50,774	2,191	1,266	3	
Connecticut	74,920	74,584	4,234	240		6
Delaware	16,414	12,973	400	. . . . . .	. . .	3
Florida	39,561	26,657	423	. . . . . .	. . .	4
Georgia	100,499	40,496	1,808	136	. . .	12
Illinois	348,278	370,473	21,695	7,090	22	
Indiana	261,013	263,361	9,881	2,694	15	
Iowa .	179,887	211,598	3,550	9,105	13	
Kansas	103,744	182,934	6,768	37,726	9	
Kentucky	183,800	155,134	5,225	622	. . .	13
Louisiana	85,032	30,484	166	39	. . .	8
Maine	50,481	73,734	2,691	1,344	6	
Maryland	106,168	99,986	4,767	. . . . . .	. . .	^
Massachusetts . . .	151,855	183,892	8,701		14	
Michigan	213,459	236,370	20,942	4,542	13	
Minnesota	104,385	142,492	15,311	1,094	7	
Mississippi	85,471	30,096	218	22	. . .	9
Missouri	261,974	236,257	4,539	18,632	. . .	16
Nebraska	80,552	108,425	9,429	4,226	5	
Nevada .	5,362	7,229	41		3	
New Hampshire . .	43,456	45,728	1,593	13	4	
New Jersey	151,493	144,344	7,904		. . .	9
New York	635,757	648,759	30,231	626	36	
North Carolina . . .	147,902	134,784	2,787	32	. . .	11
Ohio	396,455	416,054	24,356	3,496	23	
Oregon	26,522	33,291	1,677	363	3	
Pennsylvania	446,633	526,091	20,947	3,873	30	
Rhode Island	17,530	21,968	1,250	18	4	. . .
South Carolina . . .	65,825	13,736	. . . . .	. . . . . .	. . .	12
Tennessee	158,779	138,988	5,969	48		12
Texas	534,883	88,422	4,749	29,459		13
Vermont	16,788	45,192	1,460		4	
Virginia	151,977	150,438	1,678	. . . . . .	. . .	12
West Virginia . . .	79,664	77,791	669	1,064	. . .	6
Wisconsin . . .	155,232	176,553	14,277	8,552	11	. . .
Total . .	5,540,329	5,439,853	249,506	146,935	233	168

1,591 for Curtis, American; 2,418 for Cowdrey, United Labor.

	Popular Vote				Electoral Votes		
STATES	Harrison Rep.	Cleveland Dem.	Bidwell Pro.	Weaver Peo.	Cleveland and S	Harrison and M	Weaver and F
Alabama	9,197	138,138	239	85,181	11	...	...
Arkansas	46,974	87,752	'113	11,831	8	...	.
California	117,618	117,908	8,187	25,226	8	1	.
Colorado	38,620	......	1,687	53,584	...	...	4
Connecticut	77,032	82,395	4,026	809	6	..	
Delaware	18,077	18,581	564	......	3	..	...
Florida		30,143	570	4,843	4	..	
Georgia	48,305	129,386	988	42,939	13	..	
Idaho	8,799	......	219	10,430	...		3
Illinois	399,288	426,281	25,870	22,207	24		
Indiana	255,615	262,740	13,044	22,198	15		
Iowa	219,373	196,408	6,322	20,616	...	13	...
Kansas	157,241	......	4,553	163,111	...		10
Kentucky	135,420	175,424	6,385	23,503	13		
Louisiana	25,332	87,922		1,232	8	.	
Maine	62,878	48,024	3,062	2,045	...	6	...
Maryland	92,736	113,866	5,877	796	8	.	
Massachusetts . ..	202,814	176,813	7,539	3,210	...	15	...
Michigan	222,708	202,296	20,569	19,792	5	9	
Minnesota	122,736	100,579	14,017	30,398	...	9	...
Mississippi	1,406	40,237	910	10,256	9	.	
Missouri	226,762	268,628	4,298	41,183	17	.	
Montana	18,833	17,534	517	7,259	...	3	...
Nebraska	87,218	24,943	4,902	83,134	...	8	...
Nevada	2,822	711	85	7,267			3
New Hampshire .	45,658	42,081	1,297	293	...	4	
New Jersey	156,080	171,066	8,134	985	10		
New York	609,459	654,908	38,193	16,430	36	...	...
North Carolina ..	100,346	132,951	2,636	44,732	11	...	...
North Dakota ...	17,486	......	......	17,650	1	1	1
Ohio	405,187	404,115	26,012	14,852	1	22	...
Oregon	35,002	14,243	2,281	26,965		3	
Pennsylvania	516,011	452,264	25,123	8,714	...	32	...
Rhode Island	27,069	24,335	1,565	227	...	4	...
South Carolina ..	13,384	54,698		2,410	9	..	
South Dakota ...	34,888	9,081		26,512	...	4	
Tennessee	99,973	136,477	4,856	23,622	12	...	.
Texas	81,444	239,148	2,165	99,638	15	...	..
Vermont	37,992	16,325	1,424	43	...	4	..
Virginia	113,256	163,977	2,798	12,274	12	...	..
Washington	36,470	29,844	2,553	19,105	...	4	...
West Virginia ...	80,285	83,484	2,130	4,165	6	..	
Wisconsin	170,761	177,436	13,132	9,909	12	...	...
Wyoming	8,376	......	526	526	...	3	...
Total	5,186,931	5,553,142	268,361	1,030,128	277	145	22

State								
Alabama	11	8		1	2,147	6,462	130,307	54,737
Arkansas	6	6		893	839	2,006	110,103	37,512
California	1	3	1,611	1,047	2,573	1	43,373	146,170
Colorado	4		159	566	1,717	4,334	161,153	26,271
Connecticut			1,223		1,808	877	56,740	110,285
Delaware	7				355	654	13,424	16,804
Florida	13	21	1,147	793	1,778	2,708	32,736	11,288
Idaho	3	15	324	267	5,613		94,232	901
Illinois		13	453	352	179	6,390	23,192	6,824
Ind.	10	12		630	9,796	2,145	464,632	607,140
Iowa	1				3,056	4,516	305,573	323,754
Kentucky	8	6	587	136	3,192	1,209	223,741	289,293
Louisiana		8	2,114	1,905	1,921	5,114	171,810	159,541
Maine			297		4,781	1,834	217,890	218,171
Maryland			867		1,570	1,870	77,173	22,037
Massachusetts			590	295	5,918	2,507	34,688	80,465
Michigan			186	797	2,998	11,749	104,735	136,959
Minnesota	9	15			5,025	6,879	105,711	278,976
Mississippi	17	14			4,343	3,202	236,714	293,582
Missouri	8	9			485	1,071	139,626	193,501
Montana	3				2,169	2,355	63,859	5,130
Nebraska					186		363,647	304,940
Nevada					1,193	2,885	42,537	404
New Hampshire		4	228	49	779	520	115,880	102,304
New Jersey	11	10	3,985		5,614	6,373	8,377	1,938
New York		36	17,667	247	16,052	870	21,650	57,444
N. Carolina					675	578	133,675	221,367
Ohio		3	1,167	2,716	358	1,857	551,369	819,838
Oregon	9	23			5,068	977	174,488	155,222
Pennsylvania	4	4	1,683	870	99	1,000	20,686	26,335
Rhode Island	12	32	558	5	19,274	1,166	477,494	525,991
S. Carolina	15	4			1,160	828	46,662	48,779
Tennessee	3				685	1,051	133,228	728,300
Texas					3,098	5,046	14,450	37,47
Vermont	2	4	108	148	1,786	1,331	58,798	9,281
Virginia	4				733	2,129	41,225	41,042
Washington		6		346	2,350	1,668	166,268	148,773
W. Virginia		12	1,314		968	677	370,434	167,520
Wisconsin	3				1,203	4,584	64,517	13,484
Wyoming					7,509		10,637	51,127
					136		154,709	135,368
							51,646	39,153
							92,927	104,474
							165,523	268,135
							10,655	10,072
Total	**176**	**271**	**36,274**	**13,069**	**132,009**	**133,424**	**6,502,925**	**7,106,779**

POPULAR AND ELECTORAL VOTE FOR PRESIDENT IN 1900.

STATES.	McKinley, Rep.	Bryan, Dem.	Woolley, Pro.	Debs, Soc. Dem.	Maloney, Soc. L.	Barker, M.R. Pop.	Ellis, U.R.	Leonard, U.C.	Electoral McKinley, Rep.	Electoral Bryan, Dem.
Alabama	55,512	97,131	2,762			4,178				11
Arkansas	44,800	81,142	584			972	34			8
California	164,755	124,985	5,024	7,554	700	387			9	
Colorado	93,072	122,733	3,790	654	898					4
Connecticut	102,567	73,997	1,617	1,029					6	
Delaware	22,529	18,858	538	57		1,070			3	
Florida	7,314	28,007	1,039	601		4,584				4
Georgia	35,035	81,700	1,396			213				13
Idaho	26,997	29,414	857					352		3
Illinois	597,985	503,061	17,623	9,687	1,373	1,141			24	
Indiana	336,063	309,584	13,718	2,374	663	1,438			15	
Iowa	307,785	209,179	9,479	2,778	259	613			13	
Kansas	185,955	162,601	3,605	1,605				707	10	
Kentucky	227,128	235,103	3,780	646	390	1,861				13
Louisiana	14,233	53,671								8
Maine	65,435	36,822	2,585	878			47		6	
Maryland	136,212	122,271	4,582	908	391				6	
Massachusetts	238,866	156,997	6,202	9,607	2,599				15	
Michigan	316,269	211,685	11,859	2,826	903	833			14	
Minnesota	190,461	112,901	8,555	3,065	1,329				9	
Mississippi	5,753	51,706								9
Missouri	314,092	351,922	5,965	6,139	1,294	1,644	672			17
Montana	25,373	37,146	298	708		4,244	254			3
Nebraska	121,835	114,013	3,655	823		1,104			8	
Nevada	3,849	6,347								3
New Hampshire	54,803	35,489	1,270	790	2,074				4	
New Jersey	221,707	164,808	7,183	4,609	12,622	669			10	
New York	821,992	678,386	22,043	12,869					36	
North Carolina	133,081	157,752	1,006			830				11
North Dakota	35,891	20,519	731	518		110			3	
Ohio	543,918	474,882	10,203	4,847	1,638	251			23	
Oregon	46,526	33,385	2,536	1,466		203	1,284		4	
Pennsylvania	712,665	424,232	27,908	4,831	2,936	638			32	
Rhode Island	33,784	19,812	1,529		1,423				4	
South Carolina	3,579	47,233		176						9
South Dakota	54,530	39,544	1,542	410		339			4	
Tennessee	123,108	141,751	3,900	1,841	160	1,368				12
Texas	121,173	267,337	2,644	720	106	20,976				15
Utah	47,139	45,006	209			357			3	
Vermont	42,568	12,849	368						4	
Virginia	115,865	146,080	2,150	2,006						12
Washington	57,456	44,833	2,363		866				4	

INDEX

(317)

CPSIA information can be obtained
at www.ICGtesting.com
Printed in the USA
FSOW03n2012071216
28315FS